WOMEN DON'T COUNT

American Academy of Religion
Academy Series

edited by
Susan Thistlethwaite

Number 87
WOMEN DON'T COUNT

by
Pamela K. Brubaker

Pamela K. Brubaker

WOMEN DON'T COUNT
THE CHALLENGE OF WOMEN'S POVERTY TO CHRISTIAN ETHICS

Scholars Press
Atlanta, Georgia

WOMEN DON'T COUNT

by
Pamela K. Brubaker

Library of Congress Cataloging in Publication Data
Brubaker, Pamela, 1946-
    Women don't count / Pamela K. Brubaker.
        p.   cm. — (American Academy of Religion academy series ; no.
87)
    Includes bibliographical references.
    ISBN 1-55540-957-1 (alk. paper). — ISBN 1-55540-958-X (pbk.)
    1. Women in Christianity. 2. Women—Economic conditions.
3. Poverty—Religious aspects—Christianity.   4. Christian ethics.
I. Title. II. Series.
BV639.W7B78 1994
261.8'5'082—dc20   94-2380
                                                        CIP

Printed in the United States of America
on acid-free paper

Dedicated to my children,
JOHN AND CORY LOWE.

TABLE OF CONTENTS

ACKNOWLEDGMENTS

I am grateful to many people who have contributed to the completion of this study. The Womaen's Caucus and Women's Program of the Church of the Brethren, the Ecumenical Center of Union Theological Seminary, and my sister Beverly Brubaker funded my participation in the United Nations Decade for Women Conference and Forum 85. This study developed in response to some third world women at the Forum who charged first world women to undertake projects of global analysis and action for economic justice. I am grateful for the commitment, clarity, and passion of the many networks of women I encountered there, whose voices and work inform this study.

I want to thank several student colleagues and friends who gave useful suggestions and invaluable support in many different ways, in particular Elizabeth Bounds, Hyun Kyung Chung, Ada Maria Isasi-Diaz, Lois Kirkwood, Marilyn Legge, and Margaret Mayman. Church Women United, Hartford Seminary, and the National Council of Churches (USA) encouraged my research during the periods of my employment with them.

Marie Giblin and William Tabb served on my dissertation committee and offered insighful observations on some of the implications of my work. Larry Rasmussen and Beverly Harrison advised me throughout the research and writing of this study. I am grateful for their encouragement and careful critical reading of earlier drafts. Beverly Harrison has also been my advisor and mentor throughout my years at Union. Without her methodological insights and personal support this project would not have been completed.

Finally, my deep appreciation to my family, particularly my sons John and Cory Lowe, for their steadfast love and support. May they continue their commitment to women's equality and empowerment.

INTRODUCTION

TOWARDS A CHRISTIAN ETHIC THAT ADDRESSES WOMEN'S IMPOVERISHMENT

That women are poor is nothing new; that women are poor is nothing unusual.... Women have always been disproportionately poor, and many women have been poor their entire lives. But many of the social movements of the past 20 years, particularly the women's movement, have attempted to redress the social and economic inequalities suffered by women throughout history. Yet for all our "progress," for all the gains made in women's rights, there is still not only a large number of poor women in the United States - and throughout the world - but now there are more poor women than ever, and they are getting poorer.[1]

A broad convergence of concern about the impoverishment of women has emerged globally in recent years. The United Nations Decade for Women (1975-85) focused attention on the fact that the impact of the

---

[1] Vicki Kemper, "Women struggle for survival," *Sojourners* (March 1986), p. 15. Kemper's claim that women have always been disproportionately poor is not one that can be documented and may not be accurate for all societies; it is generally true, however, and succinctly describes the current situation.

1

contemporary international economic crisis has fallen disproportionately on women.[2] As a result, the economic situation of women in many developing countries actually deteriorated during the Decade. Women are among the majority of the unemployed and underemployed in the wage labor force in many countries. In addition, many women who live in poverty, often with their dependent children, work -in subsistence agricultural production, in the informal sector, or in poorly paid jobs in the formal sector.[3] The United Nations warned that if these trends continue, women will remain the majority of the world's marginalized population.[4]

---

[2] This crisis has several dimensions, which include the unmanageable debt burdens and balance of payments deficits of some third world countries, imbalances in international trade and capital flows, and instability in world financial and monetary systems.

[3] Subsistence agricultural production is food production primarily for own family/household consumption. The formal sector refers to formally organized agricultural, industrial, and service activities integrated into a market or centrally planned economy. There is not a generally agreed upon definition of "the informal sector," but this term usually refers to "unregistered, small-scale and informally organised activities," such as preparing and selling food grown on a family plot in street bazaars. ILO/INSTRAW, *Women in Economic Activity: A Global Statistical Survey*, 1985, p. 10. For a discussion of the controversy around the informal sector, see Alejandro Portes, "The Informal Sector: Definition, Controversy, and Relation to National Development," *Review* VII (Summer 1983), pp. 151-174.

[4] The primary source of this data is the United Nation's report *Review and Appraisal of Progress Achieved and Obstacles Encountered at the National Level in the Realization of the Goals and Objectives of the United Nations Decade for Women: Equality, Development, and Peace*, A/CONF.116/5, 1985. See particularly Add. 2, on "Employment." The *Review and Appraisal* document is based on responses of national governments to a United Nations questionnaire. Its compilers are aware of the difficulty of their analysis due to varied interpretations of questions by respondents and of the sketchy character of statistics gathered across the Decade. Yet even with these constraints and a rather optimistic perspective in regard to progress made, the evidence clearly pointed to women's worsening economic situation. A more recent United Nations study found little improvement in the lives of most of the world's women since the end of the Decade. Many women are still overworked and underpaid, poorly represented in political and economic decision-making, and "in far too many instances, women are the providers of last resort for their families and themselves, often in relentlessly adverse conditions." *The World's Women 1970-1990: Trends and Statistics* (New York: United Nations, 1991), p. vii.

The Purpose of This Study

The sources and dynamics making for the pauperization and marginalization of women are the animating concern of this dissertation in Christian social ethics. My goal is to demonstrate the inability of much analysis to touch the reality of women's poverty[5] because of presuppositions which render women's material and cultural realities invisible. My thesis is that the various analytic frameworks used in theological ethical and economic analysis either obscure or fail to disclose the root causes of women's impoverishment. In other words, *women don't count.*

Origins of the Study

Concern for economic justice first emerged for me during a work camp in Appalachia as a youth in the early 1960s. Participation in the civil rights movement and the study of sociology during college years in Chicago deepened this concern and broadened my understanding of race and class as factors in impoverishment. Although my experience in Chicago was primarily with poor black women and children, it was not until involvement in the women's movement in the 1970s that I began to recognize that gender is a specific factor in women's pauperization.

---

[5] For the purposes of this study, I am using the following definition of poverty: To be poor is to be unable to adequately provide the basic material human needs for subsistence - food, clothing, shelter; or to have access to essential community services - health services, pure water, sanitation, education, public transportation; or to lead a full life - participation in social activities and cultural life. To be poor is to be marginalized and powerless - to be unable to impact public decision-making or to have one's voice heard. To be poor is to have one's human dignity called into question or denied. This definition is informed by the work of the International Labor Organization, who have attempted to articulate an approach to conceptualizing poverty which will be globally relevant. For a useful discussion of some of the issues involved in defining poverty, see Kenneth Abrahams, "Poverty in Namibia," *Namibian Review Publications*, Number 5 (March 1985), pp. 1-9; and Michael Harrington, *The New American Poverty* (New York: Penguin Books, 1986).

Graduate study at Union Theological Seminary and the New School for Social Research provided opportunities to further explore the multiple sources of impoverishment and their interrelationship and to begin to understand some of the global dimensions of this problem. A turning point in my understanding came through my participation in the United Nations End of the Decade for Women Conference and Forum in Nairobi, Kenya in July of 1985. Over fifteen thousand women came to the Forum, nearly two-thirds of them from the so-called third world. During the workshops on the global economic crisis, several women gave testimony on the impact of the crisis on women in their countries.

These analyses linked women around the world in the material terms of our everyday lives, enabling women from diverse cultures to begin to understand how specific and concrete solidarity in the struggle for economic and social justice could be expressed. I heard women from Africa, Asia, and Latin America bear witness to the suffering of women and children through cuts in social programs, increased workloads of rural and urban women to provide basic needs, and the growth of sweatshops mainly employing young women. As I listened to these women, I thought of suffering people I knew of in the U.S. - farm families, including my own family of origin in southern Ohio, the growing number of poor people in New York and other cities, women workers in sweatshops I had visited in Chinatown.

The impoverishment of women in the United States has become a matter of concern not only for feminists like myself but also for mainstream economists. Lester C. Thurow has noted "a surge in inequality" in the distribution of income and wealth in the United States since the late 1970's.[6] Thurow attributes this surge to international competition, coupled with high unemployment as well as the rising proportion of female workers in the labor force, coupled with "society's economic treatment of women."

> Since women are paid much less than men and are much more likely to be part-time workers, a rising proportion of female workers automatically leads to a more unequal distribution of earnings. The average female worker makes

---

[6] Lester C. Thurow, "A Surge in Inequality," *Scientific American* 256, no. 5, (May 1987), p. 30.

52 percent of what the average male makes, and the average full-time, year-round female worker makes just 65 percent of what her male counterpart makes.

This phenomenon, together with an increasing proportion of female headed households, has led to a low-income population increasingly dependent on women's earnings: the feminization of poverty. [7]

Thurow noted that the average female worker earns hardly enough to keep a family of four above the poverty line. Moderates like Thurow recognize the problem of impoverishment of women in the U.S., but the actual scope, scale, and global character of the issue is not widely understood.

In this study I aim to expose the roots of the invisibility of women's poverty by analyzing and evaluating assumptions about women's economic reality employed in contemporary progressive economic approaches that impact Christian ethics. I will examine examples of Christian economic ethics and also the literature from the U.N. sponsored Decade for Women in order to show how methodological presuppositions derived from various theoretical frameworks used in economic analysis obscure women's cultural and material well-being. I will also examine the adequacy of existing normative theological assumptions and ethical principles as these relate to the concrete well-being of women. I propose to formulate criteria for an alternative theoretical approach to women's economic reality, drawing on literature developed by women during the Decade for Women, which more adequately illumines and engages women's reality.

---

[7] Ibid., p. 34. Although the term "feminization of poverty" is increasingly used, it has been criticized for rendering invisible the long term poverty of working class and racial ethnic women and men and for obscuring *women's* reality by emphasizing the *"feminizing"* of *poverty*. I will use the terms pauperization and marginalization or impoverishment in this study, unless feminization of poverty is used by the author I am quoting

Some Working Assumptions

Theological Methodological Assumptions

My theological ethical approach is a feminist liberationist one, which deals critically and constructively with the Christian tradition.[8] A full consideration of this method lies beyond the scope of this thesis. Here it is necessary only to clarify some of the basepoints which shape my work.

Accountability to concrete suffering. I understand this method to presume a commitment to marginated and oppressed peoples, theologically understood as the preferential option for the poor. In my method, the preferential option for the poor specifies a theological and moral commitment to the struggle for justice and liberation for poor women, as they are the majority of the poor and the poorest of the poor.[9] And since women play a critical role in the survival of poor families, a commitment to their well-being is simultaneously a commitment to the well-being of their families.

Accountability to concrete suffering is the starting point of a liberation theological ethic. The centrality of historical, human suffering in liberation theology distinguishes it from other modern theologies, as does its concern for transformation of existing reality

---

[8] Beverly W. Harrison describes this method as beginning with conscientization and sociohistorical ethical analysis, and moving to articulation and critical evaluation of the moral norms of Christian traditions and the liberation struggle itself in her essay "Theological Reflection in the Struggle for Liberation: A Feminist Perspective," *Making the Connections: Essays in Feminist Social Ethics*, ed. Carol S. Robb (Boston: Beacon Press, 1985), pp. 249-59.

[9] Margaret Farley contends that since feminism is opposed to discrimination on the grounds of sex, it is necessarily pro-woman since discrimination on a sexual basis "remains pervasively discrimination against women." Feminism aims to correct this bias *against* women by a bias *for* women, which includes "a focal concern for the well-being of women and a taking account of women's experience in coming to understand what well-being demands for women and men." "Feminist Theology and Bioethics," *Women's consciousness, Women's conscience: A Reader in Feminist Ethics*, ed. Barbara H. Andolsen, Christine E. Gudorf, Mary D. Pellauer (Minneapolis: Winston Press, 1985), p. 288.

rather than merely understanding it. Theological method is also transformed in liberation theology. In the words of Rebecca Chopp:

> Bringing suffering into the midst of reflection, liberation theology rethinks human existence, Christian tradition, and present Christian experience.... With God's liberating activity at its center, liberation theology offers a new understanding of human existence through the centrality of praxis and a new interpretation of Christianity through Christ's solidarity with those who suffer. The method of liberation theology demands that theology be a reflection on Christian praxis - a reflection aimed at interpretation, critique, and transformation.[10]

This thesis is a critical reflection on some aspects of Christian praxis for economic justice, in solidarity with those who suffer injustice.

To interpret a Christian praxis of economic justice from a liberation theological perspective, one must begin with those who suffer injustice. The option for the poor is both a moral and an epistemological assumption. The epistemological privilege of the oppressed is required for a Christian praxis of justice. As Karen Lebacqz contends:

> If justice begins with the correction of injustices, then the most important tools for understanding justice will be the stories of injustice as experienced by the oppressed and the tools of social and historical analysis that help to illumine the process by which those historical injustices arose and the meaning of them in the lives of the victims.[11]

It is in the lives of poor women of color that the interstructuring of injustices of racism, sexism, and class exploitation can be seen; it is from the standpoint of their lives that we can critique the adequacy of existing theoretical frameworks in light of the need for a critical theory of oppression. In this study, I attempt to operationalize the epistemological privilege of poor women by claiming as a primary criterion of evaluation the ability of economic and theological ethical analyses to account for the suffering of poor women.

---

[10] Rebecca S. Chopp, *The Praxis of Suffering: An Interpretation of Liberation and Political Theologies* (Maryknoll, NY: Orbis Books, 1986), pp. 3-4.

[11] Karen Lebacqz, *Justice in an Unjust World: Foundations for a Christian Approach to Justice* (Minneapolis: Augsburg, 1987), p. 150.

Biblical remembrance. A liberation theological ethic juxtaposes historical consciousness that hears the voices of the oppressed with biblical remembrance that recaptures the meaning of scripture as the oppressed understood them, according to Lebacqz.[12] This juxtaposition correlates with the retrieval of tradition characteristic of liberation theology. Narrative becomes a basic form of theology, Chopp contends, "to retrieve the Christian tradition, to narrate the dangerous memories of suffering, and to effect conversion and transformation."[13] Given the growing economic suffering of women, a biblical narrative that has been for me a metaphor of the suffering of women during the course of this study is the story of the woman who was so bent over that she could not stand upright. (Luke 13:10-17)[14]

According to the text, the woman had an illness which had left her "bent double." When Jesus saw her, he said: "Woman, you are freed from your infirmity." (Luke 13:12 RSV) He laid his hands on her and she immediately straightened up and praised God. In response to criticism for healing on the Sabbath, Jesus answered:

> You hypocrites! Does not each of you on the sabbath untie his ox or his ass from the manger, and lead it away to water it? And ought not this woman, a daughter of Abraham whom Satan bound for eighteen years, be loosed from this bond on the sabbath day? (Luke 13:15 RSV)

---

[12] Lebacqz contends that to assume the validity of such juxtapositions is not to assume "that direct parallels can be found between biblical texts and the contemporary world." Rather she argues that "historical consciousness illumines biblical remembrance ˙ and biblical remembrance in turn illumines historical consciousness." Ibid., p. 61.

[13] Chopp, p. 141.

[14] My use of this text has been as a rhetorical invocation of the memory of the solidarity of Jesus with the suffering of this woman and of her liberation from that suffering. I do not offer a historical critical interpretation of the text, but rather approach it metaphorically. For a historical critical interpretation, see Elisabeth Schussler Fiorenza, "Liberation, Unity and Equality in Community: a New Testament Case Study," *Beyond unity-in-tension: Unity, renewal and the community of women and men*, ed. Thomas F. Best (Geneva: WCC Publications, 1988), pp. 59-60. "The woman bent double," Fiorenza contends, "has become a paradigm for the situation of women, not only in society but also in the churches." Ibid., p. 60.

His criitcs were shamed and the people rejoiced at what he had done.

A feminist biblical hermeneutic illumines ways remembrance of this narrative may effect conversion and transformation today. In the words of Elisabeth Schussler Fiorenza:

> Just as Jesus, who was born with the privileges of a Jewish male, focused attention on the woman bent double and insisted that she must be healed, so Christian men must recognize the patriarchal exploitation and oppression of women in society and church. They must not only reject all theologies of subordination or of "women's special nature and place" as patriarchal ideologies, but must also relinquish their patriarchal privileges and join women in our struggle to end patriarchal exploitation and bondage.
>
> Recognizing ourselves in the story of the woman bent double, we women must identify ourselves as women deformed and exploited by societal and ecclesiastical patriarchy. Those of us who are priviieged in terms of race, class, culture and education must realize that as long as a single woman is not free, no woman is able to overcome patriarchal infirmity and bondage.... Only when we see ourselves and our daughters in the women who are today bent double in our midst, will we be able to articulate theologically a vision of God's salvation and community which enables all women to become free from patriarchal dehumanization.[15]

One task of this study is a critique of existing theological and ethical presuppositions, moral principles, and strategic proposals in an attempt to articulate criteria for a transformative theological ethical approach to the liberation of the women today bent double in our midst from cultural and material oppression - the poor third world women who are at the "bottom of the patriarchal pyramid."[16]

---

[15] Fiorenza, "Liberation, Unity and Equality in Community," p. 63.

[16] Ibid., p. 62. Fiorenza defines patriarchy as perpetrating not only sexism, but also racism and "property-class relationships" as basic structures of women's oppression. She argues that all women "are bound into a system of male privilege and domination, but impoverished third world women constitute the bottom of the oppressive patriarchal pyramid." It should be noted that some women of color argue that the concept of patriarchy is not descriptive of the oppression they experience from "their relation to the white-controlled American institutions governing their lives," in which white women participate and from which they benefit. Delores S. Williams, "The Color of Feminism," *The Journal of Religious Thought* 43, (Spring-Summer, 1986), p. 50. Given this fact, I will not use the term patriarchy here as

Some Moral Assumptions

A feminist liberationist theological ethic has implications for our understanding of moral norms. My warrants for concern for women's well-being and moral agency are derived to this point from liberation theological grounds. Warrants for this concern can also be formulated on moral philosophical grounds. Considering both warrants is important in social ethics, so as not to treat all moral claims as legitimate only in a specifically theological framework. Recognizing the legitimacy of moral claims in non-theological terms also facilitates our ability to build alliances with non-religious people who are committed to the well-being of women.

Inequality is a moral issue. My first moral-philosophical assumption is that deep inequality is a moral issue. I agree with Daniel Maguire that "the foundation of morality is the experience of the value of persons and their environment."[17] Deep inequalities are harmful to both persons and society. Those who suffer directly from inequality are devalued in fact and denied conditions necessary for their human dignity as persons.[18] Widespread inequality tears at the social fabric by undermining its moral foundations in the devaluing of those who suffer inequality. If legitimating ideologies, such as racism and sexism, develop to attempt to account for social inequalities the moral foundations of society are further undermined.

---

inclusive of racism and class oppression, unless it is used in this way in the text I am reviewing. I will generally use the term male domination, rather than patriarchy, to refer to the specific oppression of women as women.

[17] Maguire contends that this experience of the value of persons and their environment "is *the* distinctively human and humanizing experience..." Daniel Maguire, *The Moral Choice* (Minneapolis: Winston Press, 1978), p. 72.

[18] Human dignity is a foundation moral norm shared by secular and religious people. Nations subscribing to the Charter of the United Nations made specific commitments "to reaffirm faith in fundamental human rights, in the dignity and worth of the human person..." Quoted in United Nations, *Report of the World Conference of the International Women's Year* 1975, p. 2. Chapters 2 and 3 of my study will review the centrality of this norm in Roman Catholic and World Council social thought.

If one values persons, the conditions for their existence is a foundational moral issue.[19] Thus economic justice is a critical socio-ethical principle because human existence is dependent upon access to and control of resources to meet basic needs for food, shelter, and clothing. These are absolute minimum conditions for physical existence. Conditions for full human existence also include "health, bodily integrity, nonalienating labor and cultural creativity."[20] Where serious inequities in access to and control of resources are institutionalized, justice requires socio-economic transformation to equalize access and control.

Women's moral worth. My second moral assumption is that the pauperization and marginalization of women is a question basic to any normative discussion of social justice. The grounds for such a claim are the same grounds for the claim that broad inequality and economic justice are foundational ethical issues. This assumption may appear to be self-evident to some in that women are persons and members of the human community.[21] Yet appeals to justice and equality for women

---

[19] This understanding of moral foundations correlates with a liberationist view that sees material well-being rather than ontological meaning as foundational. I am grateful to Elizabeth Bounds for pointing out this correlation to me.

[20] Harrison, p. 254. For a critical discussion of approaches to economic justice, see C. Norman Bowie and Robert L. Simon, "Economic Justice," *Poverty and Economic Justice: A Philosophical Approach,* ed. Robert H. Hartman, (New York: Paulist Press, 1984), pp. 132-155. Bowie and Simon claim well-being to be a natural right and develop a contextual theory of distributive justice which takes into account different economies. While this approach has some validity, it neglects the dynamics of the international economic system which creates conditions of extreme scarcity in some places and conditions of affluence in others. Marvin Mahan Ellison has argued convincingly that *global* economic justice is a socio-ethical problem in *The Center Cannot Hold: The Search for a Global Economy of Justice,* (Washington, DC: University Press of America, 1983), pp. xix-xviii.

[21] As discussed in chapter four of this study, the United Nations affirmed the equal rights of women and men as part of its belief in fundamental human rights in its 1946 Charter and adopted The Declaration on the Elimination of Discrimination Against Women in 1967. Yet violence against women was not recognized by the United Nations as a violation of human rights until the 1993 World Human Rights Conference. This recognition resulted from the efforts of many women's organizations, which brought petitions from 124 countries bearing half a million

have often been dismissed because women's nature or situation are said to be different from men by "nature."[22] Such claims are morally indefensible because they deny the full personhood of women and therefore our right to all conditions of well-being deserving of personhood. In other words, such claims mean *women don't count*. Further, for reasons to be enumerated in the course of this study, I believe that a careful examination of women's economic reality is a critical condition for adequacy of economic ethical debate and for any prospects for global economic justice.

The pervasiveness of the denial of full moral agency and moral worth to women is illumined in an essay by Kathryn Pauly Morgan, a Canadian moral philosopher. Morgan points to four "maneuvers" in ethical theory and moral practice which can lead women to "a genuine sense of confusion and a kind of moral madness." The first, which I have already alluded to above, questions women's capacity for full moral agency through analyses of the concept of human nature. The second involves the distinction between public and private morality that is characteristic of some strands of progressive Christian ethics. In this maneuver women are assigned to the domain of private morality, and then it is presumed that only in the public domain is morality fully expressive of serious or full morality. The third maneuver consists of failing to acknowledge that "moral contortions" permeate women's lives, handicapping women with moral double-binds. The fourth theoretical maneuver occurs because of "the perceived invisibility of actual moral domains in women's lives."[23] My analysis will show that the sources of the invisibility of moral domains in women's lives are

---

signatures demanding "gender violence to be recognized as a violation of human rights." Ellen Goodman, "Women Silent Never Again," *The Plain Dealer* (Cleveland, Ohio), June 18 1993, and Associated Press, "Women bolster position in fight for rights, safety," *The Plain Dealer*, June 25, 1993).

[22] Carol Robb has a useful discussion of this problem in her "Introduction," *Making the Connections*, pp. xiv-xxi.

[23] Kathryn Pauly Morgan, "Women and Moral Madness," *Canadian Journal of Philosophy,* Supplementary Volume 13, pp 201-226.

connected to the roots of the invisibility of women's poverty in economic ethics.

I have asserted that human dignity is a foundational moral norm shared by religious and secular people. Although this norm would seem to be gender neutral, we shall see that there is some evidence that the experience of males is normative or that women are invisible in the religious traditions examined here. A critical evaluation of the anthropological presuppositions of these traditions is necessary to assess what difference taking women's experience seriously would make to this professed fundamental norm or to its implications for moral agency.[24]

Sources for This Study

The primary literary sources for this study are bodies of literature that have been in the foreground of efforts to address policy questions of economic justice specifically. My long-term intellectual interest is in arriving at effective policies. These sources include Roman Catholic, World Council, and United Nations Decade for Women documents, official and unofficial. Contemporary Roman Catholic social teaching and the social ethics of the World Council of Churches both aim to influence public policy.[25] The full scope of my concern about the marginality and invisibility of women's economic reality in progressive religious teaching is best amplified by looking at the teaching of both these bodies. Documents from the United Nations Decade for Women further the scope of this study by offering sources which take seriously women's reality. The full implications of this material will become apparent when strategic proposals are explored.

---

[24] For a useful discussion of moral agency and the moral life, see Bruce C. Birch and Larry L. Rasmussen, *Bible and Ethics in the Christian Life: Revised and Expanded Edition* (Minneapolis: Augsburg, 1989), pp. 38-62.

[25] Much literature written by individual social ethicists focuses on economic theory rather than on public policy. Wogaman's discussion of the debate in economics is one of the more perceptive of this genre. J. Philip Wogaman, *The Great Economic Debate: An Ethical Analysis* (Philadelphia: The Westminster Press, 1977).

These bodies of literature are grounded in the praxis of each of the organizations that have produced them. Praxis, simply defined, is action informed by thought. The relationship between thought and action, theory and practice, is perceived to be dialectical.[26] These bodies of literature all contain conflicting perspectives, as each is the collective voice of an institution which is itself an arena of struggle between classes, racial and ethnic groups, women and men, and the so-called first and third worlds.[27]

The praxis of these three groups is distinct and diverse. Roman Catholic social teaching is authoritative instruction from the teaching magisterium of the church to its members and to the broader society. No women participate directly in its articulation. The World Council of Churches does not speak *for* the churches, but *to* the churches which constitute the Council. Women have begun to participate and have some voice in the work of the Council. The official governmental conferences of the United Nations Decade for Women adopted action plans for use by the United Nations General Assembly and national governments, but they have no binding authority. The majority of participants in the U.N. process have been women appointed by national governments. The documents from the non-governmental forums during the decade have no official standing. Their importance for my study is that many of them were prepared by grassroots women's

---

[26] This brief definition is specifically informed by discussions of praxis in Chopp, particularly pp. 134-148 and Nancy Hartsock, "Feminist Theory and the Development of Revolutionary Strategy," *Capitalist Patriarchy and the Case for Socialist Feminism*, ed. Zillah R. Eisenstein (New York: Monthly Review Press, 1979), pp. 56-77.

[27] While the United Nations is recognized as an arena of struggle, the Roman Catholic Church or the World Council of Churches usually are not so recognized. In the second part of this study, some awareness on the part of these bodies of their role in social struggles is evident. For an insightful discussion of the contemporary Catholic church as an arena of class struggle, see William K. Tabb, "The Shoulds and the Excluded Whys: The U.S. Catholic Bishops Look at the Economy," *Churches in Struggle: Liberation Theologies and Social Change in North America*, ed. William K. Tabb (New York: Monthly Review Press, 1986), pp. 278-290, but especially p. 287.

organizations and networks which implement programs and undertake advocacy efforts.

My sources for Roman Catholic social teaching include the standard collections of papal encyclicals.[28] To illumine the social teaching, other less official pronouncements such as radio messages and published presentations to groups were surveyed, particularly for teaching on women. A wide selection of secondary literature on Catholic social teaching was also consulted.[29]

Sources for my discussion of World Council of Churches ecumenical social ethics were developed as a part of processes aimed to bring about the visible unity of the church around the world. Concern for unity here was not for its own sake but for the purpose of encouraging the church's ministry to the world.[30] My primary sources

---

[28] The collections of English translations of the social encyclicals used for this study are *Justice in the Marketplace: Collected Statements of the Vatican and the U.S. Catholic Bishops on Economic Policy, 1891-1984*, ed. David M. Byers (Washington, DC: United States Catholic Conference, 1985); *The Gospel of Peace and Justice: Catholic Social Teaching Since Pope John,* ed. Joseph Gremillion (Maryknoll, NY: Orbis Books, 1976). Other sources are identified in the notes for chapter two.

[29] Of particular importance are the study by Christine Gudorf, *Catholic Social Teaching on Liberation Themes* (Washington, DC: University Press in America, 1981); Donal Dorr, *Option for the Poor: A Hundred Years of Vatican Social Teaching* (Maryknoll: Orbis Books, 1983); Marie Giblin, *Toward Justice, Equality, and Participation* (Union Theological Seminary, unpublished dissertation, 1986), pp. 148-87; Mary E. Hobgood, *Catholic Social Teaching and Economic Theory: Paradigms in Conflict* (Philadelphia: Temple University Press, 1991). Other secondary literature is noted in the second chapter of this study.

[30] Primary sources for the history of the World Council of Churches are W.A.Visser't Hooft, *The Genesis and Formation of the World Council of Churches* (Geneva: WCC, 1982) and David Gaines, *The World Council of Churches: A Study of its Background and History,* (Peterborough, NH: Richard R. Smith, 1966). Charles S. McFarland's *Steps Towards the World Council* (New York: Fleming H. Revell, 1938) traces the development of the Universal Christian Council for Life and Work as part of the origins of the ecumenical movement. Other sources for the history and development of the social teachings are Edward Duff, *The Social Thought of the World Council of Churches* (New York: Association Press, 1956); Paul Bock, *In Search of a Responsible World Society: The Social Teachings of the*

for the discussion of ecumenical social ethics included here are the official reports of the conferences of the Life and Work movement and the various assemblies of the World Council of Churches. Reports of WCC-sponsored consultations were also consulted and a wide selection of secondary literature on ecumenical social ethics has been reviewed. The method and the content of World Council[31] and Roman Catholic social teaching differ from each other. In his study of World Council social teaching, Paul Bock made some comparisons of Roman Catholic teaching to World Council teaching. He noted that World Council documents are produced by a council representing many confessions whose authority rests on "their inherent truth or wisdom" whereas Roman Catholic documents are papal encyclicals whose authority is established doctrinally.[32]

Roger Shinn has also noted some relevant differences. He points out that Catholic teaching authority remains lodged in a hierarchy, works with some fixed doctrinal points, and traditionally uses a deductive style of ethics which makes distinctions between moral principles which are declared to be binding on the Christian conscience and prudential application of moral principles, on which there can be disagreement. In contrast, the WCC teaching is prepared by international groups of clergy and laity, does not have a common tradition with fixed points, and tends not to make distinctions between

---

World Council of Churches (Philadelphia: The Westminster Press, 1974); Martti Lindqvist, Economic Growth and the Quality of Life: An Analysis of the Debate within the World Council of Churches (Helsinki: Finnish Society for Missiology and Ecumenics, 1975); Richard D.N. Dickinson, Poor, Yet Making Many Rich (Geneva: WCC, 1982); Thomas Sieger Derr, "The Economic Thought of the World Council of Churches," This World, no.1 (Winter/Spring 1982), pp. 20-33; Roger L. Shinn, ed. "Church and Society: Ecumenical Perspectives - Essays in honour of Paul Abrecht," Ecumenical Review 37 (January 1985); and Paul Abrecht, ed. "Fifty Years of Ecumenical Social Thought," Ecumenical Review 40 (April 1988). Ans J. Van der Bent, Vital Ecumenical Concerns (Geneva: WCC, 1986) is a useful compendium of WCC statements on ecclesiological and social issues.

[31] The World Council of Churches (WCC) includes Protestant, Orthodox, Pentecostal, and Old Catholic religious bodies in its membership.

[32] Bock, pp. 27-8. Many commentators also include statements by national bodies of Catholic bishops within the rubric of Roman Catholic social teaching.

binding moral principles and prudential application of principles.[33] The World Council documents are formulated by diverse groups of people which makes the issue of participation in the Council especially relevant to the examination of its teachings.

Sources of United Nations Decade for Women literature that I employ are the official published reports of the three decade conferences and various unofficial reports of other decade meetings. Secondary literature on the Decade was also consulted.[34] Literature from non-governmental organizations and grassroots women's groups has been reproduced in various women's journals. A wide collection of this literature is also available at the International Women's Tribune Center in New York City.

The reason for using such diverse sources is rooted in my normative purpose. All of this literature purports to analyze the nature of poverty, each recognizes normative ethical dimensions to the problem, and all aim to influence the direction of public policy. Questions as to how economic well-being is understood, how women's economic reality is conceptualized, and what presuppositions and norms inform their analysis and policy proposals can be addressed to each distinct body of literature.

---

[33] Roger Shinn, "The churches' search for a peace policy," *Christianity and Crisis* (April 2, 1984), pp. 105-111. This article comparing World Council and the US Catholic Bishops documents on peace is applicable more generally to WCC and Roman Catholic social teaching.

[34] The only book length study of the Decade for Women available during this study was Arvonne S. Fraser, *The U.N. Decade for Women: Documents and Dialogue* (Boulder: Westview Press, 1987). This volume includes summaries of the major official governmental documents from the Decade for Women. Since this study was concluded, a book length study of the United Nations and women includes several chapters on the Decade for Women. See Hilkka Pietila and Jeanne Vickers, *Making Women Matter: The Role of the United Nations* (London: Zed Books, 1990), The citations for the full official reports I used for this study are in chapters one and four.

The Outline of the Study

In order to set the stage for the evaluation of the economic ethical and policy analyses that follows, the initial chapter of this study is a cross-cultural survey of the economic reality of the world's women. Here, I attempt to highlight the complexity and the diversity of women's experience resulting from the impact of the interstructuring of race, ethnicity, class, and nationality with gender. Commonalities and differences in women's economic reality are identified. The chapter aims to illumine the depth of the problem of women's pauperization and marginalization. This analysis is used to assess the adequacy of the analytic conceptualizations and the normative proposals of the ethical literature examined in the subsequent sections of the study.

The second chapter examines contemporary Roman Catholic social teaching to assess its adequacy in illumining women's economic vulnerability. I will argue that although Roman Catholic understandings of the economy and economic justice have shifted from traditional organic ones to liberal and radical ones, a similar shift did not occur in regard to its theological and moral anthropology. Static natural law understandings of women and femininity preclude a full and effective analysis of women's economic vulnerability.

In chapter three I examine the ecumenical social ethics of the World Council of Churches. I demonstrate that women's situation is at best marginal and often invisible in these documents. Here the problem is located in liberal presuppositions that preclude adequate attention to women's economic vulnerability. While the Council has moved from liberal understandings of the political economy and economic justice to radical ones, it has not made such a move in its understanding of the family/household and justice for women.

In chapter four I turn to literature from the United Nations Decade for women, including the action plans from the official governmental conferences and documents from women's organizations presented at the non-governmental forum. I argue that during the Decade there is a shift in perspectives from a liberal sex-role framework of analysis to a multidimensional structural transformative framework which attends to the interstructuring of gender, class and race.[35]

In chapter five I review selected literature representative of the different theoretical accounts of women's oppression implicit in the Decade literature. These include liberal feminism, marxism, cultural feminism and socialist feminism.[36] I assess the adequacy of each of these frameworks in accounting for the impoverishment of women, in light of the Decade's accomplishments. I contend that the multidimensional transformative perspective integrates the best insights from these frameworks to more adequately illumine and engage the pauperization and marginalization of women.

In the conclusion I explore the difference it would make to Christian economic ethics if the experience of women, particularly poor women, were its starting point. I revision the presuppositions, criteria, and normative moral and policy principles which would shape economic ethics in this case. I also suggest some implications for theological reflection, drawing on the work of third world women theologians who count women's contributions to the struggle for justice and life.

Depending on the reader's own interests, one might approach these chapters in various ways. If one is interested in approaching women's impoverishment from the perspective of Christian ethics, the study may be read as now organized. However, if one is interested in approaching Christian ethics from the perspective of feminist social theories, chapters four and five may be read after chapter one and before chapters two and three.[37]

---

[35] For further discussion of this framework, see Pamela Brubaker, "Sisterhood, Solidarity and Feminist Ethics," *Journal of Feminist Studies in Religion* 9 (Spring /Fall 1993).

[36] Carol Robb has an insightful discussion of these theories and their use in feminist ethics in her essay "A Framework for Feminist Ethics," *Women's consciousness, Women's conscience*, pp. 219-231.

[37] For a summary and some further development of this study, see Pamela Brubaker, "Economic Justice for Whom? Women Enter the Dialogue, Michael Zweig, ed., *Religion and Economic Justice* (Philadelphia: Temple University Press, 1991, pp. 95-127.

PART ONE

THE SCOPE OF THE PROBLEM

In Part One I will present a global overview of women's economic vulnerability, drawing on literature from the United Nations Decade for Women. Collective voices of women's organizations deepen the perspectives of official governmental reports.

CHAPTER ONE

WOMEN'S ECONOMIC REALITY:
DEEPENING PERSPECTIVES

This study is informed by the feminist theological ethical convictions already described. In keeping with these convictions, the study begins with the concrete suffering of women. What do we really know about women's growing economic marginalization?   What really is our problem? This chapter answers these questions with a global overview, drawing on what I take to be the most adequate available resources for such a task.[1]

The first task of this chapter is to present an overview of the insights that can be garnered from the formal sources about women's economic reality. The second task is to review the critical insights that have developed during the Decade about the inadequacies of the data and assumptions about women's economic reality. The third task is to examine dimensions of women's reality from emerging alternative perspectives - to ask what happens when women's voices enter the discussion.

---

[1] I will analyze the theoretical adequacy of these resources in chapters four and five of this study.

More Work, Fewer Benefits:
Insights Regarding Women's Vulnerability
Derived From Official Documents

Women, who are one half of the world's population, do two-thirds of its work, receive one tenth-of its income, and own less than one-hundredth of its property, reported *The State of the World's Women 1985*.[2] This statement aptly describes the economy reality of the world's women as a group. In three of the key indices of economic reality - work, income, property - the inequities between women and men are striking. In her survey of the world's women, Ruth Sivard noted that neither in the economy, education, health nor government have women attained equality with men. Women are disproportionately represented among the poor, the illiterate, the unemployed and underemployed.[3]

United Nations analysis, on which this study focuses, has called attention to the fact that large segments of the world's population have suffered pauperization, especially in developing countries, as a result of the widening gap in income inequalities between nations and within nations. Growing impoverishment and income inequality are part of an ongoing global economic crisis characterized by low or negative growth rates, the huge indebtedness of many developing countries, and cuts in social service spending. The economic situation of women in developing countries "has further deteriorated" as they are cut off from traditional sources of income and seek "new avenues of survival" in rural and

---

[2] *The State of the World's Women 1985* (Oxford: New Internationalist Publications, 1985), p. 3. This report was prepared at the request of the United Nations, using data from their surveys. This finding was first reported at mid-decade, United Nations, *Report of the World Conference of the United Nations Decade for Women*, 1981, paragraph 16. It was confirmed by data collected at the end of the decade.

[3] Ruth L. Sivard, *Women ... a world survey* (Washington, D.C.: World Priorities, 1985), p. 5. Sivard draws primarily on United Nations data.

urban areas.[4]   An assessment of projects of the United Nations Development Fund for Women indicated that "women are the poorest of the poor." Their levels of education and training are also lower than that of men within the same socio-economic group.[5]

Data gathered by the United Nations during the Decade for Women substantiate these findings. A questionnaire reviewing and appraising the position of women in their countries was returned by 121 governments.[6] Independent research by United Nations agencies during the Decade was compiled and published as well.[7] The findings of both these documents are summarized in the *Report on the State of the World's Women 1985*. The findings reveal that:

- women do almost all the world's domestic work which, together with their additional work outside the home, means most women work a double day;

- women grow around half of the world's food, but own hardly any land, find it difficult to get loans and are overlooked by agricultural advisors and projects;

- women are one third of the world's official labour force, but are concentrated in the lowest-paid occupations and are more vulnerable to unemployment than men;

- although there are some signs that the wage gap is closing slightly, women still earn less than three quarters of the wage of men doing similar work;

---

[4] United Nations, *Review and Appraisal of Progress Achieved and Obstacles Encountered at the National Level in the Realization of the Goals and Objectives of the United Nations Decade for Women: Equality, Development and Peace*, 1985, A/CONF.116/5/Add.2, "Employment," p.66; United Nations, *World Survey on the Role of Women in Development*, 1986, A/CONF.116/4/Rev.1, p. 13.

[5] *United Nations Development Fund for Women: Development Co-operation with Women*, 1985, p. 3.

[6] United Nations, *Review and Appraisal...*, 1985, A/CONF.116/5/Add.1-14.

[7] United Nations, *World Survey on the Role of Women in Development*, 1985, A/CONF.116/4.

- women provide more health care than all the health services put together and have been major beneficiaries of a new global shift in priorities towards prevention of disease and promotion of good health...[8]

Women's disadvantaged position is also reflected in the finding that they are "dramatically under-represented in the decision-making bodies of their countries," although 90% of countries have organizations to promote "the advancement of women."

The report concludes that the underlying cause of the inequality of women is that

a woman's domestic role as wife and mother - which is vital to the well-being of the whole of society, which consumes around half her time and energy - is unpaid and undervalued.[9]

That unpaid domestic work is everywhere seen as women's work was one of the few generalizations the report found to hold true throughout the world.

The extent of inequality and impoverishment experienced by the world's women is well-established by these investigations. Yet as the report indicates, there are few generalizations which are accurate cross-culturally. Women do not form a homogeneous social group.[10] The world's two and a half billion women speak nearly 3,000 different languages and live in countries where the average annual income varies from under $200 to $30,000 per capita. Women in wealthier countries have an average life span nearly thirty years longer than do women in poor countries. In some countries nine out of ten women over 25 have had no schooling at all, whereas in some others six out of ten women of university age are enrolled in higher education. In some countries women begin childbearing before age 15 and have seven or eight

---

[8] *State of the World's Women 1985*, p. 3. I have formatted the passage into sections to improve readability.

[9] Ibid.

[10] This is noted in the *Review and Appraisal* document on "Employment," para. 9, which indicated that this diversity has "serious repercussions on policy, research and action."

children, whereas in other countries the majority of women have only two children. There are also striking contrasts between women who live in rural and urban areas.[11]

In our discussion, both commonalities and differences among women will emerge. To begin to probe the economic reality of women, I will review sections of the United Nations documents which address this reality in some detail. The aim will be a fuller presentation of women's economic reality.

Paid Employment: Unequal Work and Pay

The Review and Appraisal document focused on employment observed that "during the period 1976-84 the economic status of women has undergone a profound change in most countries."[12]   Women constitute one third of the world's official labor force. There has been an increase in the number of women working in paid employment in the world's major economic regions.[13] The number of married women with one or more children working outside the household more than doubled during the previous thirty years.

Women enter the paid work force mainly because "of economic necessity and provision of basic needs of the family."[14]   Nearly one third of all households are headed by women, due to rising levels of migration and divorce.[15]   In two-parent families, the man's income alone is often inadequate to provide basic needs. The employment patterns of women are interrelated with family structure, family health, family size, and demographic issues such as migration; in other words,

---

[11] Sivard, p. 6. The third section of this chapter will discuss differences among women within nations, particularly class and race differences.

[12] "Employment," para. 3.

[13] Women's labor force participation was 31% in 1950, 35% in 1985. *State of the World's Women 1985*, p. 9.

[14] "Employment," para. 66.

[15] Sivard, p. 11.

"there is a critical interplay between the productive and reproductive roles of women."[16]

Varied participation in paid work. Labor force participation of women varies among regions of the world. According to the International Labor Organization (ILO), the highest rates of participation of women over 15 years of age are in the Union of Soviet Socialist Republics (58.4%) and other European centrally planned economies (57.8%). The lowest rates of participation are in Latin America (25%) and North Africa (8.5%). In the European market economies, 36% is the estimated participation rate of women over 15; 44.5% in North America; 38.4% in Africa; and 42.6% in Asia.[17] The fastest growing sector of employment at the time of these investigations was women's employment in free trade zones. In Malaysia, for example, 85% of the workers in the Bayan Lepas free trade zone are women ages 18 to 24.[18]

The patterns of employment of women vary between and within various types of economies. The United Kingdom, Portugal, and Denmark are cited as examples of countries with an industrial market economy. In both the United Kingdom and Denmark, women workers are highly concentrated in services, especially sales, while in Portugal women are more highly concentrated in the agricultural sector.[19]

The largest number of women in developing countries continue to work in agriculture or related occupations, although in some "newly industrializing countries" more women are moving away from family farms to wage labor and the number of landless women is increasing.[20] Pakistan and the Philippines show contrasting trends. In Pakistan the highest number of female workers is in the category of unpaid workers,

---

[16] "Employment," para. 67.

[17] Ibid., para. 32. These labor force participation rates show how many women out of every 100 women in the age-group identified are employed for pay in the labor force.

[18] *State of the World's Women*, p. 11.

[19] "Employment," para. 35, 37.

[20] Ibid., para. 43.

as it is in many other Asian countries. The participation rate of women in all sectors of the Philippine economy has increased, while in Pakistan women had shown an increase only in the service sector.[21] In other areas it was difficult to make such comparisons because of the scarcity of data provided by governments.

Women in the centrally planned economy countries are reported to have rapidly improved their qualitative contribution to the economic development of their countries. Women's participation in education, science and cultural and health services is significant in these countries. For example, in the Soviet Union 82% of the labor force in health services is women, 75% in education, and 52% in sciences.[22]

Equal pay for equal work? In many countries women are beginning to move into professions such as medicine and law, but reports show that they generally "do not have access to higher-level, higher-paying jobs involving decision making and managerial skills."[23] Two thirds of the countries replying to the United Nations questionnaire indicated that there was "equal pay for equal work" in new occupations in science and technology in their countries. However, one government confessed that this was only "theoretically;" in actuality women received only 32-41 cents for every dollar earned by a man. Another government said that as the salary scales rose, men only are hired by companies for those positions. As the report concludes, "there may be equal pay for equal work, but there is no equal work."[24]

Further, the impact of technological development may disadvantage working women more than men. Although technological development may make it possible for women to enter occupations such as the metal trade through the elimination of heavy physical work, there is evidence that "technology may push women out of the labour market or into even

---

[21] Ibid., para. 49. Pakistani women challenge this data, as will be discussed in the third section of this chapter.

[22] Ibid., para. 59.

[23] Ibid., para. 100.

[24] *Review and appraisal...*, "Science and technology," para. 28.

less skilled and lower paid jobs." The technical skills required are not equally accessible to women in many areas.[25]

Persistence of wage discrimination. Many governments report formation of policy and legislation to eliminate discrimination against women in the labor force or workplace and to ensure equality of opportunity and treatment between women and men in employment.[26] Yet the data indicates that although there has been some improvement in women's employment status, there still are "tangible and intangible" forms of discrimination against women in employment and occupation patterns. The report concludes that "the actual improvement in the status of women in employment has not measured up to expectations everywhere."[27]

In most parts of the world, marked inequalities in wages between women and men exist. In manufacturing industries women's wages have risen to about three quarters of men's. But there are national variations here. In 1982 Japan had the lowest average in manufacturing, with women earning only 43% of what men earned. Sweden had the highest average, with women earning 90% of what men earned.[28] "In some occupations, the average salary [of men] is more than twice that of women."[29]

Although many industrial market economies have legislative provisions for equal remuneration for work of equal value, "hidden discrimination based on non-technical causes" are difficult to eliminate and thus inequalities in remuneration persist. Legislation has helped reduce the gap in wages between women and men in some countries, such as Portugal. In developing countries, the majority of women are not covered by existing legislation as they work mostly in agriculture, domestic service, or family enterprises. Equal pay legislation is usually

---

[25] "Employment," para. 18.

[26] Ibid., para. 4.

[27] Ibid., para. 6, 8.

[28] *State of the World's Women*, p. 9.

[29] "Employment," para. 100.

limited to the small number of women who work in the organized sector. The socialist countries report that discrimination against women is outlawed. Pay systems are drawn up by factory management in consultation with trade union committees and are solely based on work performance.[30]

Women's work, men's work. Occupational segregation is prevalent in many countries. In developed countries women have a larger proportion of jobs in the service and sales sectors.[31] It is in the service sector in developed countries that occupational segregation is most prevalent. For instance, in Sweden more than 40% of women work in just five of the 270 occupational categories - secretary, nurse's aide, sales worker, cleaner, and children's nurse. Such jobs tend to have lower wages, lower status, longer hours, fewer or no fringe benefits, and less security.[32] Women manufacturing workers in most countries tend to be concentrated in textiles and clothing, leather and footwear, and food processing industries.[33] Countries with centrally planned economies report no "male-dominated" occupations, except for some "arduous" occupations prohibited by law to women.[34]

In developing countries agriculture is the principal employer of women, providing two thirds of the paid jobs for women in the third world in 1980. Industry and services provide roughly equal shares of the rest of the employment of women there. In all three types of employment, women are concentrated in unskilled jobs with low pay and little potential for advancement. In cash cropping women usually do the "back-breaking" work of planting, weeding, and harvesting,

---

[30] Ibid., para. 101-2, 105, 110.

[31] A growing service sector and growing female employment within that sector is characteristic of a large number of countries in industrial market, centrally planned, and developing countries. *Review and appraisal...*, "Monetary factors, services and trade," para. 40.

[32] Sivard, p. 16.

[33] "Employment," para. 16.

[34] These laws may in fact be interpreted as discriminatory by some women, but this possibility is not raised in the document.

while men usually operate whatever mechanical equipment is used. In
industry, women are concentrated in textiles, apparel and electronic
products. In the service sector, women are usually domestics or sell
food and home-grown crops in the informal sector.[35]

The informal sector is a significant factor in third world cities.
Between 20 and 70% of the urban labor force makes a living in this
sector. On the average, over 50% of poor urban populations work in
this sector. In some regions, such as West Africa, the Caribbean and
South Asia, women predominate in the informal sector. In these
regions between 70 and 90% of the farm and fishing products consumed
are bought and sold by women.

These informal trading activities are often the only way for
untrained, unskilled and often illiterate women to earn an independent
income. The formal labor market is often closed to them and they most
likely lack the capital needed to establish a formal business enterprise.[36]
Rural women do engage in a variety of income-generating activities but
their participation in the labor force is constrained by their "lack of
access to land and other resources, lack of control over labor and
income and lack of physical occupational mobility."[37]

Out of work. International Labor Organization estimates and
projections indicate that while more and more women are seeking
employment in most parts of the world, their unemployment continues
to be higher than men, except in the service sector in some countries.[38]
Unemployment rates tripled over the decade in almost all market
countries and women had "a disproportionately high share" of this
unemployment.[39] Many women also do part-time or temporary work,

---

[35] Sivard, p. 15.

[36] *State of the World's Women*, p. 11.

[37] "Employment," para. 19.

[38] *World Survey...Women in Development*, pp. 30-31. In *State of the World's
Women* this difference is attributed to the larger percentage of women in the service
sector, the low wages they receive, and the difficulty of substituting technology for
some of this work - such as teaching or nursing, p. 11.

[39] "Employment," para. 41.

or homework, because they cannot find full-time employment or lack child-care facilities.[40]   Such work is vulnerable or precarious employment, with few if any benefits and little security.

The income level of their household influences women's response to "the employment crisis in the formal sector."

- For fairly prosperous women, what seems to have determined their labour force participation rate is the outcome of the conflict between high consumption demands and the increasing costs of the services that replace domestic work, such as child care and care for dependents in general.

- For the women in households with a medium to low income, the wives of industrial workers who have been dismissed or are earning less money, the decision is usually to join the labour force.   This may push unemployment rates up.   Although hard data are not available on a global basis, it can be fairly assumed that the income they receive from their productive activities is low and unstable and that the increase in women's participation rates is likely to have produced a decrease in their average income.

- For poor women who were already active before the crisis, this has probably meant an even lower income and a heavier work-load.[41]

The impact of the economic crisis on women varies by class, region, and employment sector - agricultural, industrial, or services.

Summary.   The data gathered on women's employment status indicates that although increasing numbers of women are entering the paid labor force, their economic well-being is not assured.   The wage gap between women and men and occupational segregation persist in most industrial market economies and developing countries. Unemployment has increased and further employment opportunities seem to be limited, particularly if the global economic crisis continues.

---

[40] Sivard, p. 14.

[41] *World Survey...Women in Development*,   p. 35.   I have formatted the quotation to improve readability.

Agricultural Production: Overworked and Left Out

Women's participation in agricultural production has been significant. The *State of the World's Women* report indicates that women produce about half the world's food. In parts of Africa, rural women account for 80% of food production.[42] Yet modernization efforts have most always been directed toward men. The Food and Agriculture Organization (FAO) found that "developing countries revealed rather discouraging information about women's access to agricultural education, training, and extension services."[43]

Technology disadvantages women. The introduction of modern agricultural technology was also found to be "primarily aimed at male tasks and used almost exclusively by men, whereas women tend to be left out."[44] When technology is introduced for tasks traditionally done by women, these tasks are often taken over by men - who come to own and operate them, displacing women. In Bangladesh, for instance, rice mills have been introduced that employ only men. Local women who had long gained income by husking rice for better off families have lost this income.[45] In addition to loss of income, women who withdraw from productive work generally find their "bargaining power" both within and outside the family weakened.[46]

Women lose land with "modernization". Large scale commercialization of agriculture and the production of cash crops for export are two major trends in agricultural modernization. Neither has benefitted women as much as men, but the pattern varies from region to region. In Latin America there is a tradition of concentrated land ownership among a small elite. A shift in this pattern has begun with increasing control of prime land by multinational corporations on the

---

[42] Sivard, p. 5.

[43] *State of the World's Women*, p. 6.

[44] *World Survey...Women in Development*, p. 44.

[45] Ibid., p. 46.

[46] Ibid., p. 20.

one hand and on the other some moderate efforts at land redistribution. Traditionally men are employed as farm laborers, with women hired as extra hands at harvest time. Most women are unpaid laborers on their family's land or migrate to town for paid employment. As a result, land redistribution has not usually benefitted women. In Chile, for example, government policy aimed redistribution only at those who had been continuously employed on an estate. Since women are usually hired only at harvest time, most did not qualify to receive land.[47]

In Asia, with the exception of China, there is a condition of land scarcity and increasing landlessness. Almost all women are landless; divorce and inheritance laws prohibit their gaining access to a man's land. High-yielding varieties of seeds, fertilizers, pesticides, irrigation and tractors have been introduced as part of the agricultural development process. The seeds used require more work and it is often women who are employed on large farms to care for them. But their average earnings are significantly less than those of men.[48] In Java, for instance, 56% of women earn under 3,000 rupiants per month while only 14% of men earn so little. If these seeds are grown on family plots, most of the additional work will be done by women, without pay.[49]

In Africa, women had been guaranteed access to land under traditional land use rights. But with colonization, and now with national development projects, these rights have been largely undermined. Land most always has come into men's hands. Men are the ones who have been encouraged to grow recently introduced cash crops, even though women continue to do the great bulk of agricultural work. The FAO concludes that "despite the well-documented, crucial role that women play in food production in this region, agricultural modernization efforts have excluded them, leading to negative

---

[47] Ibid., pp. 44-5.

[48] Ibid., pp. 45-6.

[49] *State of the World's Women*, p. 7.

consequences for food production [and] the perpetuation of rural poverty..."[50]

Decline in food production results. What has been insufficiently recognized is that this exclusion of women from land use and agricultural modernization has been an important factor in the food shortages that have led to famine in Africa. Africa moved from being a net exporter of food in the 1930's to being only 90% self-sufficient in food in the 1960's. When cash crops are introduced to men, food production often declines. Men have claimed the land women had used to grow food for their families and require that women work in the men's cash crop fields rather than growing food on whatever land is left to them. Profits from cash crop production generally go only to the men. Women sometimes passively resist these changes by refusing to turn over their land to their husbands for cash crop production or neglecting the cash crops.[51]

The heavy work load of African women has also contributed to this decline in food production. Many African women work eighteen hour days. In Malawi, women do twice as much work as men on the staple crop maize, an equal amount on the cash crop cotton, and in addition do all domestic work in the home. In Burkina Faso families lost weight during the rainy season because women were too exhausted from working in the fields to cook what food was available. In Zambia the amount of food harvested depends on the amount of work women can manage in the daylight hours, not what the land can yield. After cocoa prices fell sharply, Ghanian men migrated to the cities, leaving women to do all the agricultural work alone. They substituted less nutritious cassava for the traditional yam crop because it took less time to cultivate.[52]

Effective policies require land and resources. When land and resources are made available to women, they have become more productive agriculturally. In Kenya it was found that when women

---

[50] *World Survey...Women in Development*, p. 47.

[51] *State of the World's Women*, p. 8.

[52] Ibid.

were given the same level of help as men, they produced bigger harvests. All-women cooperative farms and rural credit programs have been successful in Vietnam, Bangladesh and India. Yet the FAO charges that "policy-makers and international experts have persistently resisted the idea of all-women's cooperatives."[53] The FAO concludes that "it is virtually impossible to identify any country in which national strategies have generally benefitted women's role in agriculture."[54] Yet when women have benefitted financially from their agricultural work, their children also benefit. Studies in Bangladesh and Burkina Faso have shown that when women have extra time or money, they use it to improve the health and well-being of their children.[55]

Summary. Women's work in food production is critical to the well-being of their families and societies. Yet many women who work in agriculture are overworked and unpaid. Furthermore, agricultural modernization has left them out as technology, training, credit and land goes to men for cash crop production. However, as the *World Survey* points out, these results cannot be attributed to the modernization process itself; "rather, it is the social conditions in which modernization takes place that cause more of the benefits to accrue to men than to women."[56]

Here, as with the inequitable benefits women receive from their work in the paid labor force, "cultural values and norms on sexual roles ... have a profound effect on women's inequality..." According to United Nations analysts, these values and norms are "important variables" that support and reinforce "fundamental inequalities in the economic sphere."[57] A related factor is that much of the work women do is undercounted and underreported.

---

[53] *World Survey...Women in Development*, p. 54.

[54] Ibid., p. 53.

[55] *State of the World's Women*, p. 9.

[56] *World Survey...Women in Development*, p. 34.

[57] Ibid. An indepth discussion of the relation of sex-roles norms and political economic structures is a main theme of chapters four and five of this study.

When Women's Work Does Not Count:
Hidden Sources of Bias in Data Conceptualization
and in Theoretical Assumptions Underlying Reporting

A crucial factor in relation to women's participation in the economy is that much of the work they do is not counted, or defined as "economic activity." It is mainly in the areas of unpaid family labor and household work that this underestimation and underevaluation happens. Among the tasks excluded from the accepted definition of economic activity are work in subsistence agriculture, provision of water and fuel, animal husbandry, and producing food for family use even though such tasks are significant contributions to meeting families' basic needs.

The consequences of this exclusion were delineated by the United Nations:

> This underestimation and underevaluation has serious consequences for women and their families, for development concepts and strategies and for value systems which form the basis of socio-economic decisions. Not assigning an economic value to women's work results in undercounting and under-reporting and, therefore, the value of women's work is underestimated by society.[58]

Underestimation of women's work leads to their exclusion from development plans, such as access to extension, credit and training.

Problems in data gathering. Data gathering methods contribute to the underestimation of the amount and value of women's work. Researchers in various United Nations agencies have analyzed the extent of the underestimation of women's participation in the labor force. In a study for the International Labor Organization, Lourdes Beneria identified three key sources in the data - the definition used in determining who is an unpaid family worker, the practice of classifying data only by "main occupation," and failure to take into account market oriented activities carried out in or near the home, such as selling food and drinks or cloth and handicrafts.[59]

---

[58] "Employment," para. 10.

[59] Lourdes Beneria, "Accounting for Women's Work," *Women and Development: The Sexual Division of Labour in Rural Societies*, edited by Lourdes

In many countries a person is counted as "an unpaid family worker" only if she or he has worked a minimum of fifteen hours during the two weeks prior to a census. As women's unpaid family work, particularly in agriculture, may be seasonal she will not be counted as an active worker if the census is taken during a "slow season." Elise Boulding has reported a similar pattern of under-reporting of farm wives in the United States who are unpaid family workers, as the census is taken in mid-March - a slow season on most farms.[60]

Women's main occupation often is classified as housewife, even though they may be engaged in considerable work outside the domicile. Beneria cites a study in India which estimates that this practice reduced women's labor force participation rate from about 23% to 13%.[61] Thus the statistics cited in the previous section as to women's labor force participation need to be viewed cautiously and in the documents themselves are given only as "estimates."

The United Nations Research and Training Institute for the Advancement of Women (INSTRAW) has identified additional factors in the underestimating of women's agricultural work:

> In all regions of the world, women are performing agricultural tasks which are not usually separated from household work and therefore not assigned any economic value or recognition.... Both in developed countries, where the work of rural women is often known as "pluriactivity," and in developing countries, where it relates to subsistence agriculture, they do not generally have employment status since their work is dependent upon those who own, control and manage agricultural activity. Most women do not own land in their own right and do not control the inputs such as water, fertilizers and technology to monitor agricultural productivity. The number of work hours performed by women on most agricultural activity is under-reported for various reasons including inadequacies in: the methodology of designing household surveys, census enumeration and techniques of interviewing women.[62]

Beneria (New York: Praeger Publishers, 1982).

[60] Elise Boulding, untitled, *Women at Work*, Number One (1981), pp. 8-9.

[61] Beneria, p. 122.

[62] INSTRAW, *Women in Economic Activity: A Global Statistical Survey*, 1985, p. 11.

Women's activities in the informal sector are often linked to agriculture, particularly in developing countries. These activities include agricultural processing and storage and taking home-produced goods to market. Women's contributions to this sector are also underreported, for similar reasons.[63]

What counts as economic activity? An even more profound question has been raised about the very definition of economic activity on which labor force participation is based. Current definitions presume that

> activities that - according to the United Nations - result in goods or services which are included in the SNA [national income statistics], i.e. included in GNP [gross national product] statistics and hence related to wage or salary employment and/or entrepreneurial profit, are considered to be "economic" (and therefore labour force) activities; other activities are considered to be "non-economic" (and therefore non-labour force) activities.[64]

Such presumptions particularly underestimate labor force participation in areas where the market has not penetrated so deeply, as in much of the third world, but unpaid domestic labor in industrialized countries is also excluded by this definition.[65]

Recognizing this problem, the International Labor Organization has attempted to broaden the definition of economic activity. The Thirteenth International Conference of Labor Statisticians, meeting in 1982, acknowledged that economic activity *is* defined when measuring the economically active population in terms of production of goods and services. The definition of production was expanded so that "tending a garden, poultry, or dairy for household consumption may be considered an economic activity; other unpaid household work such as

---

[63] Ibid., p. 10.

[64] Richard Anker, "Female labour force participation in developing countries: A critique of current definitions and data collection methods," *International Labour Review* 122, (Nov.-Dec., 1983), p. 712. For an illuminating critical discussion of the UN "sna's," see Marilyn Waring, *If Women Counted: A New Feminist Economics* (San Francisco: Harper and Row, 1988).

[65] Beneria discusses this problem in her article, p. 122.

countries, most socialist countries did not participate in preparation of alternative reports. Asian socialist countries did not respond to requests for country reports for the alternative Asian report. As no European alternative report was prepared, the voices of women from European capitalist, mixed economy, and socialist countries are not represented in these alternative perspectives.

Yet even with the absence of these perspectives, the alternative reports prepared for the NGO Forum at the end of the Decade for Women represent the most inclusive account available of women's reality. This is an emerging literature - women's own analysis will continue to develop. In this section, I attend to these collective voices to identify the various types of critiques being made and the emerging issues not usually addressed as relevant to economic life that these women think need to be engaged to lessen their vulnerability.

Emerging Arab Voices: Assumptions Challenged

A review of the Decade for Women was prepared by the Women's Studies in the Arab World program at Beirut University College. A broad sketch of Arab women's reality shows that women have entered all fields of employment, but few occupy leadership positions. and that although the number of university women has increased, about 80% of Arab women are still illiterate.[79]

Some Arab women question the worth of integrating women into development. An editorial in the Women's Studies journal observes that

> new research findings from Third World countries are demonstrating empirically that the integration of women in development does not necessarily take into account their well being or their special needs. Further, some Arab researchers have even come to challenge the assumptions that there is a positive correlation between "education," "women's labor force participation," and "development."[80]

---

[79] Rose Ghurayyib, "Reviewing the Decade for Women in Arab Countries," *Al-raida* (February 1, 1985), pp. 7-9.

[80] Wafa' Stephan, "Editorial," *Al-raida*, p. 3.

Challenges to integration of women in development as a strategy for improving women's well-being are also raised by other women around the globe.

Emerging African Voices: Our Burdens Increase

Two hundred forty women representing twenty-one countries and 46 NGO's gathered for the African NGO meeting to decide on priority issues and a common approach to them.   Drought, desertification, international economic recession, the low level of industrialization and technology are among the severe problems identified as facing the continent.   The women insist that the participation and freedom of all Africa's people is critical to development.   They note that strategies for African development, particularly the Lagos Plan of Action, have called for improvement in the status of women and the need to change cultural attitudes towards women.[81]

The obstacles to African women's full participation in development are identified as:

> lack of involvement of women in planning; lack of education and human resources development; the weight of history; lack of peace (with the related problems of apartheid and refugees); lack of technology and resources in the fields of agriculture, industry and management of the environment.[82]

---

[81] Jane L. Parpart has written an appreciative, but critical review of the Lagos Plan.   While applauding the Plan's attention to women, she insists that simply calling for sexual equality is inadequate.   Specific programs which address land ownership, access to credit, payment for labor in production of family cash crops, and other critical problems are also essential.   *African Women and Development: Gender in the Lagos Plan of Action*, Michigan State University WID Series, 1985, Working Paper #87, p. 10.

[82] *African Women Link: A Development Newsletter* 1, no. 3, (1985) p. 2. South African women at Forum 85 insisted that it must be recognized that "women of South Africa suffer triple oppression - classism, racism and sexism." Lindine Mobuza of the African National Congress quoted in *Forum 85* (Nairobi), Tuesday, July 23, 1985, p. 2.

Several issues are lifted up for further attention. These include the needs of rural women, particularly as they relate to food production, access to resources, and lessening women's burden; looking anew at income generating activities for women; and a redefinition of the concept of development itself.

Questions raised by the Association of African Women for Research and Development (AAWORD) more clearly articulate some of these issues. Most critical is the question "do programmes designed for women enable them to become self-reliant or do they in fact increase their burden?" AAWORD charges that some community-based and income-generating programs promoted by international donors are "even more exploitative of women and further increased their burden." These programs are based "on the ideology of the sexual division of labor," and thus depend on women's unpaid or underpaid labor for their success.[83]

Emerging Asian Voices: Exploitation Abounds

The Asian Women's alternative report is appropriately entitled "Asian Women Speak Out!"[84] Its objective is to evaluate the Decade for Women from the perspective of equality and justice, rather than mere growth. The most important point of the report, its authors insist, is "the fact that the nature of development that the women were going to be integrated into was not questioned" during the Decade for Women. The western capitalist growth model and the new development

---

[83] "Report of the AAWORD Working Group on Women and Reproduction in Africa," *Echo* 1, no. 1 (1986), p. 6. Parpet also raises questions about these income generating projects as they organize "economically marginal handicraft and/or food production that permit women to supplement household budgets while continuing to carry the double burden of reproductive and productive labor." Parpet contends that these projects are popular because they are politically safe and do not require commitment to redistribution or more fundamental change. Parpet, p. 8.

[84] The Asian Women's Research and Action Network coordinated the preparation of this report, in consultation with the Women and Development Network of Australia, the Pacific Asian Women's Forum, and the Pacific Women's Resource Bureau. Copies of the report were distributed at Forum 85 in Nairobi.

strategies has been accepted without criticism as appropriate for the
Third World. The report charges that

> No model, neither the economic growth model nor the Marxist model, has
> addressed the problem of patriarchy. Society's acceptance of male domination
> and control of women by men has pervaded development work. Traditional
> patriarchal structures of society have not been questioned.... Women have
> become doubly oppressed, at work and at home.[85]

Furthermore, women's oppression is not examined and violence against
women is not discussed by development planners.

The majority of Asian women are poor, the report asserts. They
are more hungry, less healthy, and less literate than Asian men. Across
Asia - in both developed and developing economies - women earn less
than men, work longer hours, and are shunted into temporary,
supplementary or secondary jobs. Women in Asia wield little or no
political power, whether their countries are democracies or
authoritarian.   Marriage, property, citizenship and employment
lawsdiscriminate against them.[86]

Women from several Asian countries testified to the invisibility of
women in national statistics discussed above and added to the reasons
for this situation. Pakistani women contend that in their country men
deny that women work, even when they do, with the result that official
data is falsified. Husbands deny that their wives work and community
leaders or factory owners claim that they have no women workers when
one can see women working in the fields, on construction sites, or in
factories.   As a result only 176 women are listed as working in
agricultural and animal husbandry out of 18.3 million rural women,
many of whom actually do agricultural work.[87]

---

[85] Hema Goonatilake, "The Framework of the Alternative Asian Report, *Asian
Women Speak Out!,* p. 3.

[86] Pakistani women reported to *Depthnews Women's Features*, (May 5, 1985),
pp. 1-4, their loss of legal rights with the changes in the legal structure of their
country.

[87] *Asian Women Speak Out!*, p. 11.

The report discusses the negative impact of various development strategies on women. The creation of "free trade zones" or "export processing zones" is a central development strategy used by some developing countries. In the Philippines, single young women are recruited for employment in these zones. They make up 70% of the workforce in these zones. Their hourly wage is the lowest of any Asian country processing zone at the time of the report - 30 cents US in electronics factories and 17 cents US in garment factories. The average length of stay of a female zone worker is about three years, after which she leaves usually because of deteriorating physical and mental health from occupation disease and hazards. Indian women also testified to the poor working conditions of women in such zones in their country. They cite chemical hazards, improper ventilation, and some factory uniforms as causing respiratory ailments, deteriorating eyesight, burns, ulcers, fatal liver and kidney diseases, and miscarriages and birth defects.

Some countries send their workers abroad, as there are not enough jobs in the home country. In Sri Lanka 80% of migrant women workers are housemaids. Their income has improved the standard of living of their families. But as the alternative report points out, many have received "inhuman treatment" - beatings, rape, sexual harassment, excessive work, and low pay. Testimony from India also speaks of rape and sexual molestation of women. In most cases these sexual crimes are linked to caste and communal riots, class struggle or repression by the state in an attempt to demoralize mass movements.

Prostitution is used to develop tourist industries, particularly in Thailand and the Philippines. "The sex tourism industry is a blatant form of exploitation of women in the Third World."[88] About 10% of the Thai female population between 14 and 24 years of age work as prostitutes or masseuses. Prostitution in the Philippines is related to sex tourism and the presence of US military bases.

The report from Japan describes a new phenomenon called "Japanese sex tours come home." A sudden rise in the number of women entering Japan from countries struggling with mounting foreign

---

[88] Ibid., p. 14.

debts has been noted. "The difficult circumstances in their countries push more and more women out of their countries."[89] Organized crime syndicates are reported to be behind the Asian sex traffic, engaging in highly profitable smuggling operations which buy both women and contraband. The question of prostitution has been one of the more controversial issues during the Decade.[90] Some third world women criticize Western feminists who organize against "female sex slavery" for not analyzing or criticizing the economic circumstances which push women into prostitution or the role the state plays in pimping.[91] These reports from women in Asian countries help clarify the connections.

Emerging Latin American Voices: Subordination Continues

Representatives from thirty-nine countries meeting in November of 1984 saw little progress for Latin American women during the Decade for Women. They argue that the Decade has not been enough to end discrimination against women, pointing to the double work day of mothers, the difficulty of finding child care, and women's work in "secondary activities" with wages only 60% of men's as examples of ongoing discrimination. The women insist that inequality, oppression, and subordination continue - even though their forms may have changed. The fact that the great majority of actions undertaken during

---

[89] Ibid.

[90] Some of these critics contend that this organizing activity is a way of keeping third world women "from tapping metropolitan money." For instance, see the article by Fanbutteh Fahnbulleh in *Third World Women's News* 1, no. 1 (1986), pp. 17-22. Fahnbulleh's charges about Western feminists are based on discussions at the 1980 Mid-Decade Conference and Forum in Copenhagen.

[91] Elizabeth Bounds made similar criticisms of this first world radical feminist analysis, noting further the way such analysis denies the possibility of agency and self-determination to women who are prostitutes. Elizabeth Bounds, "Sexuality and Economic Reality: A First and Third World Comparison," paper presented at the American Academy of Religion, Chicago, Illinois, 20 November 1988.

the Decade has been initiated by women's organizations themselves is seen as hopeful.[92]

A declaration entitled "Our Struggle Continues" was issued by Caribbean and Latin American women during Forum 85. The women contend that although they had assumed responsibility for the challenges of the plan for the Decade and participate in joint and autonomous struggles, they still are "subjected to patriarchal relations which place obstacles in the path of our own liberation."[93]

The declaration charges that the conditions in which Latin and Caribbean people live are affected by the grave world economic crisis of capitalism and declare that they are not willing to pay for the effects of the economic crisis with greater suffering and humiliation. They contend that this crisis has a greater effect on women, in both the public and private spheres, as money which went to service the region's foreign debt was taken from development and social service projects, such as employment, housing, education, health and alleviation of hunger. Women usually are the majority of social service workers and poor women and their children are primary users of many of these programs.

Fempress, a Chilean news agency, reported on sources of oppression that are not openly discussed in Latin America. Abuse, battering and rape of women are an "open secret" acknowledged only by women's organizations. Many women die from illegal abortions. Women's domestic responsibilities are not shared, even when women are employed outside the home. Although legislation assumes that the man is the head of the house, in some countries more than half of the households are headed by women. The article reported that Latin women question the purpose of their integration into development by

---

[92] "Decade - Mujer," *Alternativas, Organo de Dirusion del Centro de Promocion y Accion de la Mujer, Lima, P*eru, no date.

[93] The complete text in Spanish was published in *Forum 85* (Nairobi), Friday, July 29, 1985, p. 2; an English translation summary was published in *Womanspeak: Quarterly Newsletter about Caribbean Women*, Number 18 (July/December 1985), pp. 27-28.

asking "what kind of development?" and claiming that "we women have always been an essential part of development..."[94]

Emerging U.S. Voices: Our Status Deteriorates

Alternative reports from U.S. women were prepared by The Women's Coalition for Nairobi (WCN) and the International Council of African Women (ICAW). WCN, a multi-racial coalition of women from women's, civic, labor, peace, political, and religious organizations, held hearings to investigate the status of women in the United States, with a particular focus on the condition of poor and moderate income women and women of color. The report they prepared insists that "the status of women in the United States is not improving: *our status is deteriorating.*"[95]

In support of this charge, The Women's Coalition observes the rise in poverty among women and children in the US: nine million more people, a 35% increase, sank below the poverty line between 1979 and 1983. Families headed by women are disproportionately poor, making up nearly half of all families below the poverty line and more than half of all female-maintained black and Hispanic families. The Coalition also notes that poverty rates for black women are three times those of white women and that unemployment rates for black men are three times the rate for white men.[96]

Cutbacks in government programs for the poor fall most heavily on people of color, the coalition reported. People of color have the highest

---

[94] Adriana Santa Cruz, "Ten Years of Progress - But Still more to be Achieved," *Third World Women's News*, pp. 24-26.

[95] The Women's Coalition for Nairobi, *The Effects of Racism and Militarization on Women's Equality*, 1985, p. 1. The Coalition contends that this document is essential for the work in Nairobi as it counteracts the fantasies presented by the Reagan administration delegation. Maureen Reagan, head of the official US delegation, reported "dramatic progress" for US women during the Decade in her statement to the Conference, July 16, 1985. Although she mentioned "cultural, sociological and economic barriers" to political equality for women, the only specific problems she discussed were functional illiteracy and domestic violence.

[96] Ibid., pp. 14-5.

unemployment rate, the highest poverty rate, the highest rate of homelessness and the least access to health care. Cuts in welfare, food stamp and school meal programs, and maternal and child health programs all fall more heavily on women and children.

The impact of U.S. foreign policy and U.S.-controlled multinational corporations on peoples around the world is discussed. The coalition contends that racism is "a key factor" in US economic policies at home and abroad.

> Racism has been historically profitable since the first Europeans expropriated the land from its original inhabitants, the Native Americans. Today, with violations of treaty rights and land-use, the US government continues land and resource expropriation from Native Americans. Historically, racism rationalized a slave system which provided unpaid labor for the slaveowners; today, racism is used to maintain an unequal wage gap and expanding pool of surplus labor of Afro-Americans and other people of color, and depresses the wages of all working people.... The drive for maximum profits maintains racism and sends US corporations to exploit the labor of women, children and men in the Philippines, the Caribbean, Haiti, Mexico and other countries with low-paid labor, markets and raw materials, and a political climate favorable to the transnationals.[97]

The coalition observes that women of color have even lower wages and face both racial and gender oppression. They conclude that unless the effects of racism are analyzed, hope for equality and development will be useless.

The International Council of African Women, with support from Native American, Hispanic, Filipino, Asian and African women in the United States, drafted The Women of Color Plan of Action for the Nairobi Conference and Forum. Families and children, opposition to oppression of lesbians, support for reproductive freedom, and opposition to violence against women are among their areas of concern. Their conception of violence against women includes "race and class violence" such as "housing displacement, economic exploitation, and

---

[97] Ibid., pp. 7-8.

forced sterilization" as well as "sexual violence" such as assault, battery, rape, pornography and sexual harassment on the job.[98]

The Council criticizes statistical indicators and development strategies:

> Data collection methods are largely based on the mythical Western assumption defining work: it is performed only for money and it is only located outside the home, in the "modern" sector. Governments must deal with the fact that women perform at least two roles in society - worker and caretaker. This latter role is essential to family well-being. Statistics and governments don't incorporate the contributions of women to national economies outside of their acknowledged participation in the "official" labor force. Thus, no programs are effectively planned for us and no projects adequately benefit us.[99]

They further charge that development projects and strategies have not closed "the gap between rich and poor nations, rich and poor classes within nations, and the earning capacity of women and men."

Summary: The Silence is Broken

In breaking the silence about their lives, women around the globe insist that the interstructuring of gender, race, and class oppression; patriarchal family and social relations; and the connections between prostitution, violence against women, and the political economy are particularly critical issues that intensify their economic vulnerability that are not addressed in official governmental reports.

Women are deeply critical of efforts to integrate them into development as this incorrectly presumes that women are not already contributing to development and that present development models are beneficial to women and poor people. Women are challenging the very definition and organization of work, economy, and development.

---

[98] ICAW, "Women of Color Plan of Action," *African Women Rising*, p. 4. ICAW's report also included a discussion of the deterioration of women's status similar to that of the Women's Coalition for Nairobi.

[99] Ibid., p. 2.

Common Threads Bind:
A Summary Sketch of Women's Economic Reality

The collective voices of governments, of United Nations agencies, of nongovernmental organizations, and of women's groups from around the world are beginning to give accounts of women's economic reality. What is becoming evident is that differences among women of race, ethnicity, class, culture, nationality, rural or urban location all shape women's lives and frequently divide them.

Yet common threads of suffering are identified in these sources. Women do contribute to their family's and society's well-being, but these contributions are underestimated and undervalued. Their wage labor is not equitably reimbursed and their domestic labor is unpaid. Women everywhere are held responsible for domestic labor, and men seldom share this responsibility even when women are in the paid labor force. Thus many of the world's women work a double day. Women are marginalized in public decision-making, whether in trade unions, development planning, or governmental bodies.

The findings from a series of international workshops on the impact of the world crisis on women aptly describes many women's reality:

> It is clear that the majority of the world's women have been affected by the global crisis in a fundamental and profound manner and yet the seriousness of their plight remains largely unrecognized and underestimated. In reviewing the workshop reports it is evident that despite the vast diversity in women's cultural and socio-economic conditions around the world there are *common threads of powerlessness, of marginality and of dispossession* that bind them to *their subordinate position in society.*[100]

---

[100] These workshops were held by the Society for International Development. The findings were reported in the society's newsletter, *Compass*, Number 27 (April 1986), p. 1, emphasis added. The universality of women's subordination, the report concluded, was "best exemplified in the usage of women's labour as a 'shock-absorber' for tensions resulting from unemployment and instability due to the ongoing transformation of work." This explanation of women's subordination will be evaluated in the fifth chapter of this study.

Women are beginning to organize themselves and network with each other to challenge their subordination and to improve their own lives and their communities - locally, nationally, regionally, and globally.

These accounts of women's economic reality are relevant to the work of Christian economic ethics. My thesis is that recognition of these emerging voices and their concerns is required if Christian economic ethics is to adequately address the impoverishment of women. The next step of our study is to go back and measure progressive Christian economic ethics from the resistance to invisibility that begins to emerge in the literature reviewed here.

PART TWO

INVISIBILITY OF WOMEN'S
ECONOMIC VULNERABILITY
IN PROGRESSIVE CHRISTIAN ETHICS

In Part Two I will examine the social teachings on economic life of the Roman Catholic Church and the World Council of Churches, which I take to be the most progressive Christian sources for an ethic of global economic justice, in light of the global impoverishment of women. I will demonstrate that women's economic vulnerability is at best marginal and often invisible in this teaching.

CHAPTER TWO

ROMAN CATHOLIC SOCIAL TEACHING
ON ECONOMIC LIFE
IN RELATION TO WOMEN'S REALITY

Contemporary Roman Catholic social teaching has consistently addressed questions of economic justice. Three primary social models are present in much of this teaching: 1) traditional, 2) liberal and 3) radical. For our purposes, specific theoretical assumptions about economic life in these various models need to be clarified.

Traditional social theory is grounded in natural law philosophy. A central characteristic is its understanding of society as a "single organic social fabric, organized around the 'common good.'"[1] Thus it is

---

[1] Joe Holland and Peter Henriot, S.J., *Social Analysis: Linking Faith and Justice*, Revised and Enlarged Edition (Maryknoll, NY: Orbis Books, 1983), p. 32. My discussion of these analytic frameworks also draws on Hobgood, Chapter One in *Paradigms in Conflict: Economic Theory in Catholic Social Teaching*, pp. 1-100; David Gordon, *Problems in Political Economy,* Second Edition (Lexington, MA: D.C. Heath and Company, 1977); Elaine Donovan and Mary Huff Stevenson,

difficult to identify assumptions specific to economic life. However, its general assumptions inform analysis of and proposals for economic life, particularly its insistence on the right of every person to the conditions necessary for a dignified human life and the responsibility of all to the common good. The vision of the just society in traditional theory is hierarchical; order and harmony are basic social virtues.

Assumptions about economic life in liberal social theory are grounded in neo-classical economic theory, which posits market exchange - the buying and selling of commodities and labor - as the central human economic activity. Capitalist institutions such as private ownership of the means of production and wage relations between owner and worker are conceptualized as "natural." In general, this theory contends that market exchange is an efficient and fair distribution of resources and goods. However, liberals recognize that factors such as racial or sexual discrimination may impede what is perceived as the self-correcting character of the market. Government intervention is proposed to correct such factors. Just distribution and equal opportunity are key normative criteria.

Radical social theory draws on neo-Marxian socio-economic theories, which posit production as the central human economic activity. "Class" is a central category of analysis which refers to who controls wealth within capitalist economies. Class relations are perceived to be antagonistic social relations created by wage dependency, and the fact that owners, not workers, determine the aims of production and gain advantage from workers. Radical theory rejects the liberal presupposition that there is, in fact, autonomy between the political and economic spheres and argues that without social ownership and control of the means of production, political power will always function to protect economic power and privilege. The aim of political action must, from this perspective, be the control of economic power through

---

Loud: Women and Poverty in the United States, ed. Rochelle Lefkowitz and Ann Withorn (New York: Pilgrim Press, 1986), pp. 47-60; and Howard M. Wachtel, "Looking at Poverty from Radical, Conservative and Liberal Perspectives," *Poverty and Economic Justice: A Philosophical Approach*, ed. Robert H. Hartman (New York: Paulist Press, 1984), pp. 200-13.

democratic political processes. Full and effective participation is a central normative criterion.

I contend that there has been a shift in Roman Catholic social teaching from primary reliance on traditional organic presuppositions grounded in static conceptions of natural law to a historical social analysis of the political economy informed by liberal and radical presuppositions. Although a full exposition of this claim is beyond the scope of this study, I am convinced that a radical perspective more fully accounts for and addresses the sources of economic injustice in the present political economy.[2]

While the movement to recognizing the radical obligations for economic justice overall has been constructive, this teaching has not touched the radicality of the economic vulnerability of women. I argue that a primary reason for this is the perpetuation of a static natural law conception of women's nature. I will demonstrate that this is the case even in the teachings which most consistently draw on radical social theory.

To understand the depth of this problem, it is necessary to begin our examination with the earliest documents of contemporary social teaching. The first task of this chapter is a critical review of papal and conciliar teaching since 1891 to reveal the marginality of women's economic vulnerability in this teaching. The second task is an examination of recent teaching from regional conferences of bishops in which women's economic vulnerability is highlighted to assess its adequacy in addressing the sources of women's impoverishment.

---

[2] Some of my reasons for this conviction will become apparent in the course of this study. For a full exposition of this claim, see the study by Ellison, *The Center Cannot Hold*, and Hobgood, Chapter 5, *Paradigms in Conflict*, pp. 259-89.

Organic Perspectives on Economic Life:
Leo XIII and Pius XII

Leo XIII

Modern Catholic social teaching originated with the Papal Encyclical *Rerum Novarum* (The Condition of Labor) issued by Leo XIII on May 15, 1891. Concerned with the "miserable and wretched conditions" in which many workers lived and the appeal that socialism held for them, Leo endeavored to prevent class struggle by articulating the rights and duties of workers, employers, and the state.

Property, wages, and the common good. Leo draws on natural law to articulate "the economy of duties and rights according to Christian philosophy." In this economy, "the goods of nature and the Gifts of Divine Grace belong in common and without distinction to all human kind..." But this does not constitute an argument against private property. Leo sharply criticizes "the socialists" for the abolition of private ownership as private ownership is a natural right.[3]

Both workers and employers share the right to private property. Workers' other rights include the right to work, a just wage, the right to form workers' associations, and care for the poor. The rights of employers include no crushing taxes and the right to form private societies for private advantage.

Concern for harmony and order is evident in Leo's description of the duties of workers and the poor:

> to perform entirely and conscientiously whatever work has been voluntarily and equitably agreed upon; not in any way to injure the property or to harm the person of employers; in protecting their own interests, to refrain from violence and never to engage in rioting.[4]

---

[3] *Rerum Novarum*, in *Justice in the Marketplace*, paragraphs 38-9, 10. References subsequent to the first mention of a text of papal and conciliar documents will be given by the initials of the Latin name of the text and the paragraph number.

[4] RN 30.

Some of the duties of employers are also restraints: not to treat workers "as slaves," not to impose more work than strength can endure, not to tamper with worker's savings, "either by coercion, or by fraud, or by the arts of usury..." Employers are also obliged to let workers attend to family and religious obligations.[5]

The principal duty of the employer, however, is to pay a just wage:

> Assuredly, to establish a rule of pay in accord with justice, many factors must be taken into account. But, in general, the rich and employers should remember that no laws, either human or divine, permit them for their own profit to oppress the needy and the wretched or to seek gain from another's want.[6]

Leo asks if the observance of these duties would not remove "the bitterness and causes of conflict." The church's aim in this, he asserts, is to unite "all the classes of society" in protecting the interests of workers. The state is also charged with responsibility to "show proper concern for the worker" and to support measures that would benefit the condition of workers.[7]

Leo defends natural inequalities and a natural hierarchy as a fact of human existence:

> There are great and very many natural differences among men. Neither the talents, nor the skill, nor the health, nor the capacities of all are the same, and unequal fortune follows of itself upon necessary inequality in respect to these endowments.[8]

These differences are to be accepted, as "in civil society the lowest cannot be made equal with the highest." This condition has been adapted to benefit all, Leo insists, for different aptitudes and services are required to carry on the affairs of community life. The end of civil society concerns "absolutely all members of society, since the end of

---

[5] RN 32.

[6] RN 32.

[7] RN 51.

[8] RN 26.

civil society is centered in the common good, in which latter, one and all in due proportion have a right to participate."[9]

Women, family and "nature." A sketch of Leo's conception of women's economic reality can be drawn from his discussion of the economy of rights and duties. In describing protections for workers, Leo makes clear what women's work should be:

> Certain occupations likewise are less fitted for women, who are intended by nature for work of the home - work indeed which especially protects modesty in women and accords by nature with the education of children and the well-being of the family.[10]

The male worker is to receive a "wage sufficiently large to enable him to provide comfortably for himself, his wife and his children...[11] This principle came to be called "the family wage," a principle still used in Catholic social teaching.

Leo teaches that the family wage should be large enough so that if a worker is thrifty, he could buy property. Leo thought that ownership of property would lead to "a more equitable division of goods" and lessen the gulf between the classes. Leo makes clear that this right to own property, although "bestowed on individual persons by nature, must be assigned to man in his capacity as head of a family." Through property ownership, a father can provide for his offspring and through inheritance transmit it to his children, who "in a sense continue his person." Leo further teaches that the family, like the state, is a society; it is governed by "its own proper authority, namely by that of the father."[12]

Leo defends the family against intervention by civil power, on the grounds that the family is prior to civil society. "It follows that its rights and duties are also prior and more in conformity with nature."

---

[9] RN 71. Note that this is not a claim to *equal* rights to participation, but *proportional* participation in keeping with the hierarchical ordering of society.

[10] RN 60.

[11] RN 65.

[12] RN 66, 19-21.

Leo charges that "the Socialists" replace parental care with care by the state, thus acting "against natural justice" and dissolving "the structure of the home." Leo teaches that a "properly ordered family life" contributes to the prosperity of the state.[13]

Pius XI

Pius XI's encyclical *Quadragesimo Anno* (The Reconstruction of the Social Order, May 15, 1931) is the next major document of social teaching. In light of the widespread depression and further development of class society, this encyclical called for a reconstruction of the social order in accordance with the principles of equity, just distribution, and social charity - the "union of minds and hearts."[14]

Just distribution of wealth and power. Pius generally follows the direction set by Leo in *Rerum Novarum* in regard to property, wages, and the common good. However, in response to changed conditions, he stresses the social responsibility of ownership of property and the right of the state to bring "private ownership into harmony with the needs of the common good."[15]

Pius also more directly challenges economic concentration. He contends that "the riches which are so abundantly produced in our age of industrialism ... are not rightly distributed and equitably made available to the various classes of the people." The "norms of the common good, that is, social justice" require not only just wages but also a just distribution of wealth, as both capital and labor contribute to its creation.[16]

Pius criticizes concentration of power in the hands of the state. Although the state is charged with promoting the common good, this responsibility is to be shared with "lesser and subordinate organizations"

---

[13] RN 20-1, 48.

[14] *Quadragesimo Anno*, in *Justice in the Marketplace*, para. 136.

[15] QA 49.

[16] QA 58.

such as town, industrial and professional associations. This teaching is identified as the principle of subsidiarity: decisionmaking and responsibility are to be lodged as close as possible to local communities and institutions. The state, freed from these responsibilities, can more effectively "protect and defend" the social order and strive with other nation states "to promote by wisely conceived pacts and institutions a prosperous and happy international cooperation in economic life."[17]

Pius follows Leo's teaching on the family. He advocates the family wage "for the father" as a just wage, although he contends that other family members may also help support the family. He cautions that

> to abuse the years of childhood and the limited strength of women is grossly wrong. Mothers, concentrating on household duties, should work primarily in the home or in its immediate vicinity. It is an intolerable abuse, and to be abolished at all cost, for mothers on account of the father's low wage to be forced to engage in gainful occupations outside the home to the neglect of their proper cares and duties, especially the training of children.[18]

Pius does not consider the possibility that household duties might overtax the supposedly limited strength of women. Cooking, cleaning, laundry and other such activities are usually exhausting tasks, as is work in the fields. It is doubtful that women's health is the issue at stake here.

True or false equality for women?   An examination of Pius' encyclical *Casti connubi* (On Christian Marriage, December 31, 1930) illumines his presuppositions about women.   In this encyclical he discusses and evaluates demands for the emancipation of women. Pius teaches that adherents of emancipation call for threefold change - physiological, social, and economic:

> physiological, that is to say, the woman is to be freed at her own good pleasure from the burdensome duties properly belonging to a wife as companion and mother; social, inasmuch as the wife being freed from the care of children and family, should, to the neglect of these, be able to follow her own bent and devote herself to business and even public affairs; finally

---

[17] QA 79-80, 89.

[18] QA 71.

economic, whereby the woman even without the knowledge and against the wish of her husband may be at liberty to conduct and administer her own affairs, giving her attention chiefly to these rather than to children, husband and family.[19]

Pius contends that these freedoms would mean "the debasing of the womanly character and the dignity of motherhood." In contrast to this "false equality" which he denounces, Pius affirms "a true equality" in the dignity of women and men.[20]

Pius teaches that any change in the civil rights of a married woman must always give regard to "the natural disposition and temperament of the female sex, good morality, and the welfare of the family." In addition, the "essential order of the domestic society - the authority of the husband and the obedience of the wife - is to "remain intact" as it is founded "on the authority and wisdom of God."[21] Pius fears women's economic and social independence and assumes that it would be used against the family. Thus he insists on continuing women's economic dependency.

Critical Assessment

The organic presuppositions of this early Catholic social teaching laid a foundation for criticism of the condition of workers in industrialized capitalist societies, as the common good limits individual rights to use and control of private property and profit. However organic presuppositions, particularly the concern for order and harmony and the acceptance of "natural hierarchies" as just, constrain Leo XIII and Pius XI from a systematic condemnation of capitalism or

---

[19] *Casti Connubii*, in *Seven Great Encyclicals* (Glen Rock, NJ: Paulist Press, 1939), para. 74.

[20] CC 75.

[21] CC 77.

endorsement of political action to effectively challenge concentrations of wealth and power.[22]

The basic economic solutions to "the social question" in these early teachings are just wages - defined as the family wage, opportunity for workers to become property owners, associations of workers, limited state regulation of the economy for the common good, and charity where needed. As the popes teach that women are not to be workers, these solutions are not meant to include them. A woman's economic well-being is dependent on that of her husband. If he receives an adequate family wage, presumably her well-being is assured.

But this assumption must be questioned. Although these papal teachings generally assume that a man will use his wage to support his family, they do not present specific criteria in this regard. Since the father is the authority in the family and his wife is to obey him, she does not necessarily have a voice in allocation of wages.[23]

Women's participation in the economy is to be indirect. Hence economic dependency, at least in wage labor economies, is explicitly mandated for women. Women's contribution is through domestic duties, which are exclusively their responsibility. Motherhood and domesticity are women's "function" and "mission," for which "her nature" suits her. Although women and men are equal in dignity, they are complementary in function. It is in carrying out her assigned role that women receive their dignity, according to these papal teachings.

Marie Giblin argues that this conception of the natural family "has imposed on the *whole* church, made up of many different cultures, one model of the Western nuclear family, where the wife tends the hearth

---

[22] Dorr, pp. 11-75, 252-4; Hobgood, pp. 101-131. These interpreters point out that the popes are also concerned to protect the stability of the church in a time of rapid change. Dorr contends that Pius XII, who followed Pius XI, embraced capitalism "as the best available option in his time," p. 255. I do not examine the teaching of Pius XII in this study as he issued no encyclicals of social teaching and generally followes the line of his predecessors in his teaching on women.

[23] Hartmann argues that the family wage was supported by unions as a means of maintaining male dominance within the family. Heidi Hartmann, "Capitalism, Patriarchy, and Job Segregation by Sex," *Capitalist Patriarchy and the Case for Socialist Feminism*, pp. 206-47.

and the man provides material support. This model has not been universal *even in the West*, certainly not among the poor, and it is clearly remote from the reality of families" in many non-Western cultures.[24] Yet it continues to inform Catholic teaching.

New Understandings of the Common Good:
John XXIII and Vatican II

John XXIII

John XXIII is perceived as an innovator in Catholic social teaching.[25] Christine Gudorf observes that John "modified to a degree" the static understanding of natural law characteristic of earlier teaching with his openness to distinctive characteristics of this historical period.[26] This openness enables John and his successors to rethink some of the organic presuppositions of previous teaching in regard to justice and the common good.

Just distribution and participation. In his first major social encyclical, *Mater et Magistra* (May 15, 1961) John addresses "Christianity and Social Progress." Following Pius XI, he appeals to the norm of equity both in relation to a just wage and the distribution of the goods of a society. John argues that wages cannot be set "arbitrarily at the will of the more powerful." The norms of justice and equity require a wage "sufficient to lead a life worthy of man and to fulfill family responsibilities properly."[27]

Furthermore, a "corresponding social development" should accompany economic growth so that "all classes of citizens will benefit equitably from an increase in national wealth." John proposes that a

---

[24] Giblin, p. 172.

[25] Dorr, pp. 87-116; Pawlikowski, *Justice in the Marketplace*, pp. 110-12.

[26] Gudorf, p. 16.

[27] *Mater et Magistra*, in *Gospel of Peace and Justice*, para. 71.

just distribution of goods become the criteria by which to assess economic prosperity, rather than the sum total of goods and wealth.[28]

This claim is an important new emphasis in social teaching, as is John's emphasis on the participation of workers:

> Justice is to be observed not merely in the distribution of wealth, but also in regard to the conditions under which men engage in productive activity. There is, in fact, an innate need of human nature requiring that men engaged in productive activity have an opportunity to assume responsibility and to perfect themselves by their efforts.[29]

An economic order which compromises the human dignity of workers, weakens their sense of responsibility, or limits their freedom of action is judged by John to be unjust even if its distribution of goods is just and equitable.

Natural rights and duties. In *Pacem in Terris* (Peace on Earth, April 11, 1963) John extends the teaching on human rights and duties, which "find their source, their sustenance and their inviolability in the natural law which grants or enjoins them."[30] John emphasizes the elements of a worthy standard of living:

> every man has the right to life, to bodily integrity, and to the means which are suitable for the proper development of life; these are primarily food, clothing, shelter, rest, medical care, and finally the necessary social services.[31]

Following Pius XII, John affirms that human beings also have the right "to choose freely the state of life they prefer, either to set up a family or to follow a religious vocation." "Equal rights and duties for man and woman" are specified in relation to family life. This parallelism des not follow through, however, when John addresses economic rights: "Women have the right to working conditions in accordance with their

---

[28] MM 73-4.

[29] MM 82.

[30] *Pacem in Terris*, in *Gospel of Peace and Justice*, para. 28.

[31] PT 11.

requirements and their duties as wives and mothers." No parallel claim is made for men in relation to their duties as husbands and fathers.[32]

In this encyclical, John affirms that the social order is by nature moral, with universal, absolute, and unchangeable principles. Yet he observes that "our age" does have distinctive characteristics. From a review of these characteristics, he concludes that "the conviction that all men are equal by reason of their natural dignity has generally been accepted." John notes that as women have become more conscious of their human dignity, "they will not tolerate being treated as inanimate objects or mere instruments, but claim, both in domestic and public life, the rights and duties that befit a human person."[33]

Equality for women? Overall, John's teachings on women in these social encyclicals appears to be innovative. He affirms women's participation in public life and their equality within the family. Yet his argument for working conditions which accord with family responsibilities only for women raises questions. An exploration of some of his other teaching enables us to understand that John is much more in sympathy with previous papal teaching on women than his social encyclicals indicate.

John is more accepting of women working outside the domicile and their desire for economic independence than his predecessors were:

> There has been and still is some discussion over how wise it is, from certain points of view, to employ women in certain specified types of labor and certain professions. But we have to face facts as they are and make it clear that there is an ever greater flow of women toward sources of employment, of labor, and an ever more widespread desire on their part for some kind of activity that can make them economically independent and free from want.[34]

But in addressing a group of young Catholic women about women's work, he "affirmed without hesitation that the task of woman, being

---

[32] PT 15, 19.

[33] PT 44, 41. Both these observations implicitly challenge presuppositions in earlier teaching about the justice of natural hierarchies.

[34] An Address of Pope John XXIII to the Italian Center for Women, "The Woman of Today - at Home and at Work," *The Pope Speaks* 7 (1961), p. 171.

directed immediately or remotely toward maternity, consists of everything that is a work of love, of giving, of welcoming, everything that puts one at the disposal of others ... all this finds a natural place in the feminine calling." John cautions that a careful watch must be kept unless "work unsuitable for the feminine nature should change the personality of young workers by its deleterious influence."[35] Thus John affirms motherhood as women's vocation, and from it deduced work in the service sector as the proper place for women's employment.

John also insists that outside employment does not in any way reduce the obligations of being a wife and mother. He recognizes that women are being called to an effort "perhaps greater than that of men," when he declares:

> At all times and in all circumstances they are the ones who have to be wise enough to find the resources to face their duties as wives and mothers calmly and with their eyes wide open; to make their homes warm and peaceful after the tiring labors of daily work; and not to shrink from the responsibilities involved in raising children.[36]

It is significant that the responsibilities of raising children and making a home "warm and peaceful" are not seen as part of the "tiring labors of daily work." But how else can one describe food preparation, cleaning, laundry, and the many other tasks involved in domestic labor. John "perhaps" is not only asking women to make a greater effort than men, he is *in fact* asking women to work a double day.

This teaching seems to sharply contradict John's declaration of the "equal rights and duties" of women and men in the family. In addressing several Italian women's organizations, John clarified that "equality of rights ... does not in any way imply equality of functions." To overlook this difference and the complementary functions of women and men "would be tantamount to opposing nature: the result would be

---

[35] An Address of Pope John XXIII to the Federation of Young Catholic Women, "Woman's Work," *The Pope Speaks* 6 (1960), p. 331.

[36] "The Woman of Today," *The Pope Speaks* 7, pp. 172-3.

to debase women and to remove the true foundations of her dignity."[37]

Furthermore, John asserts that this complementary relation is hierarchically ordered. In an early encyclical, John taught that "within the family, the father stands in God's place. He must lead and guide the rest by his authority and the example of his good life."[38]

John's innovations in regard to women's economic reality are not without contradictions. Although women may now have a papal blessing on their participation in the wage labor force, their employment is confined to the service sector. If married, they are required to work a double day. John's continuation of the natural law tradition on "women's nature" denies women true equality or full participation.[39]

Vatican II

The Second Vatican Council, called by John XXIII and continued by Paul VI after John's death, accelerated the innovative development of Catholic social teaching. The conciliar document of particular importance to our topic is *Gaudium et Spes*, (The Pastoral Constitution on the Church in the Modern World, December 7, 1965).

Discrimination condemned. Among the significant developments in this document are its reinterpretation of the norm of the common good from an international perspective and its condemnation of discrimination.

Every day human interdependence grows more tightly drawn and spreads by degrees over the whole world. As a result the common good, that is, the sum of those conditions of social life which allow social groups and their individual members relatively thorough and ready access to their own fulfillment, today takes on increasingly universal complexion and consequently involves rights and duties with respect to the whole human race.... At the same time, however, there is growing awareness of the exalted dignity proper to the

---

[37] Address to Several Italian Women's Associations, "Woman and Society" *The Pope Speaks* 7 (1961), p. 345.

[38] John XXIII, *Ad Petri Cathedram*, in *The Pope Speaks* 5 (1959), p. 368.

[39] For discussion of John XXIII's views on women's participation in political life, see Gudorf, pp. 311-2.

human person, since he stands above all things, and his rights and duties are universal and inviolable.[40]

The Council goes on to claim that "with respect to the fundamental rights of the person, every type of discrimination, whether social or cultural, whether based on sex, race, color, social condition, language, or religion, is to be overcome and eradicated as contrary to God's intent." As an example of such discrimination, the Council mentions "a woman who is denied the right and freedom to choose a husband, to embrace a state of life, or to acquire an education or cultural benefits equal to those recognized by men."[41]

Economic justice mandated. The Council was deeply concerned with economic injustice. Although not denying that "rightful differences exist between men," they insist that "the equal dignity of persons demands that a more humane and just condition of life be brought about." Excessive economic and social differences between groups of people "militate against social justice, equity, the dignity of the human person, as well as social and international peace."[42]

Economic injustice is identified by the Council as a problem of "special urgency."

> Again, we are at a moment in history when the development of economic life could diminish social inequalities if that development were guided and coordinated in a reasonable and human way. Yet all too often it serves only to intensify the inequalities. In some places it even results in a decline in the social status of the weak and in contempt for the poor.[43]

The Council insists that to satisfy the norms of justice and equity, "vigorous efforts must be made, without violence to the rights of persons or to the natural characteristics of each country, to remove as quickly as possible the immense economic inequalities which now

---

[40] *Gaudium et Spes*, in *Gospel of Peace and Justice*, para. 26.

[41] GS 29. For a discussion of race and culture in papal teaching, see Gudorf, pp. 129-45.

[42] GS 29.

[43] GS 63.

exist." Economic development must be "in the service of man" and under his control.[44]

No unconditional right to private property. The Council avoided interpreting natural law to affirm an unconditional right to private property. They declare that the earth and its contents are intended by God for the use of every human being and people. Various forms of ownership, "adapted to the legitimate institutions of people according to diverse and changeable circumstances" are permissible, but "the universal purpose for which created goods" are meant must be observed. Thus ownership and private control of material goods is "not opposed to the right inherent in various forms of public ownership." Expropriation of large estates is permitted, if required by the common good, but equitable compensation is to be made. A person "in extreme necessity" has the right "to take from the riches of others what he himself needs."[45]

Equality within the family? The value of human labor is affirmed by the Council. Such activity is in accordance with God's mandate "to subject to himself the earth and all that it contains, and to govern the world with justice and holiness." This mandate includes the most ordinary everyday activities:

> For while providing the substance of life for themselves and their families, men and women are performing their activities in a way which appropriately benefits society.[46]

The acknowledgement that women also provide the sustenance of their families is a new one in Catholic social teaching.

There also seems to be some innovation in the Council's other teaching on marriage and family, also identified as a problem of special urgency. The equal personal dignity of wife and husband is affirmed, in keeping with previous teaching. A breakthrough comes in the

---

[44] GS 64-6.

[45] GS 69-71.

[46] GS 34.

discussion of the family as "a kind of school of deeper humanity" when the Council contends that this "mission" requires

> the kindly communion of minds and the joint deliberation of spouses, as well as the painstaking cooperation of parents in the education of their children. The active presence of the father is highly beneficial to their formation.[47]

Never before had the "active presence" of the father been claimed as so significant to his children's well-being.

But the Council continues in a more traditional vein when it contends that "the children, especially the younger among them, need the care of their mother at home. This domestic role of hers must be safely preserved, though the legitimate social progress of women should not be underrated on that account."[48] The Council does not specify how this is to happen. In their discussion of the principles governing socio-economic life, they do insist that

> the entire process of productive work, therefore, must be adapted to the needs of the person and to the requirements of his life, above all his domestic life. Such is especially the case with respect to mothers of families, but due consideration must be given to every person's sex and age.[49]

Thus the heavier domestic responsibility still falls on mothers. Although the Council did not discuss whether this will inhibit women's "social progress," evidence presented in the first chapter of this study indicates that it does.

Discrimination against women? A similar ambiguous argument is made in the Council's discussion of the proper development of culture. The universal recognition and implementation of the right of all to a human and civic culture favorable to personal dignity and free from any discrimination on the grounds of race, sex, nationality, religious, or social conditions is advocated. The employment of women "in almost every area of life" is recognized. The Council then teaches

---

[47] GS 52.

[48] GS 52.

[49] GS 67.

that "it is appropriate that they should be able to assume their full proper role in accordance with their own nature. Everyone should acknowledge and favor the proper and necessary participation of women in cultural life."[50]

Christine Gudorf explicates the meaning of this last statement in her study of these documents:

> Taking into account the tradition on to which this document is appended, we see that these qualifications on the entry of women into public life are an affirmation of the traditional understanding of the nature of women and her primary task of motherhood.[51]

The innovations of Vatican II in regard to women's reality are limited by natural law presuppositions, as are John's.

Critical Assessment

The encyclicals of John XXIII and *Gaudium et spes* include both liberal and radical assumptions. Their conception of justice, poverty and development are primarily informed by liberal presuppositions. Just distribution and equality of opportunity are the primary criteria for justice and capitalist models of development are the main solution to poverty. Advocacy of economic rights, effective participation, and limits to private property are more in keeping with a radical perspective.[52] However, both John and the Council appealed primarily to those with power and wealth for change. Endorsement of political action by the poor and oppressed is limited.[53]

---

[50] GS 60.

[51] Gudorf, p. 314.

[52] For further discussion of the presence of both liberal and radical perspectives, see Dorr, pp. 87-138, especially 136-8; and Hobgood, pp. 148-64.

[53] Dorr contends that the Council's claim that "the limits laid down by the natural law and the Gospel must be observed" in defending against the abuses of an oppressive government "raises more questions than it solves," p. 133.

While recognizing the limits presented above of the innovations of Vatican II in regard to its teaching on women, the significance of its innovations must also be acknowledged. Opposition to discrimination on the grounds of sex is asserted, however qualified. Affirmation of the role of the father and proposals for the recognition of the demands of domestic life in the organization of production could have positive implications for more equitable responsibilities in the domicile and equal rights for women. However, until static natural law understandings of male and female nature are challenged in the way the Vatican Council challenged natural hierarchies with its advocacy of equal dignity, the full implications of these innovations can not be realized.

Authentic Human Development a Central Criterion: Paul VI and John Paul II

Paul VI

Paul VI accelerated the innovation of Catholic social teaching. John Pawlikowski observes that Paul endorsed and further developed the themes of John XXIII and Vatican II. He cites commentators who argue that Paul "overturned the methodology" of earlier social teaching. Paul's approach is more inductive than deductive, thus breaking the link between Catholicism and "a social system based on natural law."[54] Concern for development comes to the forefront with Paul's encyclicals.

Challenges to capitalist development. In *Populorum Progressio* (On the Development of Peoples, March 26, 1967) Paul contends, as does John XXIII, that development is not limited "to mere economic growth." To be authentic, it needs to be "integral ... it has to promote the good of every man and of the whole man." Paul went further and declared that "all growth is ambivalent." Although growth is essential to human development, it can imprison "man if he considers it the supreme good."[55]

---

[54] *Justice in the Marketplace*, p. 200.

[55] *Populorum Progressio*, in *Gospel of Peace and Justice*, para. 14, 19.

Paul extends the norm of equity, which John introduced into the teaching on just wages, to trade relations. Paul is concerned that efforts to assist developing countries financially and technically would be illusory "if their benefits were to be partially nullified as a consequence of the trade relations existing between rich and poor countries." Existing trade relations, Paul argue, keep the poor nations poor while the rich ones grow richer. The rule of free trade is thus no longer able to govern international relations, given the "excessive inequalities in economic power." The competitive market, although not to be abolished, is to be kept within limits of justice.[56]

Paul identifies nationalism and racism as obstacles to universal solidarity, as are "excessive social, economic, and cultural inequalities." Relationships of violence between nations are to be replaced by relations of mutual respect and friendship and interdependent collaboration. Paul contends that to struggle against misery and injustice is to promote the common good.[57]

The natural family? Paul's innovations in social teaching do not extend to his discussion of the family. Natural law arguments predominant here. A "man's true identity" is found only in his social milieu, according to Paul. The family plays a fundamental role in this. Paul admits that the influence of the family may have been excessive in certain times and places, when its influence was exercised to the detriment of fundamental personal rights. But he insists that "the natural family, monogamous and stable, such as the divine plan conceived it and as Christianity sanctified it, must remain..."[58]

Natural law presumptions and arguments also dominate Paul's encyclical *Humanae Vitae* (On the Regulation of Birth," July 25, 1968). Paul affirms that what he calls "the conjugal act" has both a unitive meaning and a procreative meaning, but argues that these can never be

---

[56] PP 57-60.

[57] PP 62, 65, 76.

[58] PP 36. The subtle cultural imperialism in presuming the monogamous, stable family to be the natural one conceived by divine plan is not apparent to Paul. For an extended discussion of this and other contradictions in Catholic social teaching on women, see Giblin, pp. 167-87.

separated as this would go against "laws inscribed in the very being of man and of woman." Thus "artificial" means of contraception are prohibited. "Natural" means which use "the natural laws and rhythms of fecundity" are permitted.[59]

Paul further supports his arguments against "artificial means of contraception" by warning that their use may cause "man... to finally lose respect for the woman and, no longer caring for her physical and psychological equilibrium, may come to the point of considering her as a mere instrument of selfish enjoyment, and no longer as his respected and beloved companion." [60]

Yet Paul does not show this same concern for women's well-being when discussing "responsible parenthood" (a euphemism for family planning) as a concern of both parents. He never mentions the heavier burden women carry during pregnancy, childbirth, and lactation, nor the heavier responsibility the church assigns women for the care of children after birth. Paul prohibits abortion, even for therapeutic reasons, without any discussion of the woman's health or well-being. In fact, Paul discusses "the generative process" without ever mentioning women as the bearers of life.[61] Women's reproductive labor is as invisible as her actual domestic labor.

Action for justice. Paul again takes up the theme of social justice in his encyclical *Octogesima Adviens* (A Call to Action, May 14, 1971), issued on the 80th anniversary of *Rerum Novarum*. He begins by noting the "flagrant inequalities" which exist in the economic, cultural, and political development of nations" and the rising from all sides of "a

---

[59] *Humanae Vitae*, in *Gospel of Peace and Justice*, paragraphs 12-13.

[60] HV17. Paul does not question whether this disregard for women may develop whether or not contraception is practiced. He does observe in a later teaching that women are "reduced to the status of passive, insignificant objects" in some work situations, in the media, in social relations and in the family. He adds "that for some men women are the easiest tool to use in expressing their impulses to violence." Paul VI, "Women in the Life of Society," *The Pope Speaks* 22, (1977) p. 23.

[61] HV 14.

yearning for more justice and a desire for a better guaranteed peace in mutual respect among individuals and peoples."[62]

Pointing to "widely varying situations" in the world, Paul contends that it is neither the mission or the ambition of the church to put forward a solution which had universal validity. Rather, Christian communities are "to analyze with objectivity the situation which is proper to their own country, to shed on it the light of the Gospel's unalterable words and to draw principles of reflection, norms of judgment and directives for action from the social teaching of the Church."[63]

Justice, equality and participation. Equality and participation are continuing themes in this encyclical. Aspirations to equality and participation are "two forms of man's dignity and freedom."[64] Paul advocates the "need to establish a greater justice in the sharing of goods, both within national communities and on the international level."

> The most important duty in the realm of justice is to allow each country to promote its own development, within the framework of a cooperation free from any spirit of domination, whether economic or political.[65]

In this regard, Paul raises concern about the growth of multinational corporations, which are more or less independent of national political powers. He fears that these "can lead to a new and abusive form of economic domination." Political power is to have as its aim "the achievement of the common good." Within the political dimension, shared responsibility and increased participation are called for. Paul

---

[62] *Octogesima Adveniens*, in *Gospel of Peace and Justice*, para. 2. This encyclical was deeply influenced by the 1968 Medellin conference of Latin American bishops, which will be discussed in the second section of this chapter.

[63] OA 4.

[64] OA 22.

[65] OA 43.

claims that this is the way human community, freedom, and solidarity develop.[66]

Equality for women? In this encyclical, Paul notes that in many countries there are demands for "a charter for women which would put an end to an actual discrimination and would establish relationships of equality in rights and of respect for their dignity..." Paul asserts that

> We do not have in mind that false equality which would deny the distinctions laid down by the Creator himself and which would be in contradiction with woman's proper role, which is of such capital importance, at the heart of the family as well within society. Developments in legislation should on the contrary be directed to protecting her proper vocation and at the same time recognizing her independence as a person, her equal rights to participate in cultural, economic, social and political life.[67]

The appeal to "woman's proper role" and the placement of this statement within a paragraph discussing conflicts and divisions softens Paul's advocacy for equal civil rights for women.

Critical assessment. Paul does not break with the tradition as much as it might at first appear. Within the family and also the church, women still have specific roles to play rooted in what is seen as their "nature." Gudorf's conclusion to her study of papal teachings on women is applicable here. She observes that although the Church "no longer affirms the inequality of the sexes," it has not changed its "understanding of male and female nature and function upon which the former judgment of inequality was made."[68] Thus women's equality and participation are limited by and seen as in contradiction to "her proper role."

Commentators have questioned the extent to which Paul's teachings facilitate the "concrete demands of the Christian faith for a just, and

---

[66] OA 44, 47.

[67] OA 13.

[68] Gudorf, p. 327. Her study ends with the papacy of Paul VI, but I contend that her conclusions are applicable to more recent social teaching.

consequently necessary, transformation of society" which he advocates.[69] Gudorf points out that Paul offers no economic or political alternative to the capitalist system which he criticizes. He also continues to rely on the "papal tradition ... of evangelization to gradually correct injustice..."[70] Ellison further elaborates this criticism when he charges Paul with "ultimately abstract[ing] the problem of underdevelopment from its political context and downplay[ing] the urgency of restructuring political and economic power relationships within Third World countries and the advanced industrialized nations..."[71]

John Paul II

John Paul II has reiterated the centrality of "man" to Catholic teaching, not man "in the abstract" but "concrete, historical man."[72] In his first social encyclical, *Laborem exercens* (On Human Work, September 14, 1981), he addresses work as key to any understanding of humanity and the "social question."[73] In so doing he returns to some of the themes of earlier social teaching, such as concern for "the worker," use of natural law arguments and a deductive approach to ethics.[74]

---

[69] OA 51. In addition to the interpreters cited in the text, see Hobgood, pp. 164-72, for a discussion of the contradictions and inconsistencies in Paul's thinking.

[70] Gudorf, p. 154.

[71] Ellison, p. 86. Dorr contends that Paul did recognize the need for political solutions in *Octogesima Adveniens* and that he emphasized the necessity of people's participation in decision-making. But he also notes Paul's hope that change would come about by consensus. Dorr, pp. 257-8.

[72] *Redemptor Hominis* (Redeemer of Man, March 4, 1979), para. 13, in *Justice in the Marketplace*. This was John Paul's first papal encyclical.

[73] *Laborem Exercens*, in Gregory Baum, *The Priority of Labor* (New York: Paulist Press, 1982), paragraph 3.

[74] Hobgood has a useful discussion of John Paul's shift in methodology, pp. 204-5.

John Paul asserts that through worker solidarity, the condition of workers has improved. "Profound changes" have been brought about in overcoming the objectification of "man" as an instrument of production. But he also insists that there is a need for "ever new movements of solidarity of the workers and with the workers" to bring social justice in various countries and between them.

Solidarity is called for whenever there is "social degrading of the subject of work, by exploitation of the workers and by the growing areas of poverty and even hunger." The "violation of the dignity of human work can cause poverty, either through unemployment or the low value put on work and the rights that flow from it." These rights include a just wage and personal security for the worker and his family.[75]

Priority of labor a normative principle. The conflict between labor and capital is of concern to John Paul. He insists that "the real conflict" between them is not a systematic class struggle and does not require the elimination of classes. John Paul contends that if the principle of the priority of labor over capital is honored and if the subjectivity of human labor and its participation in the production processes are granted - then the opposition between capital and labor will be overcome.[76]

Just wage a central criterion. John Paul situates the rights of workers within the context of human rights as a whole. The right to suitable employment for all who are capable is affirmed. The state, which John Paul designates the "indirect employer," is responsible for seeing that all have suitable employment. The direct employer is responsible for "just remuneration of the work done." John Paul insists that just remuneration is "the key problem in social ethics" in this case. The just wage is "the concrete means of verifying the justice of the whole socioeconomic system," as wages are the practical means through

---

[75] LE 8.

[76] LE 13. John Paul contends that the church has always taught the priority of labor over capital.

which most people have access to goods intended for common use.[77]

In a return to themes of earlier social teaching, John Paul relates the just wage to the "first principle of the whole ethical and social order ... the common use of goods." A just wage is one which suffices in establishing and properly maintaining a family and providing security for its future. John Paul indicates that it can be either in the form of a family wage - "a single salary given to the head of the family for his work, sufficient for the needs of the family without the spouse having to take up gainful employment outside the home" - or through social measures such as family allowances or "grants to mothers devoting themselves exclusively to their families."[78]

Re-evaluation of mother's role? John Paul discusses "a mother's role" and "woman's nature" in some detail.

> Experience confirms that there must be a social re-evaluation of the mother's role, of the toil connected with it and of the need that children have for care, love and affection in order that they may develop into responsible, morally and religiously mature and psychologically stable persons. It will rebound to the credit of society to make it possible for a mother - without inhibiting her freedom, without psychological or practical discrimination, and without penalizing her as compared with other women - to devote herself to taking care of her children and educating them in accordance with their needs, which vary with age.[79]

John Paul contends that it is "wrong from the point of view of the good of society and of the family" to abandon these tasks to take up "paid work outside the home," if it "contradicts or hinders these primary goals of the mission of a mother."

He then turns to consider the labor process in general, and insists that it must be organized and adapted so as to respect "the requirements of the person and his or her forms of life, above all life in the home..." He observes that in many societies women work in nearly every sector

---

[77] LE 16-19.

[78] LE 19.

[79] LE 19.

of life, but cautions that they must "fulfill their tasks in accordance with their own nature."

> The true advancement of women requires that labor should be structured in such a way that women do not have to pay for their advancement by abandoning what is specific to them and at the expense of the family, in which women as mothers have an irreplaceable role.[80]

It is evident that John Paul views women as having a distinctive nature destining them to motherhood and family life. There are no references here to the "irreplaceable role" of the father or "the benefits of his active presence" that Vatican II acknowledges.

Critical assessment. These reflections on work move Catholic social teaching in some new directions. Here the activity of work becomes much more central, the question of economic development secondary. John Paul's conception of work as central to human subjectivity and his efforts to develop a spirituality of work are distinctive additions to the social teaching. His assertion of the priority of labor over capital and his use of the norm of participation in the production process were welcomed by many working people and progressives.

In her study of the use of social theories in Catholic teaching on social justice, Mary Hobgood observes a mixture of organic, orthodox, and radical socio-economic theories present in *Laborem exercens*.[81]

---

[80] LE 19. In this statement, John Paul echoes Pius XII who taught that "Every woman is destined to be a mother.... The Creator has disposed to this end the entire being of woman, her organism, and even more her spirit, and above all her exquisite sensibility." *The Pope Speaks: The Teachings of Pius XII*, ed. Michael Chinigo (New York: Pantheon, 1957), p. 58.

[81] Hobgood, pp. 203-18. Hobgood argues convincingly that *Laborem exercens* retreated from more radical concerns in the teaching of John XXIII and Paul VI. She particularly notes retreat from "concern for structural analyses of economic and class systems, support for mobilizing grass roots, utopian imagination to determine the direction of social change, growing openness to solidarity with Marxist movements, and recognition of the need for reform within the church." Ibid, pp. 217-8. Dorr interprets John Paul's teaching on solidarity as strengthening the stance of the church in the struggle for justice, p. 250. This may be so, but there are clear limits to this struggle as will be evident in our discussion of John

John Paul's presuppositions about women certainly continue to be grounded in organic, natural law theory. His use of the notion of the "mission of the mother" implies that a woman is constrained by her role in the family, that is conceived as natural and therefore as obligatory.

In contrast to some earlier papal teacning, John Paul does indicate that there is "toil" connected to this role. Yet his analysis of work in the body of the encyclical does not incorporate domestic labor. Here work is conceived as agricultural or industrial and understood as "male work." Baum, who argues at first for a generic interpretation of the word "man," concludes that "the tone of the encyclical reflects a male world" and the impression is "that the worker in question is the male worker." Baum also observes that a recognition of the "institutionalized injustices" against women "in society, culture and Church" or an analysis of how women are affected by this "inferiorization" both at the workplace and at home are missing from the encyclical. [82]

Giglia Tedesco, a Catholic feminist and a member of the Italian Senate, observes that "a sort of double track emerges" in the encyclical, so that the way indicated for women contradicts the general propositions of the encyclical. Specifically, the affirmation of the subjective dimension of work is denied to most women, given the insistence that mothers are not to work outside the home. Human work, Tedesco insists, is also a women's right. [83]

Tedesco agrees with John Paul that maternity is the distinguishing mark of "feminine specificity," but argues that this has been historically misunderstood as a social value because it has been confined to the individual and family environment. Today women are demanding that the entire society educate itself to the social value of maternity and adapt its structure to this value. If women are returned to the home, as

---

Paul's encyclical on underdevelopment.

[82] Baum, pp. 7, 78-79. For a similar argument, see Phil Land, S.J., "On Human Work: What's in it for Women?" *Center of Concern* Issue 49 (July 1982), pp. 5-6.

[83] Giglia Tedesco, "Laborem exercens: A Handicap for Women," *NTC News* (Rome) Vol. 8, nos. 11-12 (November-December 1981) p. 1.

John Paul asserts, they are not freed from the "tyranny of capital" but become functional to its needs.

Tedesco points to the interrelationship between labor and women as being where a new quality of life lies.

> A social revalorization (that is the most advanced social revalorization possible in this historical moment) of maternal "tasks" is not possible by resorting to models of life based on past ideas of woman. This social revalorization of maternal "tasks" is possible by making it so in fact and not only in principle; that is by making it so that women have job access which recognizes, valorizes, and accepts their rights as mothers.... modern society precisely due to the way in which it is organized, burdens the woman with tasks and functions which are not "necessarily" connected to maternity, but are "well" substitutes for social inadequacies of society [sic]. Therefore, far from exalting maternity, these tasks and functions distort the deepest and most essential values of maternity and transform it from a "human relationship" into a "social role" which then becomes a social "handicap" for women.[84]

Tedesco concludes that these teachings on women emerge from the limitations of a Catholic culture "which is still prisoner of concepts which, during the centuries, it has elaborated 'deductively', outside their historical context." The "social handicap" that maternity has come to involve for women is not only not recognized, but papal teaching continues to legitimate the handicap.

Return to theme of development. On the twentieth anniversary of Paul VI's encyclical *Populorum Progressio*, John Paul II issued his encyclical *Sollicitudo Rei Socialis* (The Social Concerns of the Church, February 19, 1988). He returns to the earlier theme of international development, aiming to emphasize "the need for a fuller and more nuanced concept of development."[85] In issuing the encyclical, John Paul wanted to "reaffirm the continuity of the social doctrine as well as its constant renewal." "Authentic human development" is the central criterion of this encyclical.

John Paul observes that in contrast to the "widespread optimism" about the possibilities of overcoming poverty and underdevelopment at

---

[84] Ibid., pp. 1-3.

[85] *Sollicitudo Rei Socialis*, in *Origins* 17, (March 3, 1988), paragraph 4.

the time of Paul's encyclical, the present situation in regard to development is negative. As indicators of this situation, John Paul points to the widening gap between the north and the south in regard to production and distribution of basic goods and services; specific signs of underdevelopment experienced universally such as the housing crisis, and under and unemployment; and the international debt crisis, which forces debtor nations to export capital "needed for improving or at least maintaining their standard of living."[86]

Structural analysis of underdevelopment. John Paul identifies the causes of underdevelopment as political and moral. He asserts that the existence of two opposing blocks in the North - East and West - contribute to the "retardation or stagnation of the South," as each of these blocs tends toward imperialism and neo-colonialism. Arms production and trade exacerbate this situation. John Paul contends that the interdependence of developed and less-developed nations "has disastrous consequences for the weakest" when interdependence is separated from ethical requirements.[87]

In a theological reading of this situation, John Paul contends in a world in which different forms of imperialism hold sway, rather than interdependence and solidarity, is a world subject to "structures of sin." He points to two typical structures: "the all-consuming desire for profit" and "the thirst for power, with the intention of imposing one's will upon others."[88]

Organic character of "true development." John Paul asserts that "true development" must not be limited to economic development, but must recognize the "transcendent reality" of the human being, which is "being the image of God" - a fundamentally social reality as this image is "shared from the beginning by a couple, a man and a woman." Both

---

[86] SS 13-19.

[87] SS 16.

[88] SS 36, 37.

individuals and peoples must enjoy fundamental equality, which "is the basis of the right of all to share in the process of full development."[89]

True development is achieved in a "framework of solidarity and freedom." Overcoming the moral obstacles to development requires "conversion," toward interdependence, solidarity, and commitment to the common good. John Paul insists that solidarity demands that "those who are more influential because they have a greater share of goods and common services should feel responsible for the weaker and be ready to share with them all they possess." Those who are weaker are to claim their "legitimate rights" and "do what they can for the good of all." "The intermediate groups" should respect the interests of others, rather than "selfishly" insisting on their own particular interests.[90]

John Paul calls attention to the need for reform of the international trading, monetary and financial systems. Developing countries are to take up their own responsibilities and initiatives in basic education and literacy, food production, reform of political structures, and promotion of human rights. He contends that international collaboration and global solidarity are necessary for the achievement of these reforms. Autonomy and free self-determination are essential conditions for global solidarity. [91]

John Paul follows Paul VI in affirming that the church does not have technical solutions to the problem of underdevelopment. He insists that the church does not "show preference" for economic or political systems, "provided that human dignity is properly respected and promoted, and provided herself is allowed the room she needs to exercise her ministry in the world." John Paul contends that a part of the church's ministry is sharing guidelines from its social teaching. Among the guidelines he advocates for the current situation are "the option or love of preference for the poor," the "social mortgage of private property" based on the principle of "the universal destination of goods," and the right to freedom of economic initiative. John Paul

---

[89] SS 29, 33.

[90] SS 33-4, 39.

[91] SS 33-4, 39.

claims that what is at stake here is the dignity of the human person.[92]

Critical assessment. John Paul brings some new perspectives to social teaching on international development. This is the first papal encyclical to address ecological concerns. John Paul insists that "the moral character of development" must include attention to the natural world and its limited resources.[93] His perception of underdevelopment in the southern hemisphere through the lens of east/west tensions in the northern hemisphere is a distinct perspective in papal teaching and helps illumine the impact of militarization on development.

John Paul's refusal to show preference among systems and his conception of solidarity continue the papal concern for harmony and soften the preferential option for the poor. Interestingly, John Paul has been charged in the U.S. with morally equating capitalism and communism, by criticizing both systems.[94] The weaknesses of this encyclical are similar to those of *Populorom Progressio*, in that a incisive structural analysis is not followed with political proposals for structural transformation or empowerment of the marginalized. Instead John Paul follows Paul VI in looking to the powerful for change and to evangelization and conversion as primary means of change.

He also follows Paul in not addressing women's plight in any depth, making one reference to poor "working conditions (especially for women)."[95] He does not recognize male domination as a structural reality nor is there awareness of how this oppression contributes to economic injustices against women, such as the wage gap or occupational segregation. Women's experience of marginalization and pauperization is missing entirely. The proposals for economic justice elaborated will not benefit women in the manner assumed.

---

[92] SS 41-2, 47.

[93] SS 41-2, 47.

[94] Kenneth Aman, "The Pope and 'Social Concerns,'" *Christianity and Crisis* 48 (1988), p. 177. Aman defends John Paul against these charges, contending that what he said was "that both capitalism and Marxist socialism have been morally deficient. Whether the deficiency is equal or not is beside the point."

[95] SS 14.

Preferential Option for the Poor:
Alternative Conceptions From Regional Bishops

Teaching of regional conferences of bishops offers alternative conceptions to those of recent papal teaching in regard to economic life more generally and to women's reality more specifically. Latin American bishops more consistently advocate proposals for social justice in keeping with their radical structural analysis and also begin to address women's reality. The United States bishops offer a rather extensive analysis of the economic vulnerability of women and declare sexism to be sinful. Canadian bishops offer consistent radical analysis and proposals for economic life. This section will briefly review highlights of these documents to assess their usefulness in addressing the impoverishment of women.

Latin American Bishops Speak

Medellin, 1968. In the documents from the conference of bishops meeting in Medellin, Columbia, Latin American bishops spoke movingly of "a lamentable insensitivity of the privileged sectors to the misery of the marginated sectors." They contend that power is unjustly exercised by dominant sectors and that a growing awareness of their condition is developing among the oppressed sectors.[96] "A deafening cry ... for a liberation that reaches them from nowhere else" comes to the church.[97]

---

[96] I am using the official English translation of the Medellin documents, Latin American Episcopal Conference, *The Church in the Present Day Transformation of Latin America in Light of the Council* II: Conclusions (Washington, DC: US Catholic Conference, 1970), 2:2-7. There are sixteen main documents from the conference. I will refer to the document being cited by number and also note the paragraph number of the particular citation. This conference had a profound impact on the Roman Catholic church and progressive movements around the world. For further analysis of the work of the Latin American bishops at Medellin and Puebla, see Dorr, pp. 157-62, 207-10; Hobgood, pp. 174-84; and Ricardo Antoncich, *Christians in the Face of Injustice: A Latin American Reading of Catholic Social Teaching*, trans. Matthew J. O'Connell (Maryknoll, NY: Orbis Books, 1987).

[97] Medellin 14.2.

Structural injustice and empowerment. The situation in Latin America, the bishops assert, is one of "structural injustice" and "institutionalized violence" in which fundamental human rights are violated. "This situation demands all-embracing, courageous, urgent and profoundly renovating transformations." The bishops commit the church to several actions "in solidarity with the poor." These actions include defending the rights of the poor and oppressed; denouncing the excessive inequalities between rich and poor, powerful and weak; and encouraging creation and development of people's grassroots organizations "for the redress and consolidation of their rights and the search for true justice."[98] Radical and courageous action is undertaken by the bishops in keeping with their radical analysis of their situation.

Liberation for women? The bishops note that "the women [demand] their right to a legitimate equality with men..."[99] This observation is the only explicit reference to women in the Medellin documents. None address the attainment of this equality. They do not recognize the specific inequities that our earlier analysis demonstrates that women face - the double work day, occupational segregation, unpaid agricultural labor. One may conclude that although the Medellin documents provide a more adequate evaluation of the causes of underdevelopment and suggest more effective strategies for change,[100] the situation of women will not improve without a recognition of the causes of women's marginality. At their next conference, the bishops would more fully address women's situation.

---

[98] Medellin 2.22, 23, 27; 14.10.

[99] Medellin 1.1.

[100] For further documentation of this claim, see Denis Goulet, "'Development' ... or Liberation?" *International Development Review* Vol. XII, no. 3 (1971/3) pp. 6-10; and the study by Ellison.

Puebla, 1979

When the Latin American bishops met in early 1979 at Puebla de los Angeles, Mexico, they reaffirmed Medellin's preferential option for the poor, an option aimed at their "integral liberation."[101] The bishops object to the accumulation of wealth in the hands of a few, and the resulting cost of poverty for the majority that this entails. They contend that the poor lack not only material goods, but full participation in socio-political life. The bishops identify "indigenous peoples, peasants, manual laborers, marginalized urban dwellers and, in particular, the women of these social groups" as the principal groups of the poor, adding that "the women are doubly oppressed and marginalized.[102]

Women's reality addressed. A full section on women was included in the final document issued by the conference. The preparatory documents for the conference had said only that women constitute an important issue. A group of some thirty women - "Mujeres Para el Dialogo" - met at Puebla, held seminars, and prepared documents which contributed to the more substantial treatment of women in the final document. [103]

Women are discussed by the bishops under the rubric of lay agents of communion and participation. In keeping with liberation theological method, an analysis of "the situation" comes first. As this is the most detailed description of the situation of women in Catholic social teaching to date, it will be quoted extensively:

> As is well known, women have been pushed to the margins of society as the result of cultural atavisms - male predominance, unequal wages, deficient education, etc. This is manifest in their almost total absence from political, economic, and social life. To these are added new forms of marginalization in a hedonistic consumer

---

[101] Evangelization in Latin America, para. 1134, in *Puebla and Beyond: Documentary and Commentary*, John Eagleson and Philip Scharper, ed. (Maryknoll, NY: Orbis, 1979). In all subsequent references to this text, it will be designated as ELA.

[102] ELA, footnote to paragraph 1134.

[103] For an account of the work of these women, see Ada Maria Isasi-Diaz, "Silent Women Will Never Be Heard," *Missiology: An International Review* VII (1979), pp. 295-301.

society, which even go to the extreme of transforming the woman into an object of consumption.... In many of our countries female prostitution is on the increase, due either to the stifling economic situation or to the acute moral crisis. In the work sector we note the evasion of, or non-compliance with, laws that protect women. Faced with this situation, women are not always organized to demand respect for their rights. In families women are overburdened, not only with domestic tasks but with professional work as well. In quite a few cases they must assume all the responsibilities because the man has abandoned the home. We must also consider the sad situation of domestic employees. They are often subjected to maltreatment and exploitation by their employers. In the Church itself there has been an undervaluation of women and minimal participation by them in pastoral initiatives.[104]

The entry of women into tasks dealing with the construction of society and a resurgence of women's organizations are identified by the bishops as positive signs of change.

This description of women's situation is striking in that it includes the wage gap, exploitation of domestic employees, the link between prostitution and economic need, and the overburdening of women with domestic tasks in the family. No previous documents of social teaching named these realities. Although this situation is attributed primarily to "cultural atavisms," the very identification of aspects of the marginality of women is a breakthrough. Puebla represents a valuable shift in social teaching in relation to women's reality.[105]

The bishops assert that aspirations for liberation includes "the human advancement of the woman." Women are "to be present in temporal realities, contributing their specific reality as women" and participating with men in the transformation of society. The satisfaction of economic need is not to be the sole value of women's work. Work is also "an instrument for achieving personalization and building a new society." The bishops summon the Church "to contribute to the human and Christian advancement of

---

[104] ELA 834-9.

[105] Isasi-Diaz reports that the wording in this section of the document is "in some instances" identical with that used by Mujeres Para el Dialogo in their presentations and documents. Ibid. The value of the participation of women in the formation of social teaching is evident in a more adequate address of women's reality.

women," helping them to move out of their marginalized situation and equipping them "for their mission" in the church and the world.[106]

Equality in the family? The bishops affirm "the equality and dignity of the woman," as both women and men are made in God's image. "Thus the task of ruling the world, continuing the work of creation, and being God's co-creators is woman's as much as man's." However, they "underline" that "the fundamental role of the woman" is "mother, the defender of life and the home educator."[107]

The section addressing the family is similar to that in the Medellin documents, although mention of "a natural hierarchy" is omitted and egalitarian language is used throughout. The bishops assert that "the law of conjugal love is communion and participation, not domination."[108] Only their later assertion that a woman's fundamental role is that of mother indicates that women continue to bear special and additional responsibilities for the family, as there is no specific mention of fathering as a fundamental role for men nor the assertion that their participation is shaped by this role.

Critical assessment. The bishops seem then to be unable to break fully from natural law presumptions about women. In their discussion of the contribution of the social teaching of the Church "to liberation and human promotion," they note that there are "changing elements" in it "that correspond to the particular conditions of each country and each epoch." But the social teaching also contains "permanently valid elements that are grounded in an anthropology that derives from the message of Christ and in the perennial values of Christian ethics." It seems that notions of masculinity and femininity and mothering as woman's fundamental role are

---

[106] ELA, 848-9. This assertion contrasts somewhat with the assertion in another section of the conference document that "humanistically and evangelically the Church must contribute to the betterment of women, in line with their specific identity and femininity." ELA, para. 443. The second assertion is grounded in natural law assumptions.

[107] ELA 841, 846.

[108] ELA 582.

part of the permanently valid anthropology and perennial values of Christian ethics.[109]

The continuing force of these presuppositions, the refusal to raise the question of women's entry into ordained ministry,[110] the failure to articulate systematically the ways in which women are doubly oppressed and marginalized and then to develop norms and criteria to address this specific oppression and marginalization - all these elements of the Puebla documents limit an effective response to the situation of women that it so aptly describes. Neither Medellin nor Puebla adequately respond to the inequality of women they both observe.[111]

The Conference of United States Bishops, 1986

In the fall of 1986, the bishops of the United States issued a pastoral letter on economic justice. Concerned about high levels of unemployment and "harsh poverty" in a country of "great wealth," the bishops call for "economic justice for all."[112] The bishops base the church's belief about the moral dimensions of economic life in "its vision of the transcendent worth - the sacredness of human beings." The dignity of human persons,

---

[109] ELA 472. Beverly Harrison, "Sexism and the Language of Christian Ethics," *Making the Connections*, pp. 29-34, discusses how notions of masculinity and femininity are oppressive to women and men and work against their emancipation.

[110] Isasi-Diaz, pp. 300-301, reports this refusal.

[111] I would argue that this is also the case with the statement of the 1971 Synod of Bishops statement, *Justice in the World*, which I do not review here.

[112] *Economic Justice for All: Catholic Social Teaching and the U.S. Economy* (Washington, DC: United States Catholic Conference, 1986), paragraphs 15-6. In subsequent references to this text, it will be designated EJA and followed by the paragraph number of the passage cited. Two previous drafts of this letter had been circulated widely in 1984 and 1985, with suggestions and criticisms accepted by the drafting committee. Changes in the drafts which are significant to our topic will be noted. Pastoral letters on economic and social issues have been issued occasionally by US bishops since 1919. For a collection of some of these statements, see Part II of *Justice in the Marketplace*, pp. 365-475.

realized in community with others, is the criterion by which all aspects of economic life is measured.[113]

Justice and participation. The bishops extend this criterion through an analysis of the fundamental duties of social living, which they sum up as justice and participation:

> Basic justice demands the establishment of minimum levels of participation in the life of the human community for all persons.[114]

Patterns of exclusion, whether political or economic, are denounced by the bishops as "forms of social sin."

Fundamental human rights are prerequisites - minimal conditions - for life in community. The sum of these conditions make up the common good, and include rights to the fulfillment of material needs, a guarantee of fundamental freedoms and the protection of relationships that are essential to participation in the life of society. The bishops contend that political and civil rights "have been secured" in democratic countries and urge that "a new cultural consensus" be developed which recognizes economic rights.[115]

The bishops identify moral priorities for the nation. These priorities are norms to guide economic choices, not policies. The first priority is justice for all, the protection of the human rights of all, demanded by the common good. The obligation to provide justice for all means that "the poor have the single most urgent economic claim on the conscience of the nation."

> The fulfillment of the basic needs of the poor is of the highest priority. Personal decisions, policies of private and public bodies, and power relationships must all be evaluated by their effects on those who lack the minimum necessities of nutrition, housing, education and health care. In particular, this principle recognizes that meeting fundamental human needs must come before the fulfillment of desires for luxury consumer goods, for profits not conducive to the common good and for unnecessary military hardware.[116]

---

[113] EJA 28.

[114] EJA 77.

[115] EJA 79, 82.

[116] EJA 90.

This "option for the poor," which the bishops claim has deep roots in the Christian tradition, is to enable the poor "to become active participants in the life of society ... to share in and contribute to the common good."[117]

A "high social priority" is "increasing active participation in economic life by those who are presently excluded or vulnerable." Economic participation is enhanced by employment and "widespread ownership of property." The bishops challenge privileged economic power "in favor of the well-being of all." Both the domestic and international distribution of power are critically important.[118]

The strength and stability of family life is another key priority, as "the long-range future of this nation is intimately linked with the well-being of families, for the family is the most basic form of human community." Social and economic policies and the organization of work are to be evaluated "in light of their impact on the strength and stability of family life."[119]

Employment policy proposals. The bishops affirm full employment as the foundation of a just economy. The "creation of new jobs with adequate pay and decent working conditions" is the most urgent priority for the domestic economy. The bishops point out that blacks, hispanics, native Americans, young adults, and female-headed households are "represented disproportionately" among the unemployed. The personal and social costs of unemployment are judged to be morally unacceptable.[120]

The bishops observe that large numbers of women have entered the labor force, "both to put their talents and education to greater use and out of economic necessity." Female-headed households are usually dependent on the mother's income and many two-parent families need two salaries "to live in a decently human fashion."[121]

---

[117] EJA 88.

[118] EJA 91.

[119] EJA 93.

[120] EJA 136, 140, 143.

[121] EJA 144- 6.

The bishops attribute the high rate of unemployment and low pay of "racial minorities" and women in part to discrimination. They contend that lack of adequate child-care and "the unwillingness of many employers to provide flexible employment or extend fringe-benefits to part-time employees" compounds discrimination against women.[122]

Guidelines for action include fiscal and monetary policies coordinated to achieve full employment and to keep inflation under control. Targeted employment programs are also necessary. Some new strategies are suggested. These include job sharing, flex time, reduced workweek, pay equity between women and men, upgrading the pay scale and working conditions of low-paying jobs, and affirmative action policies for victims of racial or sexual discrimination.[123]

Proposals to overcome poverty. The bishops insist that dealing with poverty is a moral imperative of the highest order. They point out that poverty "is a condition experienced at some time by many people in different walks of life and in different circumstances." Many poor people work, but receive insufficient wages. Others are unable to work. Others are on the edge of poverty.[124]

The bishops note that children, women, and racial minorities are disproportionately represented among the poor. Wage discrimination is identified as a major factor in the high rates of poverty among women. Thus full time employment by itself is not a remedy for poverty among women. Women are also discriminated against in job classification and promotion. The bishops judge such discrimination to be immoral and call for efforts to overcome the effects of sexism in our society.

Women's responsibilities for child rearing are also a factor in women's poverty, according to the bishops. Women continue to have primary responsibility in this area. They usually bear the major financial burden for supporting their children in cases of divorce. Women may make career and job choices in light of these responsibilities and may not be hired or

---

[122] EJA 147.

[123] EJA 167.

[124] EJA 174.

promoted because of them either. Older women are often left in poverty, after a lifetime of homemaking and child rearing.

While most poor people are white, the rates of poverty are highest among racial minorities. Discrimination in labor markets, educational systems, and electoral politics are major obstacles keeping racial minorities from improving their economic status. This is evidence of racism, which the bishops also identify as sin.[125]

The bishops contend that the unequal distribution of wealth and income in the United States is important to a discussion of poverty. The gap between rich and poor has increased, and this gap is among the highest of industrialized countries. They insist that this inequality is of particular concern because it reflects the uneven distribution of power in American society.

The bishops declare that "fundamental changes in social and economic structures that perpetuate glaring inequalities" are required. The process of change should be one that draws all citizens, no matter what their economic status, together into one community. The most appropriate and fundamental solutions to poverty are those that enable people to take control of their lives. Elements of a strategy to combat poverty include building a healthy economy with full employment and adequate wages, removing barriers to full and equal employment for women and minorities, self-help efforts, tax reform, education for the poor, family stability, and welfare reform.[126]

Family stability. In discussing family stability, the bishops

> affirm the principle enunciated by John Paul II that society's institutions should be structured so that mothers of young children are not forced by economic necessity to leave their children for jobs outside the home.[127]

Social welfare and tax policies are to give support to "parents' decisions to care for their own children" and are to recognize "the work of parents in the home" because of its value for both the family and society. Accessible, quality child-care and parental leave policies are called for. The bishops

---

[125] EJA 181-2.

[126] EJA 187, 196-214.

[127] EJA 207.

also urge consideration of a family allowance or a children's allowance "as a possible vehicle for ensuring a floor of income support for all children and their families."[128]

U.S. role in the global economy. The bishops claim the preferential option for the poor as the central priority for global policies as well. The proposed policies include development assistance, equitable trade policies, reform of international financial institutions, appropriate foreign private investment, food self-sufficiency, non-coercive population policies, and reduction of the arms trade. The bishops urge the forgiveness of the foreign debt of some of the poorest African nations. They summarize their policy perspective as "a call for a U.S. international economic policy designed to empower people everywhere and enable them to continue to develop a sense of their own worth, improve the quality of their lives and ensure that the benefits of economic growth are shared equitably."[129]

Critical assessment. The U.S. Bishops pastoral letter contains some innovative teaching in regard to women's economic reality. Its critique of discrimination against women was strengthened through the various drafts. In the final draft such discrimination is for the first time identified as "sexism" and called "immoral."[130] Discrimination against women had been mentioned in previous social teaching but not explicitly condemned morally. The recognition of the wage gap between women and men and the impact of occupational segregation on women's economic reality is also new, as is the call for "particular attention to pay equity." The Pastoral goes beyond the Puebla documents which mentioned unequal wages, but not occupational segregation; nor was pay equity advocated there.[131]

The section on family stability, however, reflects the ambiguities characteristic of Catholic social teaching on this subject. As noted above, the bishops refer to the principle of John Paul II on mothers caring for their children. Although the remainder of the discussion of the family

---

[128] EJA 208, 215.

[129] EJA 275, 292.

[130] EJA 179.

[131] The bishops do not discuss exploitation of domestics or prostitution, which were mentioned in the Puebla documents.

consistently speaks of parents' work in the home and parental leave, the explicit affirmation of John Paul's teaching raises questions about what the bishops intend in relation to responsibilities for children. Earlier, the bishops pointed to women's responsibilities for child rearing as another factor in her impoverishment. As they do not explicitly urge fathers to take responsibility for child rearing or work in the home, they seem implicitly to accept the assignment of these tasks to women - in spite of the handicap this creates for women in relation to economic "rights."

Thus women's economic vulnerability is only partially addressed. Pay equity and child allowances may alleviate some of the particular problems women face, but the issue of their double work day remains. This is troubling not only in regard to the unjust division of labor within the family, but also in relation to the concern for participation - a central norm for the bishops in this document.[132]

Unlike the discussion of domestic poverty, women's economic reality is invisible in the analysis of the global economy. There is no recognition of women's role in food production or the special problems they face. Neither are the poor wages and working conditions third world women suffer in multinational corporations acknowledged. Nor do the bishops recognize that the poorest people who suffer because of International Monetary Fund austerity measures are predominantly women. Thus the policy goals suggested will not be met until the nature of the problem is better analyzed.

This criticism is analogous to criticism of the pastoral's methodology offered by other scholars.[133] These can be summarized as lack of a systemic social analysis, inconsistent use of socioeconomic theory, and limited application of the option for the poor. The preferential option for the poor

---

[132] Barbara Hilkert Andolsen, "A Woman's Work is Never Done: Unpaid Household Labor as a Social Justice Issue," *Women's consciousness, Women's conscience*, pp. 3-16, relates principles of Catholic social teaching to household labor.

[133] The most illuminating discussion of this document is by Hobgood, pp. 225-44.

suggests looking at society "from the perspective of its victims."[134]   A systemic analysis of the U.S. economy from the perspective of its victims would have yielded a more critical interpretation and more radical policy proposals.

The bishops challenge liberal understandings of the economy without fully going beyond these assumptions themselves. Hobgood points to a gap

> between the document's liberal policy proposals and the radical perceptions contained in the arguments for these proposals.... the bishops named the primary agents of change to be government and business. But their analysis of the way government and business actually functioned would seem to preclude the possibility of these being able to implement reform.[135]

Thus the bishops propose reforms such as pay equity, affirmative action, and full employment which are not possible within a capitalist political economy, as "racism, sexism, and cultural imperialism are systemic dimensions of our political economy" and must be treated as such.[136] As Lee Cormie clearly demonstrates, these and other evils such as militarism and deepening global poverty are not adequately illumined in the pastoral because they are not linked at the analytic level with the present concrete functioning of our political economy.[137]

---

[134] Gregory Baum, "A Canadian Perspective on the U.S. Pastoral" *Christianity and Crisis* 44 (1985), pp. 516-18.   Although both Baum's and Harrison's criticisms were made in reference to the first draft, they are applicable to the final draft as well.

[135] Hobgood, p. 239.

[136] Beverly W. Harrison, "Social Justice and Economic Orthodoxy" *Christianity and Crisis* 44 (1985), pp. 513-15. For a more detailed analysis of racism and sexism as integral dimensions of capitalism, see Linda Burnham, "Has Poverty Been Feminized in Black America?" and Pamela Sparr, "Reevaluating Feminist Economics," in *For Crying Out Loud*, pp. 61-83.

[137] Lee Cormie, "The U.S. Bishops on Capitalism," from the working papers of the American Academy of Religion, 1985, pp. 14-16.

Conference of Canadian Bishops, 1983

By contrast, the Canadian bishops clearly analyze the connections between poverty, unemployment, the growing gap between the rich and poor both in Canada and internationally and the crisis of the world capitalist system.[138] More radical strategies are suggested in response, such as promoting new forms of social ownership and control by communities and workers. Such strategies, if implemented, could benefit both poor and marginalized women and men.

But again, women's economic vulnerability would not be addressed automatically. In neither of these statements do the Canadian bishops acknowledge economic discrimination against women or women's unpaid labor. Neither do they challenge the division of labor within the family. Thus women's marginality and vulnerability could continue even with the structural transformations envisioned by the Canadian bishops.

Conclusion

Roman Catholic social teaching offers a mix of analyses of the political economy and proposals for economic justice. Almost every major document draws on traditional, liberal and radical models of economic life and social change. Although there was a shift away from traditional organic presuppositions and openness to radical policy proposals beginning with John XXIII, John Paul has regressed from the teaching of Paul VI and the Latin American bishops. Generally speaking, papal teaching has been more conservative, particularly in its policy proposals, than the regional bishops discussed here.

Along with the U.S. bishops, the popes primarily look to evangelization and conversion of the powerful for change rather than to empowerment of and solidarity with those who have been structurally marginalized. The warning of the 1971 World Synod of Bishops about "the objective obstacles

---

[138] Canadian Conference of Catholic Bishops, "Ethical Reflections on the Future of Canada's Socioeconomic Order," (December 13, 1983) *Justice in the Marketplace*, pp. 480-499; and Canadian Bishops Commission, "Alternatives to Present Economic Structures," *Origins* 12 (1983), pp. 522-27.

which social structures place in the way of conversion of hearts, or even realization of the ideal of charity" is not heeded.[139]

Though our survey demonstrates increasing concern for women's marginality, none of the documents of Catholic social teaching adequately address this reality. Earlier teaching, which John Paul has recalled, legitimates women's economic vulnerability by insisting that nature destines women to be mothers and that this role is incompatible with participation in the labor force.[140] Women's economic dependency is perpetuated, as is women's exclusive responsibility for unpaid labor.

The economic value of this labor is generally not recognized; it is usually spiritualized as nurturing or "creating the family hearth." Nor is the contribution women make in agricultural work acknowledged. This is particularly ironic in light of the consistent advocacy of "the just wage" as a central norm of social teaching. Presuppositions about both women and work prevent the application of this norm in this case.[141]

Presuppositions about work in Catholic social teaching are grounded not in natural law, but primarily follow classical and neo-classical economic theory. Work is conceived as an activity that produces goods and services for exchange in the market. Only this form of economic activity is rewarded with a wage. Thus the work women are expected to do in the home is not really work and is not worthy of inclusion in wage labor.

With John XXIII, an acceptance of women working outside the home began and there is a recognition of the desire for economic independence by some women. Yet the expectation that women are responsible for household

---

[139] "Justice in the World," in *Justice in the Marketplace*, p. 252.

[140] The reality of the lives of women who must work is not discussed, nor is the impact of economic proposals on their lives assessed. For instance, Italian women tailors in the early part of this century insisted that they could not earn a living even though they worked twelve hour days -the maximum the law allowed - at the low wages they received. "Organizing a Women's Union" (Italy, 1903), in *European Women: A Documentary History, 1789-1945* (New York: Schocken Books, 1980), pp. 27-8.

[141] I am not arguing here that "wages for housework" is a necessary or adequate norm for economic justice. Rather I am using the just wage in relation to domestic work as an illustration of the way women's economic contribution does not count in social ethics.

work and childcare remained. John recognized that this demanded more of women, but insisted that this was in keeping with women's "fundamental mission." Even recent teaching which highlights the marginality and economic vulnerability of women has not seriously challenged this contention. Assumptions about "woman's nature" legitimate social relations which contribute to women's marginality and vulnerability and mitigate the positive effects of shifts in other aspects of social teaching, such as notions about ownership of property, hierarchical organization of society, and structural change.

These assumptions also contribute to a distortion of women's moral agency. Affirmation of the equal dignity of women and men has been part of Catholic social teaching since Pius XII, but as we have seen never without qualification. As Giblin concluded in her study of these teachings, "human dignity does not really apply, because not only must their human nature be considered, but also their 'womanhood.'"[142] This is illustrative of the difference in kind maneuver which denies women full moral personhood, described by Kathryn Pauly Morgan. Theories are generated "about the nature of woman which claim that women differ from men either in degree or kind such that women are not entitled to full moral agency."[143]

More recent teaching has moved beyond the difference in degree characteristic of Thomas Aquinas, who claimed that "woman is defective and misbegotten" and therefore "naturally subject to man, because in man the discretion of reason predominates."[144] However, when claims continue to be made about the special vocation of women to motherhood, as in John Paul's recent apostolic letter on women, a difference in kind is maintained which tends to deny women full moral personhood.

A brief review of some of the main points of this letter illustrates this maneuver and more clearly illumines how notions of femininity deny women's full agency. John Paul affirms the mutuality and equality of male

---

[142] Giblin, p. 184.

[143] Morgan, p. 204. See the introduction of this study for a review of Morgan's work.

[144] Thomas Aquinas, *Summa Theologica* I. 92. 1 and 2, ed. Fathers of the English Dominican Province (London: Burns, Oates and Washbourne, Ltd., 1914).

and female, but he also maintains the notion of "that dignity and vocation that result from the specific diversity and personal originality of man and woman."

> Consequently, even the rightful opposition of women to what is expressed in the biblical words "he shall rule over you" (Gn. 3:16) must not under any condition lead to the "masculinization" of women. In the name of liberation from male "domination," women must not appropriate to themselves male characteristics contrary to their own feminine "originality."[145]

John Paul then defines femininity as receiving so as to give of self, always in response to the love of God or of husband.[146] The implication is that a woman is not to take initiative. Women's full moral agency is denied due to her "difference in kind." The limitations of the supposed mutuality of women and men is also exposed.[147]

Catholic women are challenging the denial of their full moral agency and personhood. A group of Peruvian women represent many other women when they insist that

> A woman's dignity resides in the fact that she is a human being, graced by God with the potential for realizing herself fully as a person. This self-realization must not be limited to her maternal role. The very fact that we can be mothers demands that we be given every opportunity to develop ourselves as persons.[148]

---

[145] John Paul II, *Mulieris Dignitatem* (On the Dignity and Vocation of Women, August 15, 1988), para. 10, in *Origins* 18, (1988), pp. 261-283.

[146] See especially MD 11.

[147] This also seems to be an instance of moral contortion. Morgan claims that such moral contortions can generate moral insanity, pp. 212-16. This understanding of femininity and motherhood as "receiving" also informs Catholic teaching against artificial contraception, which has created moral insanity for many faithful Catholics. John Paul also claims it as the basis for the denial of ordination to the priesthood to women, as they cannot represent Christ who *first* gave of *himself.* MD 26-7.

[148] "Reflections of Peruvian Women on the Occasion of the Visit of Pope John Paul II" (approved English translation), *Women in the Church*, The New LADOC "Keyhole" Series, no. 2 (Lima, Peru: Latin American Documentation, 1986), pp. 2-3.

In developing criteria for collaboration in "transforming from within those structures of a pluralistic society that respect and promote the dignity of the human person," the Latin American bishops at Puebla advocate "the irreplaceable responsibility of the woman, whose collaboration is indispensable for the humanization of the processes of transformation."[149]

For such collaboration to occur organic notions of women's nature must be overcome, the dynamics of women's marginalization need to be more clearly understood and empowerment strategies must be developed.

> In fidelity to its commitment to embrace a preferential option for the poor, the church cannot remain silent in the face of the intense suffering and exploitation of women. If it is to be faithful to its commitment to human liberation, the church must not ignore the sin of sexism so manifest both in the structures of society and in daily interpersonal relationships. Neither must it support patriarchy within society as a whole or in the structures of its own institution.[150]

Transformation of unjust structures and of oppressive social relations - class, gender and race - are required for movement toward full human liberation.

In the third part of this study, I will examine various analyses of women's reality in order to develop criteria for adequacy for social analysis in economic ethics. Then in the conclusion to the study, I will discuss normative proposals to more fully address women's economic vulnerability. But first a review of World Council of Churches teaching, the other primary source of progressive Christian social ethics, is necessary to reveal a different set of theoretical presuppositions which obscures women's reality.

---

[149] ELA 1206, 1219.

[150] "Reflections of Peruvian Women," p. 2.

CHAPTER THREE

THE WORLD COUNCIL OF CHURCHES: ECUMENICAL SOCIAL ETHICS AND WOMEN'S REALITY

The World Council of Churches also addresses issues of global economic justice, but with some different theoretical assumptions than most Roman Catholic social teaching. I contend that there has been a shift in World Council social teaching from a social ethic primarily informed by liberal presuppositions in which the responsible society is the central criterion to a social ethic primarily informed by radical presuppositions in which the just, participatory, sustainable society is the central criterion.[1]

In contrast to Roman Catholic social teaching, the family is seldom discussed in ecumenical social ethics. I contend that a primary reason for this absence is the liberal presuppositions of much ecumenical social

---

[1] For a discussion of these models, see chapter two of this study.

teaching.[2] As feminist social theorists point out, there is a public/private dichotomy within liberalism which separates the family from the public arena and then restricts women to the domestic arena.

> The family is based on natural ties of sentiment and blood and on the sexually ascribed status of wife and husband (mother and father). Participation in the public sphere is governed by universal, impersonal and conventional criteria of achievement, interests, rights, equality and property - liberal criteria, applicable only to men. An important consequence of this conception of private and public is that the public world, or civil society, is conceptualized and discussed in liberal theory in abstraction from, or as separate from, the private domestic sphere.[3]

As we shall see, the relationship of the family/household to the economy and the ways this shapes women's participation in the economy is not addressed in ecumenical social ethics.

In keeping with these presuppositions, both women and the family are generally discussed separately from the political economy. World Council teachings on women and the family are usually located in discussions of "community." A review of these teachings as well as the teachings on political economy illumines the contributions and limitations of ecumenical social ethics to social and economic justice for women.

---

[2] For a discussion of some of the difficulties in discussing matters that have been presumed to be "private," see Pauline Webb, "Gender as an Issue," *The Ecumenical Review* 40 (January 1988), pp. 4-15, and Thomas F. Best, "The Community Study: Where Do We Go From Here," Ibid., pp. 48-56. The consensual nature of the reports of the World Council assemblies and the tendency to see the role of women as a church-dividing issue which undermines the unity agenda of the Council are additional reasons for the lack of attention to the family within ecumenical social ethics.

[3] Carole Pateman, "Feminist Critiques of the Public/Private Dichotomy," *Feminism and Equality*, ed. Anne Phillips (New York: New York University Press, 1987), p. 106. Pateman argues that there is a second division within liberal theory between the public and private. This split is in the "public" arena; society and economy, arenas of freedom, are seen as "private" while the state and politics, an arena of coercion, are "public." This division is addressed to some extent in ecumenical social ethics.

The Gospel for All Realms of Life:
Life and Work Movement
Stockholm, 1925

First attempts at addressing issues of social and economic justice ecumenically occurred with the coming together of the Universal Christian Conference on Life and Work in Stockholm. The aim of the conference, as defined by the International Executive Committee in 1923, was

> to unite the different churches in common practical work, to furnish the Christian conscience with an organ of expression in the midst of the great spiritual movements of our time, and to insist that the principles of the Gospel be applied to the solution of contemporary social and international problems.[4]

The Conference was not to address questions of faith and order, which were the mandate of the Faith and Order movement. Rather, it was to deal with questions of "a more directly practical character."

Emerging economic ethic. Over five hundred representatives of "the greater number" of Christian communions gathered in Stockholm, Sweden in August of 1925.[5] A formal vote was not taken on any question before the conference, with the exception of the message which was sent to the churches.[6] The message began with a call to the churches to repentance and courage. The delegates then proclaimed their acceptance of "the urgent duty of applying [the] Gospel in all

---

[4] G.K.A. Bell, editor, *The Stockholm Conference 1925* (London: Oxford University Press, 1926), p. 1. Bell's volume is the official report of the conference.

[5] Protestant and Orthodox communions, mainly from Europe and North America but also from Asia, Africa, and Latin America, sent representatives to the conference. The Roman Catholic Church declined to participate. About thirty women were among the official delegate body. Several women addressed the conference.

[6] According to David Gaines, a fear that the unity of the gathering might not survive action on controversial matters led to the decision not to take formal votes. Gaines, p. 49. The message was adopted with only three or four dissenting votes.

realms of human life - industrial, social, political and international."[7] Specific principles in regard to economic life are articulated. The "soul" is declared to be of supreme value and is not to be subordinated to either "the rights of property or the mechanism of industry." Industry is not to be based entirely on the desire for profit, but should be "for the service of the community." An account for the stewardship of property is to be given to God. Capital and labor are to co-operate rather than conflict. Both employers and employed are to see their work as fulfillment of a vocation. These principles are necessary for obedience to the command of the Gospel "to do unto others even as we would they should do unto us."[8]

Specific teaching on women. No particular mention of women or their economic reality is included in the message. The only specific reference to women appears in the paragraph on social morality. "Questions which affect woman, the child, and the worker" are mentioned as among "the more intimate questions which a higher appreciation of personality raises."[9] Such wording implies that women are not conceived of as workers. It may also imply acceptance by the conference of the economic dependence of women as normative, although this is not specifically articulated.

A traditional gendered division of labor is advocated by Paula Mueller-Ottfried in her speech before the conference on "The Relation of the Sexes." Mueller-Ottfried argued that the different characteristics of "woman" and "man" contribute to "a division of work" that men "are above all active" and women "chiefly passive." She also contends that the "worth or value of woman ... as the God-given partner of man, as the fellow-disciple of Christ" is equal with the status and value of "the man." Yet she claimed that women are to be "true to her own nature"

---

[7] Bell, p. 711.

[8] Ibid., p. 712.

[9] Ibid., p. 712.

or both the family and "the Christian ideal" would lose ground.[10] This traditional understanding of male/female relations and the family, though seldom articulated so forthrightly, would continue to inform ecumenical ethics.

Critical assessment. Richard Dickinson describes the mood of this conference as "reformist at best, if not palliative in many respects."[11] Although the responsibility of Christians in relation to "the social problem" is affirmed, education and charity are the primary proposals for bringing about changes in economic life. The norms for economic life are articulated in a general way and no specific policy goals - such as a living wage or the right of workers to organize - are proposed. Yet, as W.A. Visser t' Hooft observed, Stockholm was a turning point in church history "in that the churches said together clearly that in the presence of the Cross they accepted the urgent duty of applying the Gospel of Christ in all realms of human life ... after a long period in which Christians had accepted to live in two worlds..."[12]   The

---

[10] In his commentary on the conference, Edward Shillito noted the lack of unanimity and preoccupation with "sexual questions" during the conference. Edward Shillito, *Life and Work* (London: Longmans, Green and Co., Ltd. 1926). Given this, it is likely that Mueller-Ottfried's views, which seem to be in sympathy with those of papal social teachings on women, were not held by all the delegates at the Stockholm Conference. It is significant that the only discussion of sexual questions in the official report is Mueller-Ottfried's presentation.

The ecumenical Conference on Christian Politics, Economics and Citizenship held in Britain in 1924 offered a contrasting view of women's role in the home and the sexual division of labor. Among its observations were these: "Although the theme of poets and of artists, the mother has received scant recognition in practice for her services to the community. There is no saying more trite than 'the hand that rocks the cradle rules the world,' but to many hard-worked and overburdened mothers it must have sounded as a bitter joke. *C.O.P.E.C. Commission Reports* (London: Longmans, Green and Co., 1924), Volume 3, p. 135. "The fact has often been commented on that this arrangement [division of labor by gender] reduced woman to a status of practical slavery." Ibid., Volume 4, p. 12.

[11] Dickinson, p. 43.

[12] W.A. Visser 't Hooft, "The historical significance of Stockholm 1925," *the Gospel for all realms of life: reflections on the Universal Christian Conference on Life and Work* (Geneva: WCC, 1975), p. 15.

conference was successful in helping build mutual trust and a will to cooperate among the churches.

Participation of Women in Ecumenical Organization

A continuation committee was appointed by the Stockholm conference. This was "a first step towards the formation of a more permanent ecumenical organization of the churches." The committee was to "carry on the work of the Conference and to consider how far and in what ways its practical suggestions may be made operative," to gather information in regard to co-operation among the churches, and to consider holding another conference. [13]

A resolution was adopted in 1929, urging greater representation of women on the commissions and committees of the Life and Work movement as a matter of social justice.

> Resolved - That the Continuation Committee observes with regret the small representation of the women of the Churches in its membership and in the membership of the Commissions. Women are not only active in the work of the Church, but they constitute a larger percentage of the membership of the Churches than men. We also live in a day in which there is a powerful and universal trend towards comradeship and equality between men and women in life and in work.... It is not advisable, therefore, for the Church to lag behind such an important phase of social justice...[14]

Although there were various efforts to increase the representation of women, their membership on committees did not significantly increase.

---

[13] Visser't Hooft, "the historical significance," p. 16. The Continuation Committee met regularly until 1930, at which time it was reconstituted as The Universal Christian Council for Life and Work.

[14] Minutes of the Continuation Committee, 9/5-9/19/1929, (n.p.), p. 9. This resolution was brought by a Dr. Tippy from the United States.

Oxford, 1937: Theological and Ethical Foundations

The second conference of the Life and Work movement was held in Oxford, England, in 1937.[15] The world-wide depression of the 1930's and the rise of fascism were preoccupations of the conference. According to John Bennett, this conference "projected a Christian ethic for the economic order which is even now relevant to Christian thinking in the industrialized democracies."[16]

In his introduction to the Conference report, ecumenical leader J. H. Oldham notes that the significance of the reports of the Oxford conference is that "what they say is what a large body of Christians, representatives of diverse countries and Christian traditions, were prepared ... to say together."[17] As the work of this conference was to shape the social teaching of the World Council of Churches for at least two decades, it is important to review its conclusions about economic ethics in some depth.

The message from the conference to the churches summed up its views on the Christian faith and economic life. The first duty of the church is insisting that economic activities, like every other area of human life, stand "under the judgment of Christ." Economic classes are "a barrier to human fellowship" and are not be tolerated by the

---

[15] J. H. Oldham, *The Oxford Conference: Official Report* (Chicago: Willett, Clark & Co., 1937). Delegates from over forty countries came to the conference. Three hundred delegates were official representatives of the principal churches in the United States, Great Britain, the British dominions, and Europe. There were also about 30 delegates, many of whom were Western missionaries, from the "younger churches" in Japan, China, India, Africa, and South America. Although there were instructions to the conference organizing committee to include representatives of the universities, public life, the working classes, women and youth, only twenty women were among the delegates and few, if any, members of "the working classes." There seem to be no women among the speakers, in contrast to several who spoke at Stockholm in 1925.

[16] John Bennett, "Breakthrough in Ecumenical Social Ethics: The Legacy of the Oxford Conference on Church, Community, and State (1937)," *The Ecumenical Review* 40 (April 1988), p. 134.

[17] Oldham., pp. 16-17.

Christian conscience, but "no change in the outward ordering of life [could] of itself eradicate social evil" because of "the reality of sin." Christians are asked "to bear witness within the existing economic order and to test all economic institutions in the light of their understanding of God's will."[18]

The section of the conference report on "The Economic Order" claims that the will of God is revealed in Christ as the commandment of love - "the ultimate standard of human conduct." But "a relative standard" is needed "to check human sinfulness." This standard is the principle of justice, which is defined as "the ideal harmonious relation of life to life." Justice checks "sinful tendencies" by "defining the rightful place and privilege which each life must have in the harmony of the whole and by assigning the duty of each to each."[19] Using these principles, social and economic systems which give "one man undue advantage over others" are condemned. Systems which create "luxury and pride on the one hand and want and insecurity on the other" are challenged by the principle of love of neighbor.[20]

Economic systems criticized. The conference articulated critiques of both communism and capitalism, a theme which continued with the formation of the World Council. Social justice is recognized as the aim of socialist and communist movements. But the utopianism, materialism, and disregard for the dignity of the individual are rejected as elements of the historical development of communism which conflict with the Christian truth.

Four aspects of the assumptions and operation of the economic order of the industrialized world (capitalism) affront the "moral and spiritual nature of man." These are:

> 1) the enhancement of acquisitivesness when industry was organized for purely financial results rather than "service of the community,"
> 2) inequalities between races, nationalities, and classes,
> 3) irresponsible possession of economic power, and

---

[18] Ibid., p. 58.

[19] Ibid., pp. 76-7.

[20] Ibid., p. 80.

4) the frustration of the sense of Christian vocation, particularly through unemployment.[21]

Proposals for reform of this system involve "technical issues upon which technical evidence varies," so it was not possible "to claim a moral obligation" in support of any one proposal.[22]

Middle axioms for economic ethics. The conference delegates calle for formulation of "middle axioms" - working principles which could be a common basis for Christian action. These principles are to be intermediate between the command to love neighbor as self and "the unguided intuition of the individual conscience."[23]

Standards for measuring concrete situations and proposals in the economic order are articulated in the conference report, by way of example.

1) Class divisions based upon differences of wealth are an obstacle to "right fellowship between man and man." Thus the private accumulation of wealth is to be limited and "a worthy means of livelihood" made available to every member of the community.

2) Opportunities of education for every child and youth, regardless of race and class, are required.[24] In this connection, the protection of the family as a social unit is claimed as an urgent concern.

3) Care is to be provided for persons "disabled from economic activity, whether by sickness, infirmity, or age."

---

[21] Ibid., pp. 87-91.

[22] Ibid., p. 96.

[23] Ibid., p. 219.

[24] The section of the conference report which addressed "The Church and Race" asserts that "alien or outcast peoples" claim "special regard for Christians." Among the principles formulated to guide "sentiments and public policies" is "the right of every person, whatever his race, color or present status, to conditions essential for life as a person; to education; to opportunity in his vocation, recreation and social intercourse." Ibid., p. 216. For a record of all World Council statements on race see Ans J. van der Bent, editor, *Breaking Down the Walls: World Council of Churches' Statements and Actions on Racism, 1948-1985* (Geneva: WCC, 1986).

4) "The duty and the right of men to work" is emphasized, as labor has intrinsic worth and dignity. "The workingman, whether in field or factory, is entitled to a living wage, wholesome surroundings and a recognized voice in the decisions which affect his welfare as a worker."

5) The resources of the earth are gifts of God which are to be used "with due and balanced consideration" for the needs of both the present and future generations.

The report noted that "drastic changes in economic life" are implied if these standards are taken seriously.[25]

Property rights are critically related to the application of these standards and to the ends of economic life. Several specific principles of Christian teaching on property are articulated. The first reaffirms that "without qualification" property rights are "relative and contingent only." Individual property rights are never to be maintained "without regard to their social consequences or without regard to the contribution which the community makes in the production of wealth."[26]

Clear distinctions are made between various forms of property. Personal possessions for use have more moral justification than property "in the means of production and in land," as these give power over others. "All property which represents social power stands in special need of moral scrutiny, since power to determine the lives of others is the crucial point in any scheme of justice." Small-scale productive property also needs to be scrutinized, as it could "tempt the owner, in his competition with more powerful and productive units, to exploit hisown family and the other workers employed, especially since ... the latter may be too few to organize effectively."[27]

Perhaps most striking and innovative is the assertion that

> [t]he existing system of property rights and the existing distribution of property must be criticized in the light of the largely nonmoral processes by which they have been developed, and criticism must take account of the fact that every

---

[25] Oldham, pp. 99-100.

[26] Ibid., p. 100.

[27] Ibid, pp. 100-102.

argument in defense of property rights which is valid for Christian thinking is also an argument for the widest possible distribution of these rights.[28]

In comparison to papal social teaching which does not raise the question of how the existing distribution of property came about, this contention stands out.

The delegates contend that a new period in Christian thinking about economic life has come with the possibility of economic plenty. Before this period, poverty was often due to natural causes. But with the advent of economic plenty, the abolition of poverty depends on the human organization of economic life. Thus the persistence of poverty is something for which humans were morally responsible. "More equal justice in the distribution of wealth" is called for, not "charitable paternalism."[29]

Ambiguous teaching on women. The Oxford conference is ambiguous in regard to women and their participation in economic life. The growing emancipation of women is identified as a particular instance of a beneficial consequence of the breakup of tradition. Yet "the effect of modern industry in taking both parents out of the home" is identified as a factor in the weakening of family ties.[30]

Not surprisingly, there is no analysis of women's participation in the economy. The presupposition seems to be that insofar as women participate in the economy, their participation is no different from that of men. For example, a "charge" is addressed to women and men in industry,[31] which assumes that their roles, status, and power are equal. In the Oxford documents, as in progressive economic thought of the period, the experience of men is presumed to be the experience of

---

[28] Ibid., p. 100.

[29] Ibid., p. 87.

[30] Ibid., 174, 123.

[31] "To Christian men and women in the same vocation or industry, to meet together for prayerful discussion as to how, in their particular sphere of common life, the practical problems which arise can be dealt with as God would require." Ibid., p. 223.

women. The particularities of women's experience remain invisible.[32]

Critical assessment. The work of the Oxford conference was foundational for the development of World Council social ethics.[33] The theological foundations which are laid in the discussion of the relation of love and justice, the notion of middle axioms, criticism of political economic systems, and attention to the role of the laity are continuing themes in ecumenical ethics.

The standards given as guidelines for measuring economic policies - right to employment, a living wage, a voice for workers, the conditional nature of property - are ones that could improve the economic wellbeing of many. But the strategic proposals suggested seem inadequate to implement them, particularly in regard to the insightful critique of the dynamics of industrialized capitalism. The emphasis on harmonizing interests and individual action minimize the

---

[32] This is the "vanishing act" of universalism, in which language which claims to be generic obscures the male bias of the theory. For a discussion of this, see Beverly Thiele, "Vanishing Acts in Social and Political Thought," *Feminist Challenges: Social and Political Theory*, ed. Carole Pateman and Elizabeth Gross (Boston: Northeastern University Press, 1986), pp. 30-43.

Such assumptions also characterized the companion study volumes for the Oxford conference. For instance, in the volume on theological anthropology the notion of "man" being created in "the image of God" was prominent in the descriptions of human nature. Not once was it noted by these theologians that in the Genesis passage from which this notion comes, both male and female are created in God's image. Nor was there any discussion of sexuality. Women were never named in the discussion at all; the supposedly generic term "man" presumed to include them. T.E. Jessop et al, *The Christian Understanding of Man* (Chicago: Willett Clark and Company, 1938).

Ruth L. Smith has a useful discussion of the development of universal assumptions in liberalism in regard to the work of Reinhold Niebuhr, who was an influential figure at the Oxford Conference. "Reinhold Niebuhr and History: The Elusive Liberal Critique," *Horizons* 15, (1988), pp. 283-98.

[33] For a discussion of this continuing influence, see Dickinson, p. 44; Bock, p. 60, and Paul Abrecht, "From Oxford to Vancouver" Lessons from Fifty Years of Ecumenical Work for Economic and Social Justice," *The Ecumenical Review* 40, (April 1988). Abrecht argued that "No other ethical approach or methodology has been articulated which has commanded a similar measure of ecumenical agreement or support. It remains still today an influential option in ecumenical social thought... " Ibid., p. 150.

need for confronting injustice or systemic change alluded to in some sections of the report.[34] A liberal understanding of social change in which balance is the appropriate organizing principle predominates.[35]

The Responsible Society:
Early Years of the WCC

Amsterdam, 1948

In 1948 the Life and Work movement and the Faith and Order movement joined together to form the World Council of Churches. The constituting assembly was convened at Amsterdam in late August, 1948.[36] The Amsterdam report began with a dramatic description of the current social disorder and its root cause:

> The world today is experiencing a social crisis of unparalleled proportions. The deepest root of that disorder is the refusal of men to see and admit that their responsibility to God stands over and above their loyalty to any earthly community and their obedience to any worldly power.[37]

---

[34] The need for systemic change was mentioned in the discussion of concrete standards for measuring economic life and in the discussion of the church and race.

[35] John Bennett observed in a recent interview that "the normative elements of the American Catholic bishops' recent letter on the economy are very similar to the conference's report. Ideas about property and equality, poverty and unemployment, and the whole challenge to a prevailing view of what I call 'the almost moral self-sufficiency' of the free-enterprise system are similar in both documents." David McCreary, "John Bennett on Oxford '37," *The Christian Century* (October 28, 1987), pp. 942-4. Not surprisingly, my criticisms of Oxford proposals are similar to those I made of the US Bishops' proposals.

[36] There were 351 official delegates and nearly as many alternates representing 135 denominations in 44 countries. The work of the Assembly was divided among several sections, with Section III responsible for the report on The Church and the Disorder of Society. Gaines, p. 225.

[37] W.A. Visser't Hooft, editor, *The First Assembly of the World Council of Churches: Official Report,* (London: SCM Press, Ltd, 1949), p. 74.

Two chief factors are identified as contributing to the crisis: 1) the vast concentrations of power - "which are under capitalism mainly economic and under Communism both economic and political," and 2) the domination of society by "technics." The churches' contribution to the reigning social disorder is acknowledged: the churches have been "obstacles to changes necessary in the interests of social justice and political freedom" by giving "religious sanction to the special privileges of dominant classes, races and political groups." [38]

Economic ethics and the responsible society. In examining the relation of economic and political systems, the report observes that although controls have been put on "the free play of economic forces," there are "economic necessities" which no political order can defy - such as the need for stability in the value of money, for creation of capital, and for incentives in production. Yet the Assembly reaffirmed that justice demands that "economic activities be subordinated to social ends." Insecurity, hunger and frustration of vast numbers of people by periodic inflation or depression is declared to be intolerable.[39]

Although "coherent and purposeful ordering of society" is seen as necessary, the Assembly wanted to avoid "an undue centralisation of power." Thus, several "centres of initiative in economic life" and "smaller forms of community" are encouraged. These could be in local government, within industrial organizations, trade unions, and through the development of public corporations and voluntary associations.[40]

The Assembly developed the notion of "the responsible society" as the goal for which the churches should work.

> A responsible society is one where freedom is the freedom of men who acknowledge responsibility to justice and public order, and where those who hold political authority or economic power are responsible for its exercise to God and the people whose welfare is affected by it.[41]

---

[38] Ibid., pp. 75-6.

[39] Ibid., p. 76.

[40] Ibid., p. 77. Note the similarity between this proposal and the principle of "subsidiarity" as articulated within Roman Catholic social teaching.

[41] Visser't Hooft, p. 77.

This notion is grounded in an anthropology which claims that "man is created and called to be a free being, responsible to God and his neighbor." Thus anything which deprives humanity of the possibility of acting responsibly denies God's intention for humanity.[42]

The notion of the responsible society requires "that power be made responsible to law and tradition, and be distributed as widely as possible through the whole community" and that "economic justice and the provision of equality of opportunity be established for all the members of society." The ideologies of both laissez-faire capitalism and communism are rejected by the Assembly. Christians are to seek "new, creative solutions which never allow either justice or freedom to destroy the other."[43]

Women: invisible and marginal. Women's economic and social reality is invisible in the Amsterdam reports on social and economic disorder, as it had been in the Oxford conference documents. This invisibility at Amsterdam is the more ironic, however, because one of the preparatory papers for the Assembly specifically addresses men and women at work. In this paper, Kathleen Bliss sketches the history of women's participation in the work force, delineating some of the ways that their participation differs from men's, particularly in "bourgeois society." She also identifies an increasing range of work shared by women and men in a "technical society."

Bliss unmasks some of the unspoken presumptions of World Council of Churches social thought through an analysis of the conflict within "the technical society" between the need for women's work and the need "for intelligent and responsible mothers." She argues that this problem needs to

> be approached from the end of society, since it is usually handled by Christian writers from the opposite end, of the needs of the individual. From that point of view the demands of society for women's labor are looked upon as a threat to home life, a rival claim and loyalty, to be dismissed all too often with the catch phrase "a woman's place is in the

---

[42] Ibid.

[43] Ibid., pp. 79-80.

home" and a far too easy identification of women's God-given vocation with her biological function.[44]

Bliss argues that this attitude "does less than justice to the large contribution made by women in closing the gap between the standards of nutrition, health and education in the homes of the richest and the homes of the poorest." This task of narrowing the gap is only possible, Bliss claims, in a society "where social justice is a constant aim and where women are free and willing to take their share."[45] That none of Bliss' insights on women's economic roles and contributions are reflected in the report on the disorder of society is probably related to the small number of women who were delegates to the Assembly.

While women's reality is ignored in the Assembly's socio-economic analysis, the question of the participation of women in the church is addressed.[46] A report on "The Life and Work of Women in the Church" was received by the committee on "Concerns of the Churches." Affirming that the church is made up of "women and men, created as responsible persons, together to glorify God and to do His will," the report acknowledges the gap between theory and practice. "In many countries and churches it is evident that the full co-operation of men and women has not been achieved." Insisting that the church needs contributions from all its members, the report calls for co-operation between women and men "in the Christian home, in the duties

---

[44] Kathleen Bliss, "Personal Relations in a Technical Society," *The Church and the Disorder of Society: An Ecumenical Study* (Geneva: World Council of Churches, 1948), p. 85.

[45] Ibid., p. 86.

[46] During the discussion of the report on The Life and Work of Women in the Church, Saroe Chakko, chair of the committee, noted the disappointment of some that only two women were on the Central Committee of the World Council. Visser't Hooft, p. 151. Melanie May sketches a useful history of women's participation in the World Council with a particular focus on the Amsterdam Assembly. *Bonds of Unity* (Atlanta: Scholars Press, 1989). See also Susannah Herzel, *A Voice for Women: The women's department of the World Council of Churches*, (Geneva: WCC, 1981).

of Christian citizenship, in secular occupations, and in social and community life."[47]

Critical assessment. For the next two decades, WCC work continued to embrace Amsterdam's theme of "the responsible society." Many interpreters celebrate the notion as Amsterdam's greatest contribution to World Council social teaching. Paul Abrecht contends that this "social/ethical criterion"

> proved a valuable guide to Christian thinking in the midst of the fierce theological-ideological battles of the period, helping the churches to resist the pressure from both sides for an absolute commitment in the world power struggle. It was a practical demonstration of the ability of the WCC to develop an independent ecumenical perspective for viewing the world struggle without giving up its own fundamental concern for a just and democratic society.[48]

This criterion provided a common ground for statements by the churches on social issues.

There was one dissenting voice to Amsterdam's analysis of the sources of the disorder of society. C.L. Patijin, a Dutch layman who served in his country's Parliament, in addressing the Assembly characterized the existing economic disorder as a structural disorder. Simply to declare that economic crisis to be a consequence of sin gives no specification to the structural aspect of the crisis, Patijin argued. Rather it turns "a theological truth partially into a lie."[49]

In the attempt to lay a solid theological foundation for and to maintain the unity of this new ecumenical body, in-depth structural analysis of economic reality is lacking, as are specific strategic

---

[47] Visser't Hooft, 146-7. "Certain problems relating to the life and work of women in the Church" were highlighted. These included the integration of women's voluntary organizations into the official church structure; the need to include women on church governing boards; the training, remuneration, status and security of women who were professional church workers; and "careful and objective study" of the ordination of women to the full ministry. The report was "received by the Assembly and commended to the churches for their serious consideration and appropriate action.

[48] Abrecht, pp. 150-1.

[49] Visser't Hooft, (1948), p. 167.

proposals. Instead, the Assembly attempts to find a third way between capitalism and communism.[50] Furthermore, liberal presuppositions about the autonomy of different spheres of society, the public/private dichotomy, and the need for balance are operational in the work of the Assembly.

Evanston, 1954

At the Evanston Assembly six years later, the notion of the responsible society is expanded:

> 'Responsible society' is not an alternative social or political system, but a criterion by which we judge all existing social orders and at the same time a standard to guide us in the specific choices we have to make.[51]

Justice within the responsible society is to be dynamic. In regard to economic life, justice involves "a continuous effort to overcome economic disadvantages ... which are incompatible with equal opportunity." In regard to political institutions, justice requires both protection by law against arbitrary use of power and the responsible participation by all citizens."[52]

Liberal policy proposals. Particular policy norms are identified in a discussion of the problems of economic life. Relative freedom of enterprise is advocated as the price system was seen to play a regulating role in the economy. Goals for economic life include efficient and increased production as well as a fair distribution or equity in the distribution of wealth and income. The need for assistance to the economically vulnerable is to be promoted by the churches.

---

[50] Julio de Santa Ana, a former director of the World Council Commission on the Churches' Participation in Development, contends that the notion of the responsible society was "an intention to look for a third way *between* capitalism and socialism." "The Economic Debate in the Ecumenical Movement," *The Ecumenical Review 37* (January 1985), p. 103.

[51] Visser't Hooft, editor, *The Evanston Report,* (London: SCM Press, Ltd. 1955), p. 113.

[52] Ibid., p. 115.

Decentralized decisionmaking and widely distributed power are marks of a responsible society.   Responsible initiative and hard work are praised as virtues to be developed.

More dramatic policy goals are endorsed for "economically underdeveloped areas." When the Evanston report cited findings from one of its preparatory study conferences held in India, "the responsible society" is set within a global context. Development of political institutions, land reform and rural development, industrialization, and action in relation to population growth are all identified as problems to be addressed and are recognized as world problems of concern to all the churches.[53]

In articulating the meaning of the responsible society, the role of various small groups is noted. Of these, the family is said to be "the most fundamental." The churches are called to give "strong warning against the widespread disruption of family life." The family is to be protected, as "the witness of the Christian family is all important." It is noted that "in predominantly non-Christian countries, the building of a Christian family life implies in some cases a rupture with old non-Christian family systems."[54]

Women and work. Another section of the report addresses the Christian understanding of work. Interestingly, the definition of work is challenged by a Miss Asch van Wyck who charges that the definition omits housewives and those not gainfully employed. A rewording gave the following definition: "In one aspect work is the necessary ordering of daily life so that human needs may be fulfilled and as such work

---

[53] Ibid., pp. 124-26.

[54] Ibid., p. 114. Although this report did not specify what a Christian family was, an examination of World Council materials on the family reveals it to be the Western bourgeois nuclear family. Perhaps the most illuminating work is *Sex, Love and Marriage in the Caribbean* (Geneva: WCC, 1965), the report of a World Council seminar. The Foreward to this report contends that there were efforts "to distinguish what was Christian from what was merely Western" in thinking out "the fundamental character of the Christian family" in the intercultural work of the World Council. Ibid., p. 4. Contemporary historical critical scholarship would question whether there is one normative understanding of "the Christian family."

begins every morning in farm, factory, and home."[55]   Again we observe evidence that a woman raises questions pressing for alternative perspectives on women and work, but such a perspective is not integrated into the body of teachings on economic ethics.

Critical assessment. The invisibility of women's economic reality continues in the main body of social teachings of the World Council as it had in the Life and Work Movement. In 1948, a voice for women in the World Council was created through the institution of a women's desk; but this desk was structurally marginal to the divisions responsible for the work of social justice.[56] The participation of women in Assemblies was limited, so they are marginalized in that process too.

The notion of the responsible society, as amplified at Evanston, continued to provide the conceptual framework for the development of the Council's social ethic. It is claimed that this conceptualization is independent of any one ideological camp.[57] However if one examines the criterion for policy cited above - equality of opportunity, free enterprise, equitable distribution, efficiency of production - liberal presuppositions are clearly dominant. Increasingly, as voices from third world countries are present at World Council Assemblies, the notion of the responsible society or the claim that it is a "non-ideological" conception comes under growing criticism.

---

[55] Visser't Hooft, (1955), p. 164. The original definition was not included in the report.

[56] The World Council reproduced the structure of most Protestant denominations, where women's organizations were usually located in the section of the organization dealing with internal or educational concerns. Further exploration is needed to determine that this location is rooted in the public/private split of bourgeois society. It may be that when women entered the institutional arena they were assigned responsibility for tasks traditionally related to those they had in the so-called private sphere - housekeeping and nurturance. On this topic, see Pateman, p. 117.

[57] See quote from Abrecht in discussion of the Amsterdam Assembly above.

Challenges to "The Responsible Society:"
The Middle Years of the WCC

New Delhi, 1961

In 1961 the Third Assembly of the World Council of Churches met in New Delhi, India, the first to be held in a third world nation. Twenty-nine new member churches joined the council at this assembly, most all of them from the second and third worlds. Abrecht observes that this "enlarging constituency was changing the substance and shape of ecumenism, most especially its political and social agenda."[58] Concern for economic development comes to the forefront of the agenda at the Third Assembly.

Human development the criterion. In discussing technological and social change, the Assembly declared that Christians are to advocate changes "that serve the ends of justice and freedom, that break the chains of poverty..." Efforts to increase production and raise living standards are embraced, as basic needs of many of the world's peoples are unmet or endangered. The Assembly called for a world strategy of development and the subordination of "personal, group or national interest to the well-being of all". The Assembly cautions that economic growth, though "essential, is "not sufficient in itself.... It is the whole man, and not only a part of his personality or body that must be served."[59]

Another report of the Assembly also stresses the importance of action in the arena of economic development. "Justice demands a more equitable distribution of God-given resources" and "solidarity requires that nations collaborate for the creation of wealth for their common welfare." Yet, "trade, not aid" is endorsed as the most effective means

---

[58] Abrecht, p. 154.

[59] W.A. Visser't Hooft, editor, *The New Delhi Report* (Geneva: WCC, 1962) pp. 95-6. Julio de Santa Ana contends that the concept of "human development" became a middle axiom for ecumenical ethics, beginning with the New Delhi assembly. Santa Ana, p. 103.

to further development. Effective markets for the developing countries are to be secured by international cooperation.[60]

Some delegates explicitly criticized the adequacy of the responsible society as the central ethical criterion from the perspective of the new nations then coming into being. In particular, they charged that the criteria for judging political institutions set forth by previous assemblies reflects the experience of "long established constitution states." Each nation is "to be free to develop the patterns of political life which suit its genius best and correspond to the stage of political maturity." But this freedom is not absolute. It is limited by basic moral and political requirements of national and international community. The report warns that economic dependence upon other countries or "international industries" threatens the realization of political independence of new nations and their ability to be responsible societies. [61]

Women, work, and families. Women remain invisible in the documents of the World Council that turn toward advocating economic justice on a global scale. The presumption is that development would benefit women equally with men. A sketch of women's economic reality is included in the report placed before the Assembly by the Department on Co-operation of Men and Women in Church, Family and Society. The report notes that changes within the family are occurring, although it concludes that no general pattern to such changes can be discerned.

> In some areas, the woman is left alone at the head of the family whether it be for years of migratory labour in the Copperbelt [in Africa], or for months of seasonal work as in Italy, or for the daily absence of men in the suburbs of New York. In other sections of the same societies, the man, with shorter working hours and increased leisure, is becoming more clearly aware of his opportunities and responsibilities as a father, and is more ready to share with his wife (who is often herself gainfully employed and without servants) in the day to day running of the home.[62]

---

[60] This discussion is from the report of the Committee on the Commission of the Churches in International Affairs. Visser't Hooft, 1962, pp. 275-6.

[61] Ibid., p. 100.

[62] Ibid., p. 211.

Astonishingly, it is argued that "new educational opportunities" and the growing economic independence of women have put an end to their exploitation as cheap labor. These presumably positive changes necessitate "new protective measures and new standards of morality to replace the social safeguards of the past."[63]

The report declares the "problem" of working mothers of young children "extremely complicated" and the solutions to the problem unclear. The report calls for more study on the question of working mothers, but cautions that "it is never sufficient to protest or criticize adversely." The report also affirms the "need to dignify women who remain at home to provide for husbands, children, and guests, and who are able to maintain their interest in the affairs of Church and society at large."[64]

Critical assessment. The optimistic tone of the report on global development is also observable here. Not only is the exploitation of women as cheap labor said to be a thing of the past, equality of opportunity and protective legislation are the only policy criteria advocated. The perspective of this report is pervaded by assumptions of bourgeois families in which "the wife" has the option of remaining at home. It is obvious that there are few women delegates at this Assembly, particularly women from the working classes of either the first or third world, and such assumptions went unchallenged.

---

[63] Ibid. Purdah and pre-arranged marriages were identified as the safeguards to which the report referred.

[64] Ibid., p. 215. This WCC department's concern was "the ways in which men and women may best complement and support each other, and with the discrimination which prevents women from playing their rightful part." Ibid. Although pressures from American and European women concerned with full participation of women in the church led to the creation of a women's program in the WCC organization, the department was careful to distance itself from feminism. A 1956 brochure on "Men and Women in Church and Society" asserted that "there are few women in any of the churches who are interested in fighting a feminist battle for 'women's rights' or even for 'equal opportunities.'" (Geneva: WCC, 1956), p. 12. In a later brochure, the director of the program wrote about the difficulty of "breaking the familiar patterns of paternalism and feminism" to discover what true cooperation can be. Madeleine Barot, "Cooperation of Men and Women in Church, Family and Society" (Geneva: WCC, 1964), p. 8.

World Conference on Church and Society, Geneva 1966

World Council social teaching and concern for economic development accelerated in 1966 with the calling of an International Church and Society Conference on Technology and Social Revolution.[65] The conference was to advise the churches and the World Council on their ministries in a rapidly changing world. W.A. Visser't Hooft, general secretary of the WCC, charged that the ethical criterion of the responsible society needed to be "renewed and reinterpreted in view of the need for a responsible world community and the demands for international economic justice."[66]

Humanization and economic development. The report on "Economic Development in a World Perspective" observes that changes in technology and economic organization are bringing numerous social and personal consequences. While these advances are welcomed as "a gift from God," the report cautions that "left uncontrolled they accentuate the existing unbalance between rich and poor countries (and indeed within them), which is a scandal and offence to God and men." The report insists that technology must serve human purposes.[67]

---

[65] This conference was a successor to the earlier Life and Work conferences at Stockholm and Oxford, both of which focused on questions of church and society. Over 400 participants from 80 countries and 164 churches came to the conference. Most were from the laity: economists, politicians, social workers, scientists, businessmen. About half were from Asia, Africa, and Latin America. According to Robert McAfee Brown, this was the first time at a large ecumenical gathering that lay delegates outnumbered clergy and third world Christians were granted "a major platform." *Theology in a New Key: Responding to Liberation Themes* (Philadelphia: Westminster Press, 1978), p. 39. For a summary of the conference and its significance, see John Bennett, "The Geneva Conference of 1966 as a Climatic Event," *Ecumenical Review* 37 (January 1985), pp. 26-33.

[66] *World Conference of Church and Society (Geneva 1966) - Report: Christians in the Technical and Social Revolutions of Our Time* (Geneva: WCC, 1967), p. 13. The work of the conference resulted in four reports: 1) economic and social development; 2) nature and function of the state; 3) international co-operation; and 4) "man and community."

[67] Ibid., pp. 52-5.

Christian theology is charged with the task of expounding and defending "the human" as a criterion for judging these economic and social changes. The churches are warned against uncritical enthusiasm about economic growth. The organization of work and its fruits are not ends in themselves, but should be seen as a means to the end of the well-being of "the whole man" and the ability to help others:

> an economy cannot be judged only by its overall rate of growth. All richer countries have to work out a balance of policies relating to full employment and the distribution of income among individuals, among regions, and among rich and poor countries.[68]

Noting that market economies, welfare states with mixed economies, and centrally planned economies all had been capable of rapid economic growth, the conference charged Christians "to be critical participants in the societies in which they find themselves."[69]

Economic development is defined in a way which links growth to social justice:

> Economic development is essentially a process of change whose fundamental aim is to improve the living conditions of all the people in a country. Such change is brought about by measures to increase productivity, usually through increased investment, sustained over a period of time. From the Christian viewpoint this change is part of the effort to create a truly just social order.[70]

The report denies that there is a single universal pattern of economic development. It acknowledges that in some countries economic development might demand changes in the structures of property, income, investment, expenditure, political organization and in the patterns of international relations. Latin America is singled out as an area where land reform has to be a precondition for development.[71]

---

[68] Ibid., p. 55.

[69] Ibid., p. 62.

[70] Ibid., p. 66.

[71] Ibid., pp. 66, 77.

The nature of global economic relations were of particular concern to participants and the conference. The official report declared that

> it is not enough to say that the world cannot continue to live half developed and half underdeveloped: this situation must not be allowed to continue. Therefore, all nations, particularly those endowed with great economic power, must move beyond self-interest and see their responsibility in a world perspective. The Church must say clearly and unequivocally that there is a moral imperative behind international economic development.[72]

Inequalities between nations emerged from past acceptance of a so-called natural division between poor agricultural and rich industrialized nations. The ultimate aim of the restructuring of world economic relations is "an international division of labor based on the specific contribution of fully equipped nations that trade with each other as equals."[73]

Women: marginal visibility. Again, discussion on economic justice is silent on women's economic reality. The pattern in World Council meetings of addressing the "woman question" separately is repeated, this time under the rubric of "Man and Community in Changing Societies."[74] The sub-section addressing the topic had only two women members. The ratio of women to men in the Conference as a whole was even lower than in the sub-section - only twenty-seven of the 337 delegates were women.

The analysis of the changing relations between women and men offered in the report observed changes in women's economic reality:

> In former times, the woman as wife and mother carried out the burden of household responsibilities, protected by her family. Today the old image which associated women with sexual relationship and marriage remains, but in

---

[72] Ibid., p. 80.

[73] Ibid., p. 86.

[74] A sub-section of the working group on "Man and Community in Changing Societies" was charged with speaking to the subject of "Men and Women in Changing Societies." This division of labor at the conference reflects the public/private dichotomy of liberal theory, with issues of political economy addressed separately from issues of community and family.

an urban-industrial society she frequently works outside the home, and the dependent status gives way to an as yet undefined position of codependence or interdependence.[75]

The subgroup contended that there is no one normative role for either women or men, and in contrast to those preparing the report on economic development, did not necessarily see employment of married women as a problem.[76]

The report also addresses women's unpaid work, noting that "the economic value of the work of women both at home and in the assistance given to men and husbands in other fields has not been recognized or included in the assessment of the economic product of a country." The report cites a long history of women working alongside men in agrarian societies. In these situations, detecting and correcting imbalances is necessary rather than inaugurating "non-domestic employment" for women.[77]

The delegates assert that both society and the family might benefit "from the passing of the historic masculine culture which tended to downgrade woman's capacities." Not surprisingly, the analysis focuses more on family strain than on women's lives. New conditions combined with old mores cause such strain. In some developing countries men are educated while their wives are not, thus inviting "discord and divorce." They do acknowledge that work outside the home, while men are not always encouraged to do household tasks, doubled the "wives' work."[78]

Responsible parenthood, a euphemism for family planning, is endorsed as "an integral part of the social ethic of the day."[79] Both the welfare of families and the need to balance population growth with

---

[75] *World Conference*, p. 163.

[76] That group contended that "the widespread employment of married women may conflict with the requirements of family life." Ibid., p. 65.

[77] Ibid., p. 164.

[78] Ibid., p. 167.

[79] Ibid., p. 168.

economic and human resources justify this need. The health of the mother, as well as the health of the child, motivate the spacing and number of children optimally a family might choose to have.

The plight of "unmarried mothers" is also discussed, particularly the prejudice and exploitation from which they suffer. The delegates urge that with the support of family, friends and government, single mothers "be helped to constitute a family with the children they maintain by their work."[80]

Equality and cooperation are highlighted as norms preconditional for responsible relations between women and men. The analysis concedes, though, that the church has not always embodied these norms but has helped "perpetuate unjust types of subordination of women." The churches should:

> press for the establishment by government of laws to ensure that men and women have equal right to work, status, and pay; and provide ways and means for women to participate more fully in their life and work.[81]

This charge to the churches to more fully involve women in their life and work prefigures a trend in which the World Council gives "a higher priority" to the participation of women in its own organizational life.

Critical assessment. The significance of this conference in breaking new ground in the social ethic of the World Council is obvious. While "the double day" of women employed outside the home and the undercounting of women's work had been raised in previous discussion, acknowledgement of these issues had never been integrated into the WCC's social ethic pronouncements. Yet the policy directions suggested are only partially adequate. Equal rights to work, status, and pay, and fuller participation in the life and work of the church, although very good beginnings, do not address the full scope of the problems described.

---

[80] Ibid., p. 170.

[81] Ibid., p. 177.

Interpreters have evaluated the Geneva conference as groundbreaking in other ways.[82] Robert McAfee Brown observes that it became apparent during this conference that "the real struggle" going on in the world was not between east and west or communism versus capitalism, but north vs. south, rich vs. poor, white vs. colored."[83] Paul Abrecht asserts that although the challenge and appeal of revolutionary ideas is acknowledged, the conference "did not itself endorse general revolutionary action." The radicalism of Geneva, he contends, was pragmatic - not ideological. [84] Ellison notes the receptivity of the conference

> to recasting the problem of development in terms of the dependency of the Third World upon the affluent North and that concessions were made about the need for radical, even revolutionary changes to take place within and among nations...[85]

Yet the strategic recommendations proferred give more emphasis "to persuading those in powerful positions to enlist in a cooperative venture" for global development than they did to endorsing people's movements for liberation and self-reliance.[86]

Uppsala, 1968

The Fourth Assembly of the World Council endorsed most of the conclusions of the Church and Society Conference and deepened the understanding of development. In analyzing the dynamics of world development, the Uppsala documents criticize presuppositions held in

---

[82] John Bennett is the only one of the interpreters reviewed in this study who mentioned the discussion of male/female relations or noted the small number of women in attendance. Bennett, 1985, p. 33.

[83] Brown, p. 39.

[84] Abrecht, pp. 156-7.

[85] Ellison, p. 73.

[86] Ibid., p. 74.

both developed and developing nations regarding the sort of international cooperation needed to support such development.

> They assumed that a mere transfer of capital and techniques would automatically generate self-sustained growth. But effective world development requires radical change in institutions and structures at three levels: within developing countries, within developed countries, and in the international economy.[87]

Social and economic progress "with a new dynamic of human solidarity and justice" are essential at these three levels. Equitable patterns of trade and investment must be the framework in which aid to the developing countries is set. A suggested level of aid set at least 1% of the gross national product of developed countries is recommended.

Advocacy of revolutionary change? The Uppsala documents acknowledge that social and political structures within developing countries would require revolutionary change to enable genuine participation of the masses of the people in political and economic life and to develop authentic programs of distributive justice. At the same time the teaching here is that revolutionary change ought not to be equated with violence. If ruling groups are indifferent or oppressive and resist change by using coercion or violence, then revolutionary change might take "a violent form" but such changes are "morally ambiguous."[88] The responsibility of citizens in developed countries is a different agenda - to change their political structures so that they "shed all tendencies to exploit economically or to dominate the poorer, and therefore, weaker, economies of other nations."[89]

The central moral issue in development is realizing the criterion of humanization. Development is "a process with potential for promoting

---

[87] Norman Goodall, ed. *The Uppsala Report 1968* (Geneva: WCC, 1968), p. 46.

[88] Ibid., pp. 47-48.

[89] Ibid., p. 48. The report presumes that these structures of exploitation and domination are political rather than economic. Here again liberal social theory controls the presuppositions. Radical social theorists insist that the political order is controlled by those with economic power.

social and economic justice and world community as an encounter between human beings."[90] Economic development is perceived to be an ambiguous process which may bring release from poverty for some while other defenseless groups of people are often victimized.

White racism and discrimination against women are recognized as impediments to optimal social and economic development. The church is to advocate "the redistribution of power, without discrimination of any kind, so that all men, women and young people [might] participate in the benefits of development."[91] Social policies to redress the balance between the poor and the rich are advocated, so that the technological revolution does not continue to "merely make the rich richer."

Liberal presuppositions challenged. The presuppositions of this document were challenged in assembly discussion. During debate S.L. Parmar, an Indian economist, asked whether

> Development through cooperation has suffered a serious set-back.... Have we been too naive in seeing a natural complement between the technological revolution in developed nations and the socio-political revolution in the developing? The fact is that we do not have adequate political and economic structures to bring together possibilities and needs.[92]

Parmar contends that one has to search rather diligently in history to find instances where possessing classes willingly gave up their privileges. The historical record attests invariably that what Parmar calls the "have nots" have "to wrest their rights through agrarian movements, workers movements, trade-union activity and so on." He also argued that the welfare state fails to assure "the full welfare" of minorities in North America or immigrant workers in Western Europe. Parmar asked if "a projection of this two-group welfare state idea" to the world would lead to anything except "a projection of the elements of inequality and injustice it contains?"[93]

---

[90] Ibid., p. 49.

[91] Ibid., pp. 49-50.

[92] Ibid., p. 42.

[93] Ibid.

Discrimination against women condemned? It is fair to say that at Uppsala women's economic reality is no longer invisible in World Council social ethics, but it is marginal to the central economic teaching as women are marginal in the formation of the documents. "Established patterns in church, family and society which deny the full human rights of women stand condemned"[94] in this teaching, but by not identifying and analyzing such patterns or proposing policies for change the report leaves the impression that serious problems in this area do not exist. Furthermore, the assertion of the report on "new styles of living" that "true partnership" between men and women is not only possible but becoming a reality softens the charges of discrimination against women.[95]

Critical assessment. Although there are challenges to the criterion of the responsible society, the liberal presuppositions which informed this concept also informed the concept of development formulated during this period. Several interpreters criticize the emerging development philosophy of the World Council for its idealism. In 1970, Arent Theodor van Leeuwen observed that the "essential weakness" of this philosophy is that "it deals with the economic issues of world development without the political context of international power relations. "A lofty Christian idealism" results, one which "hardly touches the hard facts of a revolutionary world."[96]

Beatriz Melano Couch also noted "the liberal idealism" of the World Council and its unwillingness "to advocate a political rupture

---

[94] Ibid., p. 92.

[95] Ibid., p. 92. The sacralization of the family in ecumenical ethics is illustrated in the assertion of the WCC Department on Cooperation of Men and Women that "the family is the privileged community to which is given the grace of conjugal love, the mystery of a unity wherein the physical bonds and the spiritual bonds reinforce each other in order perfectly to fulfill the command of the Saviour: 'Love one another.'" Barot, p. 8.

[96] Arend Theodor van Leeuwen, *Development Through Revolution* (New York: Charles Scribner's Sons, 1970), p. 112.

with the sources of oppression."[97] Ellison contends that the Council evinces a "pervasive reluctance to question an ecumenical philosophy based on a presumed harmony of interests and goals among classes and nations..."[98] This liberal idealism also informs the Council's teachings on women, as "the hard facts" of their lives are rarely touched either. The public/private dichotomy of liberal theory and the sacralization of the family prevent an indepth analysis of the discrimination and oppression many women face in all areas of life.

Just, Participatory, Sustainable Society:
Recent World Council Social Ethics

Nairobi, 1975

At the Fifth Assembly of the World Council the notion of the "just, participatory, sustainable society replaced the "responsible society" as the central social ethical criterion. With the articulation of this criterion, the Council began to move away from its liberal presuppositions. The importance of power relations in decisions about development was a central concern of the Assembly.

Development, power, and poverty. The Assembly defined power as "the capability to orient and to implement decisions ... of economic, political, ideological, and/or military nature..." An assessment of the different components which constitute power could only be made "in concrete historical, geographical, and socio-political situations."[99]

The desire to control resources is identified as "a basic reason for the exercise of economic power and the establishment of exploitative structures of domination and dependence." Colonialism is "the classic

---

[97] Beatriz Melano Couch, "New Visions of the Church in Latin America: A Protestant View," *The Emergent Gospel: Theology from the Underside of History*, Sergio Torres and Virginia Fabella, editors (Maryknoll, NY: Orbis Books, 1978), p. 204.

[98] Ellison, p. 77.

[99] David M. Paton, ed. *Breaking Barriers: Nairobi 1975* (Grand Rapids: Eerdmans, 1976), pp. 129-30.

form of such domination." Neo-colonialism, which results in rich countries exploiting poorer countries more indirectly, exists even though colonialism is rare. Transnational corporations - "tnc's" as they are called - are identified as one form of neo-colonialism. Their aim is "to take advantage of the cheap labour that is available in the host countries and to draw out profits from them, making use of the immense control they exercise over world trade and prices." The operations of tnc's in the poorer countries is usually with the approval of national governments and often in active collaboration with local private business enterprises. But the type of goods produced are for "an elite class," the technology used is inappropriate to needs of poorer countries, and the employment created and the incomes generated are "to the advantage of the higher income groups in the host countries."[100]

Another section of the report addresses increasing ambiguities of development. It recognizes that although many new initiatives have been undertaken "to promote the development concern," it is more difficult than ever before to "articulate our understanding of the development concept and consequently to decide on the patterns of participation in the development process." Some of the uncertainty is due to a rejection of the "certainties of the past." The report affirms that development must be a liberating process aiming toward social justice, self-reliance and growth.[101]

Sustainability is added to the list of norms for responsible development. For developed countries this means "a sustainable core of economic activity relating to patterns of indigenous resource consumption... in a far longer time frame than suggested by trends in current commodity markets." A reallocation of power in control of world trade in essential resources and increased participation by

---

[100] Ibid., pp. 130-1.

[101] Ibid., p. 122. In making this affirmation, the report cited the findings of the WCC-sponsored consultation on "Ecumenical Assistance to Development Projects," 26-31 January, 1970, in Montreux, Switzerland. While this consultation played a significant role in shifting the development paradigm of the World Council, it did not discuss women in development, evidently presuming their participation was the same as men's. For a report of the consultation, see Pamela Gruber, editor, *Fetters of Injustice* (Geneva: WCC, 1970).

workers in decision-making are also required. For developing countries, sustainability includes "emphasis on production for essential human needs and avoidance on technological dependence on industrialized countries." The basic goal remains that "nobody should increase his (sic) affluence until everybody has his essentials."[102]

The Assembly questioned the "logic of the market." "'Growth' in an economic order based on the so-called 'free market' system" is declared to have "a built-in exploitative tendency where resources are unevenly distributed." Thus, Christians are to "examine carefully the patterns of utilization, control, and ownership of resources."[103] Expenditure of resources on armaments is also challenged, both for diverting resources from development but also for increasing concentration of economic power and contributing to oppressive political structures.

For the first time in WCC Assembly documents, the church's concern for development is explicitly linked to and identified as rooted in its concern for the poor. The question of development now becomes how the church expresses its solidarity with the poor and struggles with them for "liberation and justice." Now that the church has learned that poverty is caused mostly by unjust structures that concentrate resources in the hands of a few, the Assembly asserted that it must express its solidarity by opposing such unjust structures. Thus economic and social goals, pattern of resource ownership and decision-making processes, locally, nationally and internationally, are to be examined and those patterns oppressive to the poor rejected so that "the creative powers of people to satisfy their needs and decide their destiny" might be released.[104]

---

[102] Paton, p. 128. Lundqvist has a useful discussion of the principles of self-reliance, growth, justice and sustainability in his work *Economic Growth and the Quality of Life*. He contends that the principle of self-reliance gives development its "specific content." Ibid., p. 103. Santa Ana argues that to press for technological self-reliance "without trying to overcome a nation's economic dependence" is to fall again into "the idealistic temptation" facing the World Council. Santa Ana, p. 105.

[103] Goodall, p. 123.

[104] Ibid., pp. 122-3.

A fundamental element in the struggle against poverty and for development is defined as "people's power," which consists of awareness of the situation of dependence and domination, clarity of goals, and commitment to organize and act together. People's power is critical to the creation of self-reliance. The struggle for human rights and the movement for liberation of women are identified as "contributions of historical importance."[105]

The role and power of the churches is examined. As social institutions, churches are engaged at "all levels of social life." Churches have been both legitimators of dominant ideology and participants in struggles from liberation from oppression. The delegates noted that "confrontations with powers and the handling of power" are inevitable in any struggle against injustice and oppression. In the past, churches have underestimated the struggle required.

Sexism as a structure of injustice. An entire working group of the Assembly was devoted to "Structures of Injustice and Struggles for Liberation." The church is called to "follow Christ on the same path committed to the cause of the poor, oppressed, and rejected..."[106] The analysis of the group focuses on human rights understood in a foundational sense. The conditions under which human rights are denied, they argue, are created by "unjust social structures." Work for human rights means "at the most basic level" work towards a society without unjust structures.

What is distinctive in this teaching is the integration of economic criteria for what constitutes human rights. Those highlighted include

1) the right to basic guarantees for life ... including the right to work, to adequate food, to guaranteed health care, to decent housing, and to education and full development;
2) the rights to self determination and to cultural identity, and the rights of minorities;
3) the rights to participate in decision-making within the community;
4) the right to dissent;
5) the right to personal dignity;

---

[105] Ibid., p. 133.

[106] Ibid., pp. 100-101.

6) the right to religious freedom.[107]

Women's disadvantaged situation in relation to these rights is acknowledged. In the discussion of basic guarantees for life, the report contends that "because women [had] the lowest status in most world communities their special needs must be recognized."[108] Women could also make "a special contribution regarding participatory decision-making" because of their experience of oppression and liberation.

Sexism and racism are described as structures of injustice, in addition to the unjust economic structures already described. Racism had been given attention in the social ethics of prior World Council Assemblies, but this was the first time that sexism had been formally identified.[109] The Assembly proclaimed that "the concerns of women must be included in every aspect of the deliberations of the World Council of Churches."[110] Discrimination against women is related to all forms of discrimination and the liberation of women is linked to the liberation of all oppressed people.

---

[107] Ibid., pp. 103-106.

[108] Ibid., p. 103. Reinhild Traitler has recounted how slowly the social justice agencies of the Council came to this realization. She was told by her colleagues in the Commission on the Churches' Participation in Development that "in view of the really demonic nature of the powers we were dealing with, [women's liberation] was an emotional 'belly-ache.' Only later (and very gradually) did we all come to realize that the women among the poorest of the poor are still the poorest of all. The extent of suffering is always in inverse proportion to the measure of power and rights that one has. We gradually realized that in many third-world countries women have little power and fewer rights." "An Oikoumene of Women?" *The Ecumenical Review* 40 (April 1988), p. 179.

[109] A WCC consultation on "Sexism in the 1970's: Discrimination Against Women" was held in West Berlin in 1974. One hundred and seventy women from fifty countries gathered for this groundbreaking consultation. The findings and recommendations of this consultation were brought to the Nairobi Assembly, and inform the report on structural injustices. *Sexism in the 1970's: Discrimination Against Women* (Geneva: WCC, 1975) is the official report of this consultation.

[110] Paton, p. 107.

Three specific areas needing change are identified: theology, participation, and relationship.   The World Council is called "to recognize the dimensions of powerlessness that affect women in the political, economic, social and ecclesial areas of life." Funds for self-development and self-help programs for women are to be provided.[111]

The delegates reaffirmed a long-standing condemnation of "racism in all its forms both within and outside the Church," recognizing that "where racism is involved women are the most disadvantaged group of all." The task of resisting racism is a particular priority because racist structures are reinforcing each other internationally and being reinforced by economic and military power and the fear of loss of privilege by the affluent world.[112]   The report calls upon all those who benefit from economic exploitation, whether or not they are directly involved, to bring pressure on oppressive bodies to change existing structures into just ones.

Critical assessment. Both Brown and Ellison have observed that the Nairobi Assembly clearly acknowledges the structural roots of injustice.[113]   Previous assemblies had noted these structural roots, but did not question the possibility of liberal models of development to overcome them.   The Nairobi Assembly seriously challenges these liberal models of development - particularly those based on logic of the "free market" - and advocates development based on social justice, self-reliance, and growth. The Nairobi documents also focus on the nature of power, a subject which the churches has often ignored.

The analysis of power, particularly in relation to economic life, illuminates the dominance/dependence relations of first and third world while also pointing to patterns of exploitation within nations.   Rather than looking to those with power and privilege for change, the Nairobi social teaching looks to those who bear the brunt of oppression to be the agents to end oppression.

---

[111] Ibid., pp. 107-9, 115. The report cited the work begun during the UN sponsored International Women's Year in regard to participation of women.

[112] Ibid, pp. 110, 112-13.

[113] Ellison, p. 78; Brown, p. 48.

Although these structural approaches more adequately illumine the sources of injustice, some interpreters have pointed out that they neglect important cultural sources. Mercy Oduyoye's comments about a World Council study on poverty are relevant to the discussion at Nairobi:

> The social, cultural and religious factors have been completely ignored or, at best, inadequately dealt with. Economics, the making and use of wealth, may be the basis of human organization into societies but ethical considerations - the way human beings relate one to another - and culture constitute the context in which economics function. There is a mutual relationship of all three aspects of life together.... To focus exclusively on the misuse of economic and political power is inacceptable and indeed misleading.[114]

Although the Assembly analysis of structural injustice links politics and economics, their lack of attention to culture perpetuates the partial analysis characteristic of a liberal perspective which presumes politics, economics, and culture to be autonomous spheres.

The integration of women into the ethical analysis of structures of injustice broadens the conception of what oppression and liberation involves. The identification of sexism as a structure of injustice is a breakthrough in World Council understanding of the situation of women. However, the analysis of both sexism and racism would be strengthened if cultural processes were more fully explored.

The focus on the structural roots of injustice, the specific targeting of transnational corporations as agents of exploitation, and the identification of the poor as agents of transformation indicates that there has been a paradigm shift in the social ethic of the World Council from a liberal perspective to a radical perspective. Frequent attacks on the World Council - particularly in relation to its Programme to Combat Racism and its active opposition to policies of tnc's - by conservative groups such as the Institute for Religion and Democracy and the

---

[114] Mercy Oduyoye, "Comments from Three Continents: Africa," *The Poverty Makers*, David Millwood (Geneva: WCC, 1977), pp. 61-2.

Readers' Digest - add support to the belief that the World Council has made an ideological shift to human liberation.[115]

Thomas Derr, writing shortly before the Sixth Assembly of the WCC, traced a shift in the economic thought of the Council. He concluded that "the ecumenical movement has gradually shifted toward the radical, and the ideology of the radical, thus unbalancing ecumenical statements and actions." Derr called for a return "to ecumenical evenhandedness and caution in treating economic systems," and a move away from what he called "ideological solutions."[116] However, the World Council did not retreat from its radical understanding of ecumenical ethics as the appropriate expression of its normative understanding of the Christian faith.

Vancouver, 1983

The sixth Assembly of the World Council was an innovative one. The delegate body was nearly one-third women, compared to 22% at Nairobi in 1975 and only 9% at Uppsala in 1968. Almost half the delegates were from the laity, compared to one-quarter in 1968. The process of the assembly had been organized so as to be participatory, utilizing the gifts and experiences of all the delegates rather than featuring continuous substantial addresses by leading figures.[117]

---

[115] Paul Abrecht has written about the tensions this shift has caused among WCC member churches. He raises four questions to what he calls liberation ecumenism: 1) the political and economic difficulties socialist countries are experiencing, 2) the difficulty in coping with the challenge of the scientific-technical world-view, 3) the problem of political freedom and justice, 4) its utopianism. Abrecht, pp. 164-6. While these are serious questions, I do not believe they invalidate a liberation perspective or indicate that a liberal perspective more adequately addresses the current economic crisis.

[116] Thomas Sieger Derr, "The Economic Thought of the World Council of Churches," *This World* (Winter/Spring 1982), p. 31. Among the editors of this journal are men linked with the Institute for Religion and Democracy.

[117] The work of the assembly was organized into issue groups. David Gill, ed. *Gathered for Life - Official Report VI Assembly of the World Council of Churches* (Geneva: WCC, 1983), p. 18.

Participation was one of the themes for in-depth discussion during the assembly. The report declared that full life is possible only through participation. "Real participation means becoming truly human."[118] A list of factors that impede participation included illiteracy; hunger, malnutrition and inadequate health care; unjust power structures; economic, political and religious domination and military intervention; and discrimination according to race, sex, and class.

At the Vancouver Assembly the participation of women in the church finally became a matter of priority. The report observed that although women constitute "the largest part of congregations," structures of power within and without the churches "inhibit their growth and full participation." Churches are called to provide greater opportunities for the participation of women through skills training and advocacy. Women are encouraged to participate in justice and peace issues.[119]

Untangling webs of oppression. The Vancouver documents describe a web of oppression and injustice such that racism, sexism, class domination, the denial of people's rights, and caste oppression are "woven together." Racism is aggravated by international systems backed by powerful economic and military factors. The Assembly called churches to "be in solidarity with the poor, oppressed, and discriminated against, in order to empower their movements and organizations."[120] Economic domination is rejected because it "suppress[es] the socio-economic rights of people, such as the basic needs of families, communities, and the rights of workers." Recommendations are made to the churches for combatting unjust economic structures. These include reflection on "a new economic paradigm aiming at a just, participatory and sustainable society,"

---

[118] Ibid., p. 54.

[119] Ibid., p. 58. This report did not mention that the WCC Central Committee at its 1981 meeting rejected the recommendation from the Community of Women and Men study that 50% of the members of the sub-units and committees of the WCC be women. For a discussion of this, see Traitler, p. 180.

[120] Ibid., p. 91.

analysis of their own complicity in oppressive economic structures, and examination of their own investment policies.[121]

The definition of sexism employed makes some of the connections in the web of oppression explicit:

> Just as any attitude, action or structure that treats people as inferior because of race is racism, so any domination or exclusion based on sex is sexism. Behind many of the diverse manifestations of sexism are economic factors leading to exploitation and manipulation.[122]

Recognizing that the division of labor between women and men has changed considerably, the report acknowledges that "women still have a long way to go in the struggle for equality." Sex tourism and violence against women are named as "reprehensible forms of sexism."[123]

The Vancouver report draws upon and commends an earlier WCC consultation on "The Community of Women and Men in the Church," which had "contributed to identifying the root causes of the oppression of women" and developed an understanding of power as empowerment, that is allowing the oppressed "to stand up for themselves and to be full partners in the struggle for justice and dignity..."[124]

---

[121] Gill, p. 90. The Advisory Group on Economic Matters, established in 1979 by the Commission on the Churches' Participation in Development, has been working at the development of a political economic paradigm that would support a just, participatory, and sustainable society. A useful summary of the work of this group over the past decade has been compiled by Catherine Mulholland, *Ecumenical Reflections on Political Economy* (Geneva: WCC, 1988), especially pp. 3-8. While some very useful work has been done in transcending the limitations of liberal perspectives on political economy, the group has not addressed the challenges from the UN Women's Decade as to what constitutes economic activity.

[122] Gill, p. 87.

[123] Ibid.

[124] For a detailed report from the consultation, see Constance Parvey, ed. *The Community of Women and Men in the Church* (Philadelphia: Fortress Press, 1983). This 1981 consultation in Sheffield, England, was the culmination of the study on "The Community of Women and Men in the Church, initiated by a recommendation at the Nairobi Assembly. Study groups from around the world sent reports of their work to the consultation. For a critical discussion of the study

While the work of this consultation was far-reaching, its focus is primarily on life within the church. Third world women at the consultation declared that

> we feel we cannot confine our concerns to speaking of wholeness and community within the church. There is a large struggle for the realization of human wholeness, for liberation from widespread oppression that is classist and racist, and in this struggle our sisters and brothers from other faiths are caught up as well.[125]

The recommendation from the consultation for action against sex tourism and prostitution is one effort to reach beyond the life of the church. But the consultation was not able to speak directly to issues of family violence and sexual assault. Constance Parvey, staff for the study, insists that "issues of sexuality are part of the socialized conspiracy of silence in the churches."[126]

Condemnation of sexism and proposals for strategies to overcome the oppression of women are included in the Assembly documents. Even so, many dimensions of economic justice are addressed without a systemic analysis of women's participation in the economy. An illustration of this is the invisibility of women in the statement adopted on international food disorders. The causes of this disorder are

---

and consultation, see May, *Bonds of Unity*. May presents the study as "an 'insurrection of subjugated knowledges" against the effects of theological discourse on unity formulated by the Commission on Faith and Order," the sponsor of the study. Ibid., p. 12.

[125] This statement was published in Betty Thompson, *A Chance to Change: Women and Men in the Church* (Philadelphia: Fortress Press, 1982), p. 72. Thompson's book reports and expands the discussion of the consultation. Her chapter "The Third World Speaks Out" gives a useful summary of the debate. The issue of the relation of the church and the world is an ongoing struggle in Faith and Order, the locus of the Community of Women and Men study.

[126] Constance Parvey, "The Community Study: its Mixed Messages for the Churches," *Beyond unity-in tension*, p. 39. This article is an illuminating account of the potential contribution of this study to the churches and their resistance to receiving the study.

analyzed without mention of the role of women in food production or of the distinctive problems women producers face.[127]

Disagreement over family relations. Nor are the analyses of gender relations in the various reports without ambiguity, particularly as these matters relate to changing family roles. The report on "healing and shared life in community" notes that "in most situations male dominance remains the mode of social organization," although its manifestations vary from one culture to another. Parental responsibility is identified as "a focal point in gauging the significance of change in the role of women and men." The report contends that uneasiness about changing sex roles is manifested in relation to the nurture of children and the role of mothers and fathers in nurturing and care giving. No conclusion is reached and further study is called for, remembering biblical principles that "justify a desire for change."[128]

The report on "learning in community" reflected resistance to any change:

> The fundamental responsibility of the Church is clear and not controversial, namely to support the complete family consisting of parents, united in marriage and faithful to each other...[129]

Even so, the church is also asked to recognize "the social reality of other forms of family life" and to explore new notions of "mothering," "fathering," personal relationships and parenting. Clearly the recommendations of these two groups reflect a lack of agreement in the

---

[127] Gill, p. 145. The critical role of African women in domestic food production and the problems faced by these women farmers are documented in chapter one of this study.

[128] Ibid., p. 68. These biblical principles are not identified in the report, but mention of them implies that churches are to be open to change in gender roles within the family.

[129] Ibid., p. 95.

World Council about the desirability of changing roles of women and men within the family.[130]

Conclusion

Shifts in ecumenical ethics can be traced in part by noting changes in central criterion from the gospel for all realms in the Life and Work Movement; to the responsible society in the early years of the World Council; from human development during the period of transition in the 1960's; to the just, participatory, sustainable society.[131] Shifts in presuppositions, ethical norms, and strategic proposals have accompanied these changes.

A significant shift has been the movement from liberal presuppositions about social change to more radical ones. This involved a move from concern for balance in earlier teaching to the option for the poor and oppressed in more recent teaching. Parallel to this has been a move from appealing to the powerful to bring about change characteristic of liberal perspectives to supporting people's movements for change. Understandings of justice have shifted from a liberal concern for distributive justice to a more radical understanding of justice as social justice, which stresses participation. Finally, there has been a shift from primary use of neoclassical economic models - market oriented and private initiative and ownership, to radical political economic models - participatory planning and social control of productive sectors.

Clearly, there have been some gains in the understanding of women's economic reality in the developing social teachings of the World Council. As we have seen, women's experience and economic

---

[130] The 1981 consultation on "The Community of Women and Men in the Church" discussed transitions in male and female roles and family life. It also recommended a WCC study on marriage and partnership.

[131] The Vancouver Assembly issued a call to the churches to covenant together for justice, peace, and the integrity of creation. The materials produced by this program have not been included in this study, although I have examined them. This new call does not significantly change my evaluation of World Council social ethics.

reality had been invisible in the teaching of the Life and Work Movement that first addressed issues of economic justice. Women themselves were marginal within the movement.

With the formation of the WCC in 1948, women's participation in the ecumenical movement became an agenda item. But it was still presumed in the Council's social teaching that economic reality was the same for both women and men and that the normative changes toward economic justice would impact them equally. Not surprisingly, women's experience continued to be invisible in the social teachings of the Council until the Uppsala Assembly in 1968, when discrimination against women was first acknowledged in a social justice context.

With the 1975 Nairobi Assembly evidence of challenge to the relevance and impact of earlier economic ethics in terms of women's economic reality begins to emerge. The struggle has been ongoing to integrate women and their perspectives into the work of the Council. Although more women participate now than at any previous period, there is still not parity for women - particularly on the Central Committee and in certain divisions of the Council.

The World Council Ecumenical Decade of the Churches in Solidarity with Women (1988-1998) offers the possibility for overcoming this marginalization. Its goals are:

1. Empowering women to challenge oppressive structures in the global community, their country and their church.
2. Affirming - through shared leadership and decision-making, theology and spirituality - the decisive contributions of women in churches and communities.
3. Giving visibility to women's perspectives and actions in the work and struggle for justice, peace, and the integrity of creation.
4. Enabling the churches to free themselves from racism, sexism and classism; from teachings and practices that discriminate against women.
5. Encouraging the churches to take actions in solidarity with women.[132]

---

[132] Sub-Unit on Women in Church and Society, "Ecumenical Decade 1988-1998: Churches in Solidarity with Women," (Geneva: World Council of Churches, 1988), p. 1. Also *Women in a Changing World* no. 23 (June 1987). The WCC is taking some solidarity actions addressing issues of critical importance to women. For instance, the WCC sponsored a meeting of Asian lawyers and human-rights activists which is pressing for an Asian Commission on Women's Human Rights to offer a feminist perspective on women's human-rights violations, including domestic

The emphasis on empowerment, participation and solidarity is significant. Yet it is also significant that none of these purposes raises the possibility of oppressive structures in family organization or the need to address them.[133]

Protestant and Orthodox churches in the Council still sacralize traditional family relations, reflecting a de facto private/public dichotomy, and do not treat family relations as an arena of justice. Family relations have rarely been discussed in relation to issues of justice, in contrast to dominant Roman Catholic social teaching.[134]

Although the World Council has moved away from liberal presuppositions in its analysis of the political economy, some liberal presuppositions still inform its ethics. The public/private dichotomy and the universalism which is also characteristic of liberalism precludes a fully adequate social analysis or formulation of effective policies for overcoming women's economic vulnerability.[135]

---

violence and the impoverishment of women. *Ecumenical Press Service*, Year 56/issue 03 (16-20 January 1989) #51.

[133] Women from around the globe have testified to the oppressiveness of patriarchal family relations in their cultures. In addition to resources from chapters four and five of this study, see the "Final Document: Intercontinental Women's Conference," Virginia Fabella and Mercy Oduyoye, eds., *With Passion and Compassion: Third World Women Doing Theology* (Maryknoll, NY: Orbis Books, 1988), p. 185. Some women's groups are taking action in regard to family life: "Education and Cultural Movement to develop a democratic family life" is the first program of Korean church women for the Ecumenical Decade. Shin Sun, "A Vision of the Women's Committee," *In God's Image* (June 1988), p. 5. We must not, however, forget the concern for family survival and liberation, articulated by Delores Williams for the African-American community in "The Color of Feminism." These two concerns are not mutually exclusive, but remind us again of the importance of self-determination of groups of women in setting the agenda for change in their communities.

[134] See discussion in chapter two of this study.

[135] Beverly Harrison does an illuminating critique of Reinhold Niebuhr, himself a critic of liberalism, on this topic in her essay "Sexism and the Language of Christian Ethics." She notes that Niebuhr "never questioned the dualism embedded in liberal political ideology between the 'private' sphere, that is, the arena of those interpersonal, humane relations of the family, and the 'public'

The connection between women's work in the household and their labor force participation is seldom analyzed, largely because of acceptance of the public/private dichotomy. The universalism operative in thinking about the "public" arena exacerbates this, as women's socioeconomic participation is assumed to be same as men's. Thus any roots of women's oppression in the capacity to bear children or the assumed "naturalness" of childrearing and domestic labor as women's role are not analyzed. [136] Consequently, women's double work day, occupational segregation, and other specific aspects of women's economic vulnerability are not addressed.

These presuppositions also distort women's moral agency through the invisibility of moral domains. Kathryn Pauly Morgan points particularly to maternal practice and domestic labor as two of the domains in women's lives "which are not usually accorded moral worth and significance." [137] The reality of women's lives has been invisible in most of the Council's social ethics. There has been little if any analysis of domestic labor or maternal practice in the social ethics of the World Council. Women's moral agency in these domains has been rendered invisible.

The human as a central ethical criterion in ecumenical ethics seems to be relevant only to the political and economic domains, the "public" arena. We have noted that women's experience in this arena has been

---

sphere, those 'impersonal relations' of institutions and collectivities. He did not notice that the public/private split legitimized both a capitalist mode of political-economic organization and female subjugation in personal or domestic life. That the broader social injustices toward women that he noticed at the collective level were only extensions of the dynamic operating in the supposedly blissful arena of the family never occurred to him." Ibid., pp. 27-8.

[136] This is one of the limits of "the web of oppression" metaphor, especially when there is only a description of oppression and not an analysis of the roots of oppression or the linkages between oppressions. The assertion that sexism is exclusion or discrimination because of sex and racism is exclusion or discrimination because of race needs to be followed by an analysis of why it is that women are the victims of sexism and people of color the victims of racism.

[137] Morgan, p. 221. See the introduction to this study for further discussion of Morgan's work on women's moral agency.

erroneously assumed to be the same as that of men. Thus women's moral agency is again rendered invisible.[138]   World Council presuppositions about human dignity are grounded in male experience, among other reasons because of the invisibility of women's moral domains.[139]

There is a critical need for appropriation of a historical structural perspective that demystifies this public/private dichotomy and critically examines women's work in domestic and economic life. Relations in the family, sexuality, and the gendered division of labor also need to be incorporated into socio-ethical analysis. Unless the traditional gender based division of labor is challenged and the public/private dichotomy overcome with a wholistic theological and social ethical analysis of politics, economics and culture, we can not begin to adequately envision a just, participatory, sustainable society or create an effective praxis of solidarity with women. In the next part of this study, I turn to an examination of resources for a more adequate analysis of women's reality with an aim to proposing criteria of adequacy for social analysis in economic ethics.

---

[138] This is also a variation of the second maneuver Morgan describes, that of assigning woman to "the private sphere" and then asserting that "the public sphere" is the sphere of true morality. The World Council seems to presume this, rather than directly asserting it.

[139] An additional reason is that until the emergence of feminist theology, theological anthropology was grounded in male experience. I point this out in reference to the documents for the 1937 Oxford conference. The classic analysis of this bias was done by Valerie Saiving, "The Human Situation: A Feminine View," originally published in 1960 and reprinted in *Womanspirit Rising: A Feminist Reader in Religion*, edited by Carol P. Christ and Judith Plaskow (San Francisco: Harper and Row, 1979).

PART THREE

ECONOMIC ETHICS AS IF
WOMEN COUNTED

In Part Three I will examine literature from movements which specifically address women's reality from a global perspective. My aim is to discover theoretical resources that adequately address the impoverishment of women for use in progressive economic ethics.

CHAPTER FOUR

MOVING TOWARDS VISIBILITY: GOVERNMENTAL PERSPECTIVES AND THE RISING VOICES OF WOMEN

The United Nations Decade for Women, 1975-85, created opportunities for women from around the world to come together to analyze their situation and to propose policies for improving their condition. The primary sites for dialogue were the three world conferences held during the Decade.[1] Each event included an official United Nations conference attended by governmental delegates and a non-governmental tribune or forum, open to anyone and from which more radical voices came. The documents from these conferences, especially the 1985 forum, are useful sources for those who want to more adequately understand the impoverishment of women, as they represent the work of the largest, most diverse group of women ever assembled.

---

[1] As was pointed out in the introduction,United Nations conferences are sites of struggle between nations, individually and in blocs, and between governments and non-governmental organizations. The documents from these conferences often include contradictory statements, reflecting differing views of participants. For a discussion of some of the dynamics of these conferences, see Fraser, pp. 9-13.

The value of these documents for our study is precisely that they were created by such a large and diverse body of women specifically addressing the global situation of women, not that they are secular in origin. There has never been an occasion like this for Roman Catholic women. Similar occasions within the World Council of Churches have had fewer participants and were less diverse, like the 1974 Berlin consultation on Sexism, or have focused more specifically on theological and ecclesiastical questions, like the 1983 Sheffield consultation on The Community of Women and Men in the Church.[2]

During the Decade, increasing attention was brought to bear on understandings of women's work, women's role in development, and the relation between development and the impoverishment of women.[3] These themes are critical to our discussion of women's economic vulnerability and well-being, as they illuminate women's participation in the economy and the impact of economic development on women. The scope of these documents requires us to treat them from the standpoint of the theoretical frameworks that inform the varying analyses and engagements of women's oppression and economic vulnerability they offer.

Theoretical frameworks. In her review of the Decade, Arvonne S. Fraser notes two perspectives in the documents, which she describes "as a feminist perspective and a developing world perspective."[4] This dual characterization is not precise enough, however, as there is more than one feminist perspective and more than one perspective on development present in the literature. Drawing on the work of authors in the Women in International Development (WID) series, I characterize

---

[2] For further discussion of these consultations, see chapter 3 of this study.

[3] For further discussion of the impact of the Decade on these themes see, for instance, Maria Riley, "Women's Work -The New Equation," *Center Focus*, Issue 71 (March 1986), pp. 5-6, the report of the Post-Nairobi Donors' Meeting on Women and Development, December 16-19, 1985, and the introduction to the DAWN volume, Gita Sen with Caren Grown, *Development, Crises, and Alternative Visions: Third World Women's Perspectives* (New York: Monthly Review Press, 1986), pp. 11-15, as well as the sources discussed in chapter one of this study.

[4] Fraser, p. 25.

the two dominant perspectives in the Decade documents as liberal sex-role and radical structural.[5] As we shall see, by the end of the Decade a third perspective has emerged which is more fully articulated during Forum '85, the meeting of non-governmental organizations.

Liberal feminists perceive the roots of women's oppression in their lack of equal civil rights and lack of access to educational and employment opportunities. The liberal program for change involves a direct attack on discrimination on the grounds of sex. Some liberal theorists focus on sex-role stereotyping and others on extending human rights to women; both views are present in the Decade documents.

Although basic social institutions do not currently work in the best interests of women, liberal feminists believe that they can be reformed to do so. They share the belief of neo-classical and developmentalist theorists that capitalist development is basically beneficial and only requires reforms to overcome discrimination against women.[6]

---

[5] These authors characterize the two perspectives in the literature on women and development as 1) "liberal, reformist, or ideological" and 2) "marxist, nationalist, or utopian" which "sees a structural basis for women's situation." Rita Gallin, Patricia Whittier, and Margaret Graham, *Research and Policy: An Analysis of the Working Papers on Women in International Development*, WID Forum 85-V (East Lansing: Michigan State University, December 1985), p. 3. These two perspectives are streams of the liberal and radical social models described in chapter two of this study.

Susan Tiano notes the debate between Marxist feminists, "who argue that capitalism is the major source of women's oppression," and socialist feminists, who emphasize "the mutual interdependence between class- and gender-based systems of domination" and who "consider the abolition of capitalism to be a necessary but insufficient condition for women's liberation." *The Separation of Women's Remunerated and Household Work: Theoretical Perspectives on "Women in Development,"* Working Papers on Women in International Development, no. 2 (East Lansing: Michigan State University, December 1981), p. 17. The technical debates among theorists on the left as to roots and dynamics of the oppression of women are beyond the scope of our discussion here, but will be referred to at relevant points in the discussion. Both socialist feminist and cultural feminist perspectives are also present at times in the Decade documents, but they are not dominant early on. All of these theoretical perspectives will be discussed in more depth in the next chapter of this study.

[6] My discussion of these theoretical perspectives also draws on the discussion of theories of development in relation to the subordination of women by Carolyn Elliott, "Theories of Development," *Signs* 3 (Autumn 1977), pp 1 - 8; and the

The most characteristic liberal theory of development is "developmentalism," a view that the poverty of developing countries is due to "a lag" in their economic development which can be overcome with modernization and industrialization. Modernization is desirable although it entails costs as well as benefits. On this view, the impact of social changes will be unevenly distributed throughout a society. Some liberal analysts recognize that "disadvantaged groups" such as women, minorities, and the poor tend to bear disproportionate costs of socioeconomic development but look chiefly to cultural sex-role stereotypes and inadequate education as the reasons women are at competitive disadvantage in the labor market.[7] In this view, strategies for change are usually consensual and emphasize reforms within existing systems - such as improved education and training to integrate women into development.[8]

The second perspective in the Decade documents perceives exploitation and oppression as structural features of international capitalism and points out the inadequacy of analyses like liberalism that isolate sexual inequality from other socio-economic inequalities.[9] Out of the broad Marxist theoretical tradition it is that stream known as dependency theory that is a dominant perspective in the debate about global economic development.

Dependency theorists argue, in contrast to developmentalists, that "developing" countries have been underdeveloped by the developed countries during the colonial and neo-colonial periods. They understand development to exacerbate and reproduce class relations and insist that exploitative class relations have now come to exist between nations as well as internally. The overdeveloped countries at the center of the international economic system control and exploit the dependent,

---

work of Alison Jaggar and Paula Rothenberg Struhl, *Feminist Frameworks*, (New York: McGraw-Hill, 1978) and the Second Edition, 1984.

[7] Gallin, et al, p. 3; Tiano, pp. 5-7.

[8] Gallin et al, pp. 4-5.

[9] Ibid., p. 3.

underdeveloped countries at the periphery.[10]   In this perspective, the development of a new international economic order based on equity, sovereign equality, interdependence and common interest and cooperation is the primary program for overcoming underdevelopment, and thus the inequality of women.[11]

For my purposes a broad differentiation between "liberal sex-role" and "structural" will describe the two dominant frameworks used early on in the official United Nations documents to analyze the oppression of women.   The goal of the liberal   perspective is equality, conceptualized as legal equality and equal educational and employment opportunity.   In this view, governments and ngo's are the primary change agents through consensual strategies. The goal of the structural perspective is the creation of a   new international economic order through negotiation between developed and developing countries.

I contend that during the Decade there is a shift in the documents from these dual perspectives to a multi-dimensional structural perspective, which deepens the sex-role analysis and insists that gender relations as well as class relations must be transformed.[12]   This emerging perspective interrelates sex, race and class oppression, has structural transformation as its goal, and looks to grassroots organizations for change through empowerment and effective participation.   These strategies are more conflictive than consensual.

---

[10] See Ellison, pp. 30-43, for an exposition of the dependency paradigm.

[11] These are the principles articulated in the United Nations call for a new international economic order. The claim to the "inalienable right to nationalization" as an expression of "full and permanent sovereignty" over "natural resources, wealth and all economic activities" has been a point of contention between the developed and developing countries.   United Nations, *Report of the World Conference of the International Women's Year,* 1975, pp. 5-6.

[12] An Australian theorist argues that "the sex-role concept" needs to be demystified so as "to shift the theoretical perspective to relationships of control, of domination and subordination [as] these are the factors ultimately that determine the broad outlines of the behaviour described by role theorists." Clare Burton, *Subordination: Feminism and Social Theory,* (Sydney: George Allen and Unwin, 1985), p. xiv. Yet, as noted, there is disagreement as to which structures and relations account for the inequality of women - class or gender. This question will be discussed in more detail in our next chapter.

Strategies are characterized as conflictive when "profound changes affecting social relations of production and personal relations of domestic units" are proposed. Such strategies "cannot be undertaken without conflict."[13]

A review of these perspectives is necessary for our task of appropriating theoretical resources for a Christian ethic that adequately addresses women's impoverishment. Critical analysis and examination of implications of these approaches are deferred to the following chapters. Here my aim is to explicate these frameworks and to show movement during the Decade towards convergence of strands of analyses into a multidimensional structural perspective.

Aiming for Equality:
Governmental Action On Behalf of Women

International Women's Year,
Mexico City 1975

The rights of women have been on the agenda of the United Nations since its founding in 1946. The United Nations Charter affirmed the equal rights of women and men in its preamble as a part of its faith in "fundamental human rights" and the equal rights "of nations large and small."[14] The United Nations Commission on the Status of Women was created in 1947 to promote women's economic, political, civil and educational rights.

The Commission drafted conventions affirming women's political rights and the legal rights of married women, which were adopted by the General Assembly during the 1950's. These conventions are legally binding on any country who sign them, and resulted in several countries giving women the vote. The Declaration on the Elimination of Discrimination Against Women was adopted by the General Assembly in 1967.

---

[13] Gallin et al, pp. 4-5.

[14] Quoted in Fraser, p. 1. For a fuller discussion of the United Nations and rights for women, see Fraser, pp. 1-8.

Women's organizations with consultative status to the commission first proposed the idea of an international women's year. In proclaiming 1975 International Women's Year, the General Assembly charged that the year be devoted to action "promoting equality between men and women, ensuring the integration of women in the total development effort, and increasing the contribution of women to the strengthening of world peace."[15] A conference was convened for International Women's Year in Mexico City, with the theme "Equality, Development, and Peace." Six thousand women and men came to Mexico City to participate. One hundred twenty five of the 133 member nations of the UN sent delegates to the conference, sixty percent of whom were women.

World Plan of Action:
Proposed Solutions to Inequality

A World Plan of Action, prepared by the Commission (representatives of national governments) in consultation with non-governmental groups, was presented to the Conference delegates. The introduction to the Plan, as adopted, declared that the objective of International Women's Year is "to define a society in which women participate in a real and full sense in economic, social and political life and to devise strategies whereby such societies could develop."[16] The purpose of the Plan is "mainly to stimulate national and international action to solve the problems of under-development, and of the socio-economic structure which places women in an inferior position."

Both liberal and structural perspectives are interwoven in the introduction to the Plan. Indicative of a liberal sex-role perspective are the cluster of statements on equality. The Plan declared that achievement of equality for women implies equal rights, opportunities, and responsibilities. For this to happen, a change in social attitudes is

---

[15] General Assembly Resolution 3010 (XXVII) of 18 December 1972.

[16] United Nations, *Report of the World Conference of the International Women's Year*, 1975, para. 14.

necessary, especially in regard to the sharing of responsibilities by women and men for children and the home.

Structural change is called for, but within the bounds of the liberal agenda:

> Changes in social and economic structures should be promoted which would make possible the full equality of women and their free access to all types of development, without discrimination of any kind, and to all types of education and employment.[17]

Development is "the most important means of furthering equality of the sexes..." The Plan asserts that women are to be integrated into development through "widening of their activities to embrace all aspects of social, economic, political and cultural life." A more equitable distribution of "the benefits of development" is advocated.[18]

A structural perspective is present in statements calling for an end to exploitation and for a new international economic order. Efforts to achieve equality without socio-economic changes are challenged:

> Commitment on the part of Governments to the ideals of equality and integration of women in society cannot be fully effective outside the larger context of commitment to transform fundamental relationships within a society in order to ensure a system that excludes the possibility of exploitation.[19]

Any effort to improve the situation of women "must be an integral part of the global project for the establishment of a new economic order."[20]

Proposed solutions. Guidelines for national action are presented for a ten year period, as part of a long term process to meet the goals of International Women's Year. Minimum objectives to be achieved during the first five years of the Plan are identified. These include increase in literacy and civic education, equal educational access,

---

[17] Ibid., para. 29.

[18] Ibid., para. 21-2.

[19] Ibid., para. 30.

[20] Ibid., para. 8.

increased employment opportunities, comprehensive measures for health education and services, parity in civil, social and political rights; greater participation in policy-making, and recognition of the "economic value of women's work in the home in domestic food production and marketing and voluntary activities not remunerated."[21] The Plan urges the formation of women's bureaus with adequate budget and staff as well as constitutional and legal changes guaranteeing equality and eliminating discrimination. Most all of these proposed solutions are consensual strategies, reforms within existing institutions. This liberal perspective is also evident in most of the specific proposals for change.

Legislation to end inequality. Several legislative iniatives are proposed in the World Plan. A major objective of the Plan is

> to ensure that women shall have, in law and in fact, equal rights and opportunities with men to vote and to participate in public and political life at the national, local and community levels, and that they shall be made aware of their responsibilities as citizens and of the problems affecting society and affecting them directly as women.[22]

Governments are to establish strategies, goals and time-tables for increasing the number of women in both appointive and elective public offices and other public positions at all levels.

Employment practices are another area requiring legislation

> to achieve equality of opportunity and treatment for women workers and their integration in the labour force in accordance with the accepted international standards recognizing the right to work, to equal pay for equal work, to equal conditions of work and advancement.[23]

The Plan observes that women frequently experience discrimination in working conditions, hiring practices, pay, and promotion. Women's employment opportunities are also limited by family responsibilities and cultural constraints. Legislation, attitudinal change, and creation of a

---

[21] Ibid., para. 46.

[22] Ibid., para. 59.

[23] Ibid., para. 88.

variety of economic roles are key strategies for overcoming discrimination.

Integration into economic development. The delegates contend that creation of varied economic roles would not only enhance employment of women, but also address problems of unemployment and underemployment.   Self-help activities and self-employment are recommended, particularly in rural areas.   Training in community development and entrepreneurial skills should be extended both to women and men.   Governments are urged to develop co-operatives and small-scale industries.

> Essential to the effective implementation of such programmes is the provision of adequate training in co-operatives and entrepreneurial skills, access to credit and necessary seed capital for improved tools, assistance with marketing, the provision of adequate rural social services and amenities, decentralized development of towns in rural areas and basic infrastructural arrangements, such as child care arrangements, transportation and conveniently situated water supplies.[24]

Increased participation of rural women in formulating national development plans is also recommended.

The Plan recognizes the particular needs of women workers. Governments, employers and trade unions all are to assure women workers rights to "maternity protection, including maternity leave with a guarantee of returning to their former employment, and to nursing breaks." Arguments that such rights constitute "unequal treatment of the sexes" are rejected.[25]

The delegates commend approaches that facilitate combining work and family responsibilities. These include reduction or staggering of work hours, flextime, part-time work for both women and men, child-care facilities, parental leave, and communal kitchens. The rights of part-time workers are to be fully protected.

It is recommended that trade unions adopt policies to increase the participation of women at every level. Unions are to promote equality

---

[24] Ibid., para. 95.

[25] Ibid., para. 100.

of opportunity for jobs and training for women workers and leadership training for women. Trade unions are urged to play a leading role in developing new and constructive approaches to workers' problems, particularly the problems of women workers.

Action for family well-being. Noting that "[t]he institution of the family" is changing in its economic, social and cultural functions," the Plan urges action to ensure "the dignity, equality and security of each of its members," providing "conditions conducive to the balanced development of the child as an individual and as a social being."[26]

The role of both women and men in the development process is "to be considered in terms of their contribution to the family as well as to society and the national economy." The delegates assert that extending higher status to the role of parent, spouse and homemaker would enhance the personal dignity of a man and a woman, though it is conceded that "household activities that are necessary for family life have generally been perceived as having a low economic and social prestige."[27]

The Plan suggests that the family is "an important agent of social, political and cultural change," with the reassessment of the functions and roles traditionally allotted to each sex within the family "in the light of changing conditions." A specific policy recommendation is advanced for social security programmes to include child and family allowances so that the economic stability of family members might be strengthened.[28] The right to "freely and responsibly determine the number and spacing" of children is a further condition of "real equality" between the sexes. The delegates insist that without this right, "women are disadvantaged in their attempt to benefit from other reforms."[29]

Global action for equality. A section of the World Plan on "Global action" recommended that 1975-85 be designated the United

---

[26] Ibid., para. 124.

[27] Ibid., para. 125.

[28] Ibid., para. 126, 134.

[29] Ibid., para. 19.

Nations Decade for Women and Development and that all organizations of the United Nations system take separate and joint action to implement the recommendations of the Plan. It mandates that women be involved fully in policy-making at international and national levels. High priority is to be given to the preparation and adoption of the convention on the elimination of discrimination against women, with effective procedures for its implementation.

Summary. General debate during the Conference evidenced a variety of perspectives among delegates, particularly around themes of a new international economic order and the relation of legislation and participation. Some argued that achievement of a new international economic order is a prerequisite to achievement of equality for women; others argued that although these goals are related, action for equality can not wait for the establishment of a more equitable economic order. Some argued that legislative action, though important in promoting participation, would not necessarily guarantee women's effective role in development. Pressures to implement legislation are needed, as well as active efforts to create opportunities for participation.[30]

As is evident, the debate is primarily between 1) liberals advocating changes in sex-roles and equal opportunity through attitude change and legislation and 2) radicals advocating socio-economic structural change. The proposed solutions for specifically addressing women's inequality are primarily liberal, although the Plan of Action does mandate that proposals for legislation and integration are to be part of the establishment of a new international economic order. These same perspectives inform the anti-discrimination convention mandated by the Plan of Action.

---

[30] Report (1975), pp. 134-36.

New Visibility for Women's Rights: Convention on the Elimination of Discrimination Against Women

The Convention on the Elimination of All Forms of Discrimination Against Women was adopted by the General Assembly of the United Nations on December 19, 1979. Fraser calls this "the most concise and useful document adopted during the Decade." She describes it as "essentially an international bill of rights for women, setting forth internationally accepted principles and the measures needed to achieve equality between women and men." The Convention builds on the Declaration on the Elimination of Discrimination Against Women, which was adopted by the United Nations General Assembly in 1967. The Convention, unlike the Declaration, is legally binding on those countries which ratify it.[31]

Equal rights for women. The Convention began by noting that one of the purposes of the United Nations, as stated in its Charter, is "to promote universal respect for human rights and fundamental freedoms, without distinction of any kind, including any distinction as to sex." Discrimination against women continues, it observed, despite the conventions and other instruments which promote equality of rights of women and men. The Convention charged that discrimination against women

> violates the principles of equality of rights and respect for human dignity, is an obstacle to the participation of women, on equal terms with men, in the political, social, economic, and cultural life of their countries, hampers the growth of the prosperity of society and the family and makes more difficult the

---

[31] Fraser, p. 123. As of October, 1986, 91 countries had ratified the Convention; by mid-1993, 122 countries have ratified. The United States has not ratified the Convention, although there is some expectation it may ratify during the Clinton administration. The International Women's Rights Action Watch (IWRAW) was formed after the Nairobi End of the Decade conference "to monitor, analyze and encourage law and policy reform in accordance with the principles" of the Convention. Information on the Convention is available from IWRAW, Women, Public Policy and Development Project; Humphrey Institute of Public Affairs, University of Minnesota.

full development of the potentialities of women in the service of their countries and of humanity...[32]

Particular concern is expressed for women in situations of poverty, who have the least access to food, health, training, education and opportunities for employment.

The assertions of the Mexico City Plan of Action that establishment of a new international economic order based on equity and justice, the eradication of apartheid and other forms of racial and cultural domination, and the strengthening of international peace and security all contribute to the attainment of equality for women are reaffirmed. The contribution of women to family welfare and social development is noted, as is the "social significance of maternity." The Convention mandates that women's role in procreation is not to be a basis for discrimination, as the upbringing of children requires women, men, and society as a whole sharing responsibility. "A change in the traditional role of men as well as the role of women in society and in the family" is necessary to achieve full equality between women and men.[33]

Discrimination condemned. The first sixteen articles of the Convention define discrimination, condemn it in all its forms, and articulate particular strategies for overcoming discrimination. For the purposes of the Convention, discrimination is defined as

> any distinction, exclusion or restriction made on the basis of sex which has the effect or purpose of impairing or nullifying the recognition, enjoyment or exercise by women, irrespective of their marital status, on a basis of equality of men and women, of human rights and fundamental freedoms in the political, economic, social, cultural, civil or any other field.[34]

All appropriate means that will without unnecessary delay create policies of eliminating discrimination against women are mandated.

---

[32] The full text of the Convention is in the Minutes of the General Assembly, Thirty-fourth Session (1979), pp. 193-198. A condensed version of the Convention is in Fraser, pp. 130-6. I am using the text as printed in the Minutes. Ibid., p. 194.

[33] Minutes, p. 194.

[34] Minutes, p. 194. This definition of discrimination illumines its roots in liberal theory, with its emphasis on both sex roles and human rights.

The Convention stipulates that affirmative action programs aimed at accelerating de facto equality between women and men are not to be considered discriminatory.   Such programs are to be discontinued "when the objectives of equality of opportunity and treatment have been achieved."   Nor are measures aimed at protecting maternity to be considered discriminatory.   Equal rights of women with men in the fields of education, employment, health care, in marriage and family relations, and before the law are affirmed.   Appropriate measures are to be taken to guarantee the application of Convention principles to women in rural areas.   Measures are also to be taken "to suppress all forms of traffic in women and exploitation of prostitution of women."[35]

Implementation procedures.   The closing articles of the Convention establish procedures for its implementation.   A Committee on the Elimination of Discrimination Against Women (CEDAW) was established, consisting of members elected by secret ballot from a list nominated by State Parties.   Governments ratifying the Convention are to agree to implement the principles of equality, to report their progress to CEDAW within a year of ratification, and to report again every four years thereafter.

Critical assessment.   The Convention has the status of an international treaty for those states that sign it.   Thus it carries more weight than the plans or strategies adopted at the initial Decade conferences and continues to be a significant source of internationally recognized principles for the elimination of discrimination against women.   Its comprehensiveness in addressing areas not often identified as relevant to public policy is valuable - it mandates equality within the family as well as in education, employment, health, and public life.

Yet the Convention makes no effort to identify the roots of women's oppression.   Its presumption is that elimination of legal discrimination will adequately ensure equality between women and men, thus keeping within the bounds of the liberal agenda.   The possibility of hierarchical relations of domination and subordination (patriarchy) between men and women is not raised.   Thus issues such as violence against women, particularly domestic violence, are not addressed by the

---

[35] Minutes, p. 195.

Convention. These issues are raised in later Decade conferences as attempts are made to identify the roots of women's inequality.

From Equality to Empowerment:
Broadening the Scope of Action

The Mid-Decade Conference
Copenhagen 1980

The mid-decade conference brought together over thirteen hundred delegates from 145 countries in Copenhagen, Denmark. To the themes equality, development and peace were added programs of action on employment, health, and education. Most importantly, over 8,000 women attended the nongovernmental forum.

Roots of inequality. The Copenhagen Programme of Action[36] includes a section on "the roots of inequality of women: the problem of development and equality of participation of women and men in development." It observes that the causes of inequality "are directly linked with a complex historical process," derived from economic, political, cultural and social factors. Forms of inequality are as varied as the conditions of the world community.[37]

Both structural and liberal perspectives inform this analysis, as is evident in the following statements. In most countries, the inequality of women comes "to a very large extent from mass poverty and general

---

[36] This document was adopted on July 30, 1980, by a roll call vote of 94 to 4, with 22 abstentions. Australia, Canada, Israel and the United States voted against the Programme of Action, all citing attacks against Israel in the paragraphs of the Programme which equated zionism and racism and called for its elimination. Most of the countries who abstained were from western Europe. They also noted what they saw as the unnecessary politicization of the conference. Most all those countries voting against or abstaining noted their support of the other sections of the Programme. *Report of the World Conference of the United Nations Decade for Women: Equality, Development and Peace, Copenhagen, 14 to 30 July 1980*, United Nations, pp. 197-207.

[37] United Nations, *Report of the World Conference of the United Nations Decade for Women: Equality, Development and Peace*, Copenhagen, 14 to 30 July 1980, para. 10.

backwardness ... caused by underdevelopment which is a product of imperialism, colonialism, neo-colonialism and also of unjust international economic relations." Women's "unfavourable status" is aggravated in both developed and underdeveloped countries "by *de facto* discrimination on the grounds of sex."[38]

However, the account of the roots of the inequality of women moved well beyond the sex role and structural frameworks. The analysis targets the division of labor between the sexes as a basic factor in the "unequal share of women in development." The division, justified by women's childbearing function, has "mainly restricted women to the domestic sphere and has unduly burdened them." The result is that women are treated as inferior and "unequal in their activities outside the domestic sphere." Their access to resources and participation in decision-making has been limited, "and in many instances institutionalized inequality in the status of women and men has also resulted."[39]

The Programme further argued that the predominant economic analyses of labor and capital

> insufficiently trace the linkages between production systems in world economies and women's work as producers and reproducers.... Women are not simply discriminated against by the productive systems, but subject to the discrimination that arises by virtue of being the reproductive force.[40]

In many countries there has been little recognition of the actual or potential contribution of women to economic activity. Priority in employment has often been given to men in economic activities outside the household.

The delegates charge that women suffer from "dual oppression" on the basis of their sex and social class, through "cumulative processes of discrimination within and outside the family. Poverty and

---

[38] Ibid., para. 12.

[39] Ibid., para. 11.

[40] Ibid., para. 13.

underdevelopment have sharpened these inequities."[41] The effects of cumulative processes of discrimination and underdevelopment are "strikingly apparent" in the world profile of women: although only one third of the "official labour force, they perform nearly two thirds of all working hours, receive only one tenth of the world income and own less than 1 per cent of world property."[42]

This analysis, which moves beyond liberal and structural perspectives, is typical of a socialist feminist framework. As already noted, this framework points to the sexual division of labor and the dual oppression of women by sex and class and criticizes any structural account which points only to the role of systems of production in the subordination of women.

Yet even this more inclusive framework in the Copenhagen Programme does not identify the discrimination women face on the basis of sex/gender as patriarchy or male domination. The report notes that "in a group of countries [such discrimination] is called sexism."[43] The reasons for caution in naming male dominance as a problem are most likely political, and not conceptual. The interests of governments in maintaining male dominance tempers any analysis of the oppression of women. Arvonne Fraser describes the potentially explosive impact of adding gender to the discussion of power and status, which she identifies as the underlying questions in meetings on development. Gender "personalizes" the discussion of power and relationships between nations; changing relations between the sexes would affect "virtually every delegate and every power structure in the world."[44]

---

[41] Ibid., para. 15.

[42] Ibid, para 16. This profile, which was also cited at the beginning of this study, was able to be drawn because of the statistical work that had been initiated by the 1975 Plan of Action.

[43] Ibid., p. 7, footnote.

[44] Fraser, pp. 78-79. Charlotte Bunch observes, as does Fraser, the attempts of male delegates during the Copenhagen conference to keep control of the women delegates from their countries - both during formal debate and informal discussions. Fraser, p. 81; Bunch, *Bringing the Global Home* (Denver: Antelope Publications, 1985), pp. 6-7.

Equality, power and participation. A shift in perspectives is also evident at other points of the Copenhagen Programme. For example, the definition of equality moves beyond a liberal understanding of equality before the law : "The attainment of equality presupposes equality of access to resources and the power to participate equally and effectively in their allocation and in decision-making at various levels."[45] This recognition of power as an aspect of participation is a breakthrough in the Decade documents.

There is also a move away from nearly exclusive reliance on governmental action to improve the situation of women. The role of non-governmental organizations, especially grassroots organizations, in developing the self-reliance of women and obtaining "real access to resources and power" is highlighted.[46] These strategies contrast with government programs in the 1975 Plan which are restricted "to welfare activities traditionally associated with women," which tend to reinforce stereotypes of women's roles as limited to caretakers.[47]

Violence against women. Some issues which were absent from the 1975 Plan of Action are included in the Programme for Action. Domestic and sexual violence are explicitly mentioned, the result of the efforts of organized women's groups.[48] The programme proposes that legislation to "prevent domestic and sexual violence against women" be enacted and implemented as part of national strategies for accelerating the full participation of women in social and economic development.[49] There is no analysis of the causes of such violence; research into its causes and extent is called for as a priority area for action on health.

---

[45] Report (1980), para. 3.

[46] Ibid., para. 100-105.

[47] See Fraser, pp. 81 and 88, for her analysis of a move to self-reliance of women in the Programme of Action. From my reading of this document, I think she overstates the degree of the shift at this time. I find a clear analysis of the dependency of women and the need for self-reliance in the 1985 Forward Looking Strategies document.

[48] Fraser, p. 87.

[49] Report(1980), para. 65.

Prevention of "mutilation practices which damage women's bodies and health" is also given a priority in the health area.[50]

Earlier principles reaffirmed. The need to integrate women in all aspects of development is reaffirmed, as are the principles of the right of women to work, to receive equal pay for work of equal value, and to be provided with equal opportunities for training and education that had been "clearly stated in the World Plan of Action."[51] The full participation of women in development requires "adequate and equitable access to health, nutrition and other social services including family planning and child care facilities." The Programme also reaffirmed the joint responsibility of men and women for the welfare of the family in general and the care of their children, as called for by the 1975 Plan of Action.[52]

Critical assessment. The Copenhagen Programme of Action deepens the analysis of the inequality of women in observing the dual

---

[50] Ibid., para. 162. Fran Hosken, the US woman who edits WIN news, began a campaign against female circumcision practices in Africa. This was a controversial campaign, as some Africans saw it is another instance of cultural imperialism. See Fraser, pp. 75-6, for a discussion of this campaign. At the 1985 Forum workshops on the practice were "organized and controlled by African women," who have been working to eradicate female circumcision practices. According to a report in the *ISIS International, Supplement n. 4*, the message from the workshops in Nairobi was that "what is needed from our western sisters is not a denigrating, we-know-better approach, but the realization that mutilation of women is the actual order of the day. In the west it manifests itself in economics, psychological, and spiritual mutilation; in Africa, it includes the physical. Let us then unite..." Ibid., p. 20.

[51] *Report* (1980), para. 46. The Programme extended these principles to the informal sector, Ibid., para. 133. In actuality, it is "equal pay for equal work" which was stated in the 1975 Plan of Action. At the 1985 Conference, the US delegation would note the difference between the concept of equal pay for equal work and equal pay for work of equal value. The 1985 delegation said that the US only supported the first, and not the second.

[52] Ibid., para. 47. Under the section on "priority areas requiring special attention," the plight of female-headed households is noted. As there are no men in these households to share responsibilities, the Programme urges that "Governments should ensure that women who alone are responsible for their families receive a level of income sufficient to support themselves and their families in dignity and independence." Ibid., para. 208-9.

oppression of women by both gender and class and in noting the inadequacies of economic analyses which do not take account of both production and reproduction. In raising issues of power and violence, the Programme moves beyond the liberal agenda of much of the 1975 Plan of Action.

However, the Programme of Action affirmed the liberal agenda of the earlier Plan for legislation, changes in sex roles, and the integration of women into economic development. While the 1980 Programme moved to pointing beyond governments to grass-roots organizations as agents of change, it does not go so far as to question the nature of the economic development into which women are to be integrated.

End of the Decade Conference
Nairobi 1985

One hundred sixty countries sent 2,100 delegates to the conference that concluded the decade. Its purpose was to review and appraise the Decade For Women and adopt strategies looking to the year 2000. Most significantly, over 14,000 women participated in Forum '85, the nongovernmental conference. More than two-thirds of these women were from the Third World, a remarkable shift for the Decade.

After much debate and negotiation, the conference delegates adopted the Nairobi Forward Looking Strategies for the Advancement of Women by consensus. This procedural act is significant, as neither of the two earlier conference documents had achieved such a consensus.[53] An international mandate for the advancement of women had been issued, although the document has no legal binding power.

The official Nairobi document once again exhibits different theoretical perspectives, as do the earlier ones. However, in contrast to the Plan of Action (1975) and the Programme of Action (1980), the

---

[53] The offending phrase equating zionism to racism replaced zionism with the words "and other forms of racism and racial discrimination," a compromise acceptable to the United States and its supporters who had voted against the 1980 Programme because of the equation of zionism with racism.

Forward Looking Strategies (FLS) raises questions as to the nature of the economic development into which women are to be integrated. The basic approach in the FLS is to identify obstacles to the progress of women and strategies to overcome these obstacles.[54]

Milestones of Oppression:
Obstacles to the Progress of Women

The report declares that the overwhelming obstacles, in practice, are caused by "varying combinations of political and economic as well as social and cultural factors." These obstacles are historical factors which limit women's access to employment, health and education, and other resources. They also inhibit "the effective integration of women into the decision-making process."[55] Sex-role and structural perspectives are interrelated in the discussion of these obstacles, with the effect that both gender and class are seen as critical factors in women's inequality.[56]

Devaluation of women's productive and reproductive roles results in women's "secondary" status and low priority for promotion of women's participation in development. Belief in a physiological basis for assigning women domestic tasks and judgments about their inferior

---

[54] Responses from questionnaires filled out by governments as a part of the review and appraisal carried out by the United Nations were the basis for identification of obstacles. For a fuller discussion of the process, see chapter one of this study.

[55] *Report of the World Conference to Review and Appraise the Achievements of the United Nations Decade for Women: Equality, Development, and Peace, Nairobi, 15-26 July 1985*, United Nations, para. 18.

[56] These factors are also identified in a survey conducted by the NGO Planning Committee of 140 organizations from around the world to identify common problems of the world's women. Sixty-five of these non-governmental organizations are international, 72 national; 40% are located in "industrialized" countries and 60% in "the developing world." Three major obstacles to women's progress are identified: "1) deteriorating economic conditions which, in many countries, reached crisis proportions in recent years; 2) lack of education and poor dissemination of information; 3) and repressive traditional practices and the cultural attitudes of women and men. " The findings of the survey are reported in *co-action*, the newsletter of the UNESCO Co-operative Action Programme (1985-6), p. 16.

capacities to those of men perpetuates inequality and inhibits structural and attitudinal changes needed to eliminate inequality.[57]

> The complexity and multidimensional aspects of changing sex roles and norms and the difficulty of determining the specific structural and organizational requirements of such a change have hindered the formulation of measures to alter sex roles and to develop appropriate perspectives on the image of women in society. Thus, despite gains made by a few women, for the majority subordination in the labour force and in society has continued, though the exploitative conditions under which women often work has become more visible.[58]

"Structural constraints imposed by a socio-economic framework in which women are second-class persons" limits progress and women's "double burden" of domestic tasks and labor force participation remains.[59]

Some of these structural constraints are delineated in a discussion of factors of political economy:

> The effective participation of women in development has also been impeded by the difficult international situation, the debt crisis, poverty, continued population growth, rising divorce rates, increasing migration, and the growing incidence of female-headed households. Yet, neither the actual expansion of employment for women nor the recognition that women constitute a significant proportion of producers has been accompanied by social adjustments to ease women's burden of child and household care. The economic recession led to a reduction in investments, particularly in those services that allow greater social sharing of the social and economic costs of child care and housework.[60]

In the least developed countries scarce national resources and the problems of mass poverty compel governments to concentrate "on alleviating the poverty of both women and men rather than on equality issues for women." But the FLS contend that because "women's secondary position" increases "their vulnerability to marginalization,"

---

[57] Report (1985), para 45.

[58] Ibid., para. 101.

[59] Ibid., para. 18.

[60] Ibid., para. 102.

those women in the "lowest socio-economic strata" are most likely "the poorest of the poor" and should be a priority. Further, since women are "an essential productive force in all economies," efforts to "raise their status" should be intensified in times of economic recession. The advancement of women is "without doubt a pre-condition for the establishment of a humane and progressive society."[61]

Three Inseparable Goals for the Advancement of Women: Equality, Development, and Peace

The goals of equality, development and peace are reaffirmed in the FLS. The "unity, inseparability and interdependence" of these objectives in relation to "the advancement of women and their full integration in economic, political, social and cultural development" is reiterated. The FLS are "a practical and effective guide for global action on a long-term basis and within the context of the broader goals and objectives of a new international economic order."[62] As is evident, goals and strategies are drawn from both liberal and radical structural agendas. Empowerment of women emerges as a significant new strategy which deepens and broadens these agendas.

The FLS insist that to attain these goals a sharing of responsibility by women and men has to emerge in society as a whole so "that women play a central role as intellectuals, policy-makers, decision-makers, planners, and contributers and beneficiaries of development." The "strengths and capabilities" of women, including "their great contribution to the welfare of families and to the development of society, must be fully acknowledged and valued."[63] Specific obstacles and strategies are identified for each of the three goals.

Power-sharing basic to equality. "Unjust international economic relations" and "*de facto* discrimination on the grounds of sex" are identified as major obstacles to the equality of women. Women

---

[61] Ibid., para. 19, 39.

[62] Ibid., para. 37-8.

[63] Ibid., para. 15.

experience discrimination "in terms of denial of equal access to the power structure that controls society and determines development issues and peace initiatives." "Race, colour, and ethnicity" are identified as a basis for "compound discrimination" against women in some countries.   Socio-economic inequalities help determine women's knowledge of and access to the law so that all women do not benefit equally from legal changes. Fear of recrimination and intimidation also keep some women from exercising their full legal rights.[64]

Basic strategies proposed for achieving equality include the establishment and enforcement of "a comprehensive legal base for the equality of women and men" on the basis of human dignity. Legislative changes will be most effective "within a supportive framework promoting simultaneous changes in the economic, social, political and cultural spheres, which can help bring about a social transformation. "The "sharing of power on equal terms with men must be a major strategy" for the attainment of "true equality."[65]

Equality before the law in conditions and opportunities of employment, including remuneration and adequate social security, are reiterated as basic strategies, as they had been in the previous Decade documents. The sharing of domestic responsibilities by all members of the family is reaffirmed, but now linked to "equal recognition of women's informal and invisible economic contributions in the mainstream of society ... as complementary strategies   for the elimination of women's secondary status, which   has fostered discrimination."[66]

Power-sharing basic to development. Both the continuation of "women's stereotyped reproductive and productive roles" and structural factors in the global political economy such as trade restrictions and blockades are identified as obstacles to "the effective integration of

---

[64] Ibid., para. 44, 46-8.

[65] Ibid., para. 51.

[66] Ibid., para. 54, 59.

women in the process of development."[67]   Another major obstacle
identified here is the exclusion of women from policy and decision
making, such that the choices about development are "largely male-
dominated." Furthermore, the issue of women in development has been
perceived as a problem of social welfare; women are seen as a cost to
society rather than actual or potential contributers to development. As
such, the issue receives low priority.[68]

Proposed strategies for development offered here include some new
emphases. The FLS contends that development "must be characterized
by the search for economic and social objectives and goals that
guarantee the effective participation of the entire population, especially
women." It is imperative that needed structural changes be brought
about to achieve these goals. An equitable distribution of income is to
be promoted and absolute poverty, experienced disproportionately by
women and children, is to be eradicated by eliminating hunger and
malnutrition and working toward the construction of more just
societies.[69]

The need for women to possess an equal share of power is
reasserted in this discussion of the development process, as it had been
in the section on equality. Women must share both in "guiding
development efforts and in benefitting from them." Actual and potential
impacts of macro-economic processes on women are to be assessed and
modifications made "to ensure that women are not adversely effected."
In developing human resources, the need to avoid further increases in
women's work-load is emphasized, especially in regard to the
development of policies responding to the "economic and debt crisis."[70]

---

[67] Although the US delegation voted for adoption of the FLS as a whole, it
"reserved its position" on paragraphs in this section which listed structural economic
factors as impeding the advancement of women. Ibid., para. 93-4.

[68] Ibid., para. 105.

[69] Ibid., para. 109.

[70] Ibid., para. 112. The need to avoid increasing women's work load is in
contrast to the call to "ameliorate the hard working conditions and unreasonably
heavy work load ... of many women" in the Mexico City Plan of Action. *Report,*
1975, para. 18. This shift reflects, in part, the negative impact of the global

Governmental and non-governmental efforts are to focus on enhancing the self-reliance of women. Since economic independence is "a necessary pre-condition" for self-reliance, efforts are to focus "on increasing women's access to gainful activities" through grass-roots participatory processes. In order to effectively mobilize resources for women, the link "between the advancement of women and socio-economic and political development" must be understood.[71]

A moral dimension to development. Implicit in some of these proposals are questions about the nature of the economic development into which women are to be integrated. Such discontent is more explicit in the "substantive background" section of the FLS. There it is asserted that development requires

> a moral dimension to ensure that it is just and responsive to the needs and rights of the individual and that science and technology are applied within a social and economic framework that ensures environmental safety for all life forms on our planet.[72]

The FLS contend that women's perspective on development is critical as it is "in the interest of human enrichment and progress" to include their concept of equality, their choices between alternative development strategies and their approach to peace in "the social fabric."[73]

Violence against women and world peace. The FLS treatment of the issues of world peace in relation to women are for the most part prosaic. For example, obstacles to "universal and durable peace" include hostility and lack of tolerance and respect for different cultures and traditions, economic injustice, and the arms race. However, for the first time, the Decade documents include "domestic violence and violence against women" in the list of human rights abuses. It is recognized that violence against women exists "in various forms in

---

economic and debt crisis on efforts to improve the situation of women, i.e. all we can do is hold steady.

[71] Ibid., para. 113, 119.

[72] Ibid., para. 12.

[73] Ibid., para. 16.

everyday life in all societies" and includes beatings, mutilation, burnings, and sexual abuse and rape. Legal and other measures to prevent violence and to aid its victims are encouraged.[74]

Furthermore, it is asserted that issues of women and peace and the meaning of peace for women can not be separated "from the broader question of relationships between women and men in all spheres of life and in the family." Action at family and neighborhood levels, as well as at national and international levels, is necessary to ensure "a peaceful social environment."[75]

Critical Assessment

Our review makes clear that in FLS a shift has occurred away from earlier Decade documents primary concern for legal equality to the need for women's empowerment. The necessity for equal power for women is advocated in regard to attainment of equality, development and peace. This shift is also evident in the recognition of the crucial role of nongovernmental organizations and grassroots organizations of women as change agents. Early on the FLS argue that

> Success will depend in large measure upon whether or not women can unite to help each other to change their poor material circumstances and secondary status and to obtain the time, energy and experience required to participate in political life. At the same time, improvements in health and educational status, legal and constitutional provisions and networking will increase the effectiveness of the political action taken by women so that they can obtain a much greater share in political decision-making than before.[76]

Alliances are also to be built "across sexual lines" to overcome structural obstacles to the advancement of women.

Earlier Decade documents perceived the situation of women primarily as "a welfare problem" whereas here the stress is on recognizing and valuing the contributions of women to the development

---

[74] Ibid., para. 245, 258.

[75] Ibid., para. 257.

[76] *Report* (1985), para. 33.

process. The necessity of the self-reliance of women and strategies to facilitate that self-reliance are also given prominence.

Recognition that gender, race, and class structures interact to affect women adversely is articulated more clearly than earlier. Sex-role and structural frameworks are integrated in an analysis of the oppression of women. The moral quality and the nature of development is questioned, at least subtly.

So there are gains in the formal documents in identifying the perspectives, actors, and elements of analysis needed for an adequate address of women's inequality. But deeper analysis and challenges to existing power structures was provided by groups at Forum 85.

Challenges to Power Structures:
Third World Women Speak at Forum 85

The shift in paradigm apparent in the *Forward Looking Strategies* is even more evident at the non-governmental Forum, where for the first time during the decade the majority of women are from the third world. In particular, clear challenges are voiced to assumptions about what constitutes economic development, to the effects of systems of male domination including violence against women, and to the questionable role of the state. The need for genuine empowerment and organization of women is strongly voiced. By this measure, strategies of some Forum groups tend to be conflictive, rather than consensual.

Among the forum participants it is recognized that the nature of the official conferences exerts pressure toward consensual strategies. As one Forum participant observes in regard to these governmental conferences:

> ... the *official delegations* often were representative of national governments where women's issues and women's rights have marginal official visibilty, where national policies are tied to a patriarchal system that continues to keep women "in their place" and where danger to women's physical self remains a constant. Thus, if women's situations are to change, it will be by women from all strata, from the "bottom up" agitating and organizing for the change - not

necessarily from wonderful proclamations in the "Forward-looking Strategies".[78]

By contrast, the 14,000 some women at the Forum are not constrained in their ability to challenge patriarchal systems, the state, or internal class structures. Few of these women are accountable to governments; many are accountable to groups of women whom they represented at the Forum. Their experience and perspective are from the underside. Participants in this and previous Decade conferences observe that Forum 85 attests that an international women's movement has been created and is developing a common agenda. A Mexican journalist noted that:

> More and more, women are pointing out that to speak about national liberation, pacifism or new alternatives to development, we have to deal with feminism. I think this comes partly as a result of the networking that women have done since 1980 until now, and of the incorporation of very diverse types of women into the feminist movement that has expanded the scope of what women's struggle and liberation is.[79]

An Indian participant countered charges that feminism is a western concept:

> We believe that the Forum at Nairobi has established beyond all doubt that the women's movement is at this point in time truly "global" in character and not "white-western" as some would claim and like to believe. All of us from the Third World felt that the agenda truly reflected our priorities and many of the discussions were very relevant to Third World problems.[80]

---

[78] Safiya Bandele, "The UN World Conference and World Forum on Women," *African Women Rising* 2 (Winter-Spring) p. 12.

[79] Claudia Hinojosa, "Forum 80, Forum 85: Things Have Changed," *Connexions*, No. 17-18 (Summer/Fall 1985), p. 7. The main sources for thorough reports on Forum '85 include *Connexions*, No. 17-18; *The International Women's Studies Institute in Kenya,* San Francisco: IWSI, 1985; International Women's Tribune Center, *Images of Nairobi*, Decade for Women Information Resources #5, New York: IWTC, 1986; and Caroline Pezzullo for the NGO Planning Committee, *For the Record ... Forum '85*, New York: IWTC, 1986.

[80] Sundari Ravindran, "Looking forward from Nairobi," *ISIS International*, Women's Journal Supplement no. 4, p. 18.

An African researcher commented on the international character of the women's movement and the challenge facing it:

> Nairobi witnessed the maturity of the international women's movement. It should categorically be stated that this is a social movement without precedent.... there is no such notion as "Western Women." The presence of a relatively large number of women of colour who are from and or reside in Europe and North America shifted the old conflict between "Third World" and "Western" women to its proper terrain, that of a simultaneous concern with class, gender, and race. This then is the challenge facing feminism. Can it deal with all these issues without putting a hierarchy and prioritizing one issue over the other?[81]

As these women attest, the women's movement emerged at Forum 85 as an international, multiracial, multicultural web of networks coming together to challenge entrenched interrelated structures of domination and exploitation.

Many acknowledged that the DAWN network modelled such an approach with their preconference study book and the series of workshops they sponsored at the Forum. DAWN, an acronym for Development Alternatives with Women for a New Era, is "a wide network of women from many different regions, races and political ideologies"[82] concerned to find more equitable development processes.

---

[81] Zenebeworke Tadesse, "Editorial," *Echo*, Bilingual Quarterly Newsletter of the Association of African Women for Research and Development (AAWORD) Vol. 1, no. 1, (1986) p. 2. Tadesse noted that although relatively large numbers of grassroots women were present, and not just "their spokespersons" as in the past, "... it is overwhelming when one faces the fact that those 'who were brought' to the Nairobi Forum are the better off and not 'the very poor.' Thus the class issue became a more glaring reality" and remains a continuing challenge to the international women's movement.

[82] The DAWN project was initiated by The Institute of Social Studies Trust, a non-profit research and advocacy organization in New Delhi, India. Collaborating organizations included the African Association of Women for Research and Development (AAWORD), Senegal; the Women and Development Unit of the University of the West Indies (WAND), Barbados; the Asian and Pacific Development Center (APDC), Malaysia; and the Chr. Michelsen Institute (CMI), Norway. A global advisory council, made up of representatives from these organizations and other researchers and activists, guided the project, which was funded by the Ford Foundation. DAWN, pp. 9-10.

It must be stated that the DAWN panels provided a solid and integrated framework within which to view women's issues: they made it very clear that women's problems were a part of, and resulted from, an inequitable world order characterized by gross inequities of gender, race and class.[83]

The collaborative processes it uses and the potential for its theoretical perspective to be "a unifying territory" are identified as its "most powerful attributes."[84] For our purposes of developing criteria of adequacy for social analysis and proposals for change, we will examine the main points of this work and note other groups at the Forum who gave supporting views.

Interlinked Crises:
Development Processes Criticized

The DAWN project aimed to clarify the nature and meaning of the links between "development, social and economic crisis, the subordination of women, and feminism," based on the experience of women during the Decade. DAWN asserts that a major learning has been "the need to question in a more fundamental way the underlying processes of development into which we have been attempting to integrate women."[85]

Throughout the Decade it had been assumed that "women's main problem in the Third World has been insufficient participation in an otherwise benevolent process of growth and development." An increase in the participation of women in development and in their shares in

---

[83] Ravindran, p. 21. A few women at the Forum criticized DAWN for not "naming the enemy" as capitalism or imperialism, for "an unwillingness to take a political stance, and for encouraging "unity around gender issues across class differences." Gita Sen responded for DAWN by questioning whether "not naming names vitiated or distorted analysis" and asserting that "if we refuse to learn and dialogue with older organizations [more traditional women's organizations], all we do is marginalize ourselves." IWSI, pp. 21-2.

[84] Ravindran, p. 21.

[85] DAWN, p. 11. See the last half of the first chapter of my study for an account of some of the regional reports by women at the Forum which include questions about the nature of development into which women are being integrated.

land, resources, employment and income relative to men had been seen "as both necessary and sufficient to effect dramatic changes in their economic and social position." DAWN insists that "our experiences now lead us to challenge this belief."[86]

DAWN contends that it can no longer be assumed that the development process in most Third World countries is "inherently benign to the people living there." They argue that the consequences of long term economic dynamics which are inimical or indifferent to the interests and needs of poor people are manifest in "interlinked crises." "Massive and growing impoverishment and inequality" within nations and between nations continues relentlessly. Food insecurity is most evident in famine-stricken regions of Africa, but other countries are vulnerable to food shortages. The debt crisis, which keeps debtor nations exporting capital to service loans with unusually high interest rates. is a critical instance of world financial and monetary disarray. Environmental degradation, such as continuing deforestation in subsaharan Africa, the Amazon basin in Latin America, and forested areas of India, and population growth which outstrips available resources are other instances of these interlinked crises. DAWN identifies increased militarization, domestic repression, and foreign aggression as national and international policy reactions to these crises. Worse, "a growing sense of hopelessness, even lack of concern, about the Third World's poor in international donor and agency circles" is also evident.[87]

DAWN insists that new strategies for survival will not be successful

if women continue to suffer from decreased access to resources and increased demands on their labour time.... Rather than see women crushed further under the burden of their traditional work in unchanging divisions of labour, we argue that if human survival is now the world's most pressing problem, and if women are crucial to that survival, then the empowerment of women is

---

[86] Ibid., p. 11. Note that the strategy for integrating women into development which DAWN is questioning is a consensual strategy.

[87] Ibid., p. 12.

essential for the emergence of new, creative, and cooperative solutions to the crisis.[88]

Furthermore, DAWN argues that "equality for women is impossible within the existing economic, political and cultural processes that reserve resources, power and control for small sections of people." But they also assert that development is not possible without greater equity for and participation by women.[89]

Gender and class in development experience. DAWN contends that perspectives of poor and oppressed women offer "a unique and powerful vantage point" to examine the effects of development programs and strategies. Three considerations make such an approach critical. First, women are the majority of the poor, the underemployed and the socially and economically disadvantaged. Failure to assess strategies from this perspective means poverty is not really addressed. Second, women's contributions as workers and managers of human welfare, although underremunerated and undervalued, is key to the survival ability of households, communities and nations. Third, women work in all sectors (both traditional and modern) and so can assess the impact of development on a wide range of economic activities:

> ... the vantage point of poor women ... enables us not only to evaluate the extent to which development strategies benefit or harm the poorest and most oppressed sections of the people, but also to judge their impact on a range of sectors and activities crucial to socioeconomic development and human welfare. [90]

---

[88] Ibid., p. 13.

[89] Ibid., p. 14. "Unequal access to resources, control over production, trade, finance, and money, and across nations, genders, regions, and classes" are identified as the structural roots of poverty. Ibid., p. 73.

[90] Ibid., pp. 16-17. Loretta Hobbs extends this argument in light of the Forum workshops to argue that "the goals of full equality and development for women are not realizable without re-evaluating these goals through the eyes and experiences of the world's most oppressed women." Equality, Development, and Peace through Our Eyes, *African Women Rising* 2 (Winter-Spring 1986), p. 3.

The issues raised by an analysis that begins with the poorest and oppressed women, members of the project insisted, are relevant to both Third World and more industrialized countries.

DAWN contends that "women's experience with processes of economic growth, commercialization, and market expansion are determined by both gender and class," that is to say that women's experience is shaped by their position in gender hierarchies and by their relation to the means of production - whether they own or control land or capital. Political and economic structures are "highly inequitable" between nations, classes, genders and ethnic groups. Although these structures often are "the historical legacy of colonial domination," postcolonial development processes and strategies have in fact exacerbated the inequities, and "in some instances even worsened the levels of absolute poverty." DAWN asserts that since "the interests of powerful nations and classes, both internationally and nationally, are enmeshed in these structures," these nations and classes often have "a vested interest in their persistence." As a result, "the survival of large sections of the population in the Third World has become increasingly uncertain and vulnerable."[91]

DAWN stresses that this vulnerability is further reinforced for women

> by systems of male domination that, on the one hand, deny or limit their access to and control over such productive resources as land and labour and to political participation, and on the other hand, impose sexual divisions of labour that allocate to them the most onerous, labour-intensive, poorly rewarded tasks inside and outside the home, as well as the longest hours of work.[92]

Traditional gender-based subordination further curtails women's physical mobility.

DAWN recognizes that "the specifics of subordination" vary considerably across regions, historical time periods, and classes. Thus, although women "of both the propertied and the working classes" are subordinate to men, the nature of that subordination differs. "For poor

---

[91] Ibid., pp. 18-19.

[92] Ibid., p. 19.

women it may take the form of longer and harder work, while for richer women it may appear as controls on physical mobility and sexuality."[93] Further, although traditional systems of gender subordination have been transformed by forces of economic growth, DAWN presumes that "subordination itself persists, although in some cases more impersonal forces in the labour market replace the direct control of women within patriarchal households."[94]

Gender-based subordination of women is reinforced by religious beliefs, cultural practices, and educational systems that assign women lesser status and power. The collective also points to threats of sexual violence as means to control and restrict women's physical mobility and to punish women "who flouted social norms." Forms of sexual mutilation are practiced to ensure male control of female sexuality. Public spaces in many societies are physically dominated by men. "Thus the cultural subordination of women has reinforced male control of resources and power, and the divisions of labour that have enshrined male privileges." When development programs have negative effects, these are invariably felt more acutely by women.[95]

Colonial roots of women's marginalization. Analysis of the heritage of colonialism is an important ingredient in DAWN's effort to enhance understanding of the negative impact development processes have had on poor women. DAWN identifies two broad effects of colonial rule on Third World countries:

> On the one hand, it introduced private property, commercial production and export orientation, and geared production in agriculture, industry, services, and trade to the above. On the other hand, and as a result, large sections of the population were alienated from adequate or stable resources, income, or employment. In particular, the basic needs of food, health, housing, and the like became increasingly marginal to the main orientation of the production structures.[96]

---

[93] Ibid., p. 19.

[94] Ibid., p. 21.

[95] Ibid., pp. 19-21.

[96] Ibid., p. 24.

These two trends have very specific consequences for women. Women's access to resources was often reduced more by expansion of private property and commercialization than was men's access. Further, their role as providers of basic needs was downgraded by the marginalization of the basic requirements for decent life as production for the market became dominant.

DAWN insists that most third world countries still retain many of the main features of the colonial era. The inequities within and among nations created and accentuated by colonialism have proved most difficult to overcome. Thus, primary export enclaves geared to production of cash crops such as coffee or cocoa persist, justified on the grounds of comparative cost advantages. "Effective control over production, allocation, and distribution decisions" is usually "in the hands of multinational corporations that subordinate national interests to their own global profit and growth strategies."[97] Thus, first world economic hegemony persists in new forms. Although DAWN does not oppose export expansion, per se, the collective argues that under extreme inequalities in land holding and income, export promotion will likely "worsen existing inequalities," including gender inequalities.[98]

---

[97] Ibid, p. 25. DAWN does not give nearly as much attention to a discussion of multinationals as it does to agricultural production. Other groups at the Forum presented rather full analyses of the impact of these corporations. In their analysis of multinationals, The Women's Coalition for Nairobi assert that "a closer look at TNC's reveals the effect they have on the lives of women in both developing and developed countries. This is vital to understanding the links between the misery of the most oppressed and the exploitation of all working women." WCN, p. 16.

The World Council of Churches facilitated a workshop on "Women Organizing in Transnational Companies," which was reported on in the special issues of *Connexions* on the Forum. (No. 17-18, Summer/Fall, 1985, 29-31) For more extensive analyses of the impact of multinationals on women see Marilee Karl, "Integrating Women into Multinational Development," *Women in Development: A resource guide for organization and action*, Boston: New Society Publishers, 1984, pp. 23-57, and Swatsi Mitter, *Common Fate, Common Bond: Women in the Global Economy* (London: Pluto Press, 1986). Mitter's book will be reviewed in the next chapter of this study.

[98] DAWN, p. 27.

Women Living for Others:
Crisis in Reproduction

DAWN's thesis that the development strategies so far pursued have produced multiple crises is further amplified in their work. They assert that both the world economic system and the structures through which the majority of the world's populations reproduce themselves, that is meet their basic needs, are in crisis.[99] Analytically, DAWN rejects the assumption that a growing economy necessarily is one that is meeting basic needs or "reproducing human life."

DAWN contends that the economic system and the structures of reproduction are interrelated, but for purposes of evaluating the moral import of the economy, must be examined separately.

> Since most people are part of a larger economic system - regional, national, or international - their own reproduction is not independent of the healthy functioning of the larger system. But the two are by no means congruent. The economic system may show vigour and dynamism while people's basic needs remain unmet, or even worsen. On the other hand, the basic needs of the poor may be met although the growth rate and the per capita income remain low.[100]

Economic growth does not ensure that people's basic needs will be met.

State policies toward the agrarian sector, employment, direct expenditures aimed at basic needs fulfillment, and poverty elimination are crucial to reproduction of human beings. DAWN insists that without explicit policies to meet the basic needs of the poor, "economic growth will improve the conditions of human reproduction *only* if it increases the employment and real incomes of the population at

---

[99] DAWN defines reproduction as "the process by which human beings meet their basic needs and survive from one day to the next." Ibid., p. 43.

[100] DAWN, p. 43. These crises, particularly the crisis in the world economic system, was noted in the official Decade documents. For further discussion of the crisis and its impact on women, see chapter one of this study and the previous section of this chapter.

large."[101] Otherwise, many people will not have the resources needed to supply their basic needs.

Poor women are at the center of what has been called a "generalized reproduction crisis in the provision of 'basic' needs," as they are the principal providers of those needs. In many parts of the third world women are the main producers of food crops; they "almost universally" process and cook the food. Women, particularly poorer women, are also often responsible for water and fuel collection. The reproduction crisis is reflected in the trade-offs among different basic needs that women are having to make in regard to use of such resources as their time, cash income, or land they control.[102]

For women without cash income or access to land, their labor time and that of their children is the only resource they control. In coping with the growing crisis their work hours have increased dramatically. In some instances, they have had to switch to less nutritious food that is less time consuming to produce and prepare. This has affected the nutritional status of poor women and children, as women usually eat after men and sometimes boys do. Their increased work burdens and poor nutrition has led "to an absolute and a relative decline in women's nutritional and morbidity status."

Thus "women, as the main workers in basic needs provision are central to an understanding of the linkages in the reproduction crisis ... and they must be the key potential actors in any resolution of the crisis." Women in some countries have already organized themselves to respond to the crisis.[103] For instance, in India women have organized against forest contractors to maintain their access to fuel. "Harambee" groups in Kenya have organized themselves to better meet needs for water and fuel.

---

[101] Ibid.

[102] Ibid, pp. 50-51

[103] Ibid., p. 51.

Women Pay More: The Debt Crisis

Analyses of the crisis in the world financial and monetary system and its impact on women is central to DAWN's interpretation of the pauperization of women. The current debt crisis has its root in the "recycling of petrodollars" from commercial banks through lending to third world countries after 1973. With the slowing down of world trade and fluctuation in interest rates, it has become all but impossible for many third world countries to repay their debts. The World Bank and the International Monetary Fund have negotiated "structural adjustment packages" which require reduction in national budgets for social services and basic needs with debtor nations, which are having a detrimental effect on many of the people in these countries. The export promotion programs which are to bring in foreign currency, especially in agriculture, are reducing domestic food availability to the poor as available land is being used to grow crops for export. As more of the debtor nation's funds go to service their debt, cutbacks in consumer goods imports and in domestic subsidies for basic needs are made.[104] ·

The structural adjustment packages that have been accepted by debtor nations under World Bank and International Monetary Fund pressure have a number of effects on women. Women may gain some employment opportunities in export oriented industrial and agricultural production, but are generally offered poor working conditions, low pay, and high job insecurity. The informal sector may grow, as more women are forced to earn an income to meet consumption needs. Women will bring homegrown and prepared food and handicrafts to street bazaars, but as indicated in the first chapter of this study the conditions of this employment tend to be insecure with low pay and few, if any, benefits.

---

[104] Ibid., pp. 52-4. They contend that "the onus of adjustment to imbalances in international payments falls entirely on deficit countries" in the system agreed to at the end of the second world war. The structural roots of the third world's balance of payments crisis is rooted in the exposure to private capital flows which integrated the third world into the international market "and the large outflows resulting there from" that were negotiated during the postcolonial period.

A second major impact of debt extension is cuts in social services expenditures in debtor nations, at a time when demand for the services is increasing because of growing poverty and unemployment. This usually leads to an increase in the work burden of women in the home, such as health care for family members which formerly would have been provided in clinics and hospitals. It may also lead to a reduction in their own access to services such as health and education. The school dropout rate of young girls increases, as they are needed to assist in home tasks or to supplement the family income. The impact of social service cutbacks in the United States is cited, as "it provides the clearest illustration of the negative impact of governmental policies on women and the poor."[105] The impact on third world women will be even worse, as they start "from a much lower level of basic needs fulfillment."[106]

Women's Broken Bodies:
Militarization and Violence

DAWN researchers remind us that twenty-one million lives have been taken in armed conflict since 1945, most of them in the third world and most of them civilian casualties. Women, children, the aged and the infirm are the majority both of these civilian casualties and of the refugees resulting from armed conflict. This increase in global violence is related to 1) growth in arms production and trade, 2) a growing potential for armed conflict as weapons and tensions increase, 3) a growing number of military controlled governments in response to

---

[105] For a description of the situation in the United States, see chapter one, section two, of this study. Particular effects included significant rises in unemployment, poverty, hunger, and homelessness

[106] Ibid., pp. 55-59.

resistance to the structural adjustment packages,[107] and 4) mushrooming of a culture of violence against women.[108]

Powerful social forces - national chauvinism, racism and sexism - are being unleashed "that subdue the most oppressed sections of society and dissipate their ability to resist the policies being pursued." For women the dimensions of the crisis

> include growing violence within the home, attacks on their civil status, physical mobility and work outside the home, and attacks on their control over reproduction. Simultaneously there has been rapid growth in the dehumanization and sexual objectification of women in the media, as well as sex tourism and prostitution abetted by governments concerned with generating foreign exchange earnings.[109]

The Alternative Asian Report extends this analysis of violence against women: "Women are bought, burned and beaten. They are objects of violence at home and in the streets, in military camps and in jails." Women are to be chaste and pure because ethnic, religious and cultural identity often is linked to the strictness of their morals; they "suffer dire consequences" when they are perceived as not being chaste.

The report also observes the links between the economy and abuse of women. Women are responsible for reproducing the labor force needed for national economic development. "They are used and abused to bring in the tourists and the foreign exchange. Their bodies are shaped and reshaped to sell consumer products." Women's bodies are

---

[107] As people suffer from higher prices, less income, and fewer social services as a result of the terms of the packages which are geared to production for export to earn foreign currency for debt service, they protest. In several countries military governments have come to power to control the unrest, as was the case in Latin America in the seventies and early eighties. As DAWN and others at the Forum indicate, national elites often benefit from export production. They also want to remain eligible for more loans so support the structural adjustment packages.

[108] Ibid., p. 60. The statistics DAWN cites are from two United Nations reports (1982 and 1983) and Ruth Sivard, *World Military and Social Expenditures*, Washington, DC, 1980 - 1983.

[109] DAWN, p. 67.

also used "as testing grounds" for new drugs and contraceptives or as "dumping grounds" for banned ones.[110]

The Women's Coalition for Nairobi, an interracial US women's coalition, speaks particularly of the links between violence against women and militarization.

> The tolerance of serious social problems such as battered and abused women, rape, violence in the family, etc. can also be understood in relation to the larger picture, and serves to desensitize us to the government's international and domestic violence.[111]

The Coalition argues that focusing on violence against women in isolation from "the basic causes of the deterioration of the quality of our lives," results in concern for this issue "degenerating into sensationalism, fear and diversion from basic solutions."

DAWN suggests that militarism represents in some ways "the ultimate depths of class biased and male dominated cultures." Yet it also brings forth "the most courageous and tenacious resistance from women," such as the mothers of the disappeared in Latin America, women in the resistance movement in the Philippines, and the women's peace movement in Europe. However, DAWN cautions that for poor third world women, peace and the struggle against violence cannot be separated from the struggle for economic justice, basic needs, national liberation, and patterns of economic development oriented towards these goals.

> Peace cannot be separated from development just as equality cannot, because the conditions that breed violence, war, and inequality are themselves often the results of development strategies harmful or irrelevant to the poor and to women.[112]

Creation of a just economic order is a priority.

---

[110] *Asian Women Speak Out*, p.13.

[111] *The Effects of Racism and Militarization on Women's Equality*, p 20.

[112] DAWN, pp. 66-67.

Tradition a "Double-edged Sword" for Women:
Cultural Crisis

As I have noted in my earlier discussion, efforts to return women to "their 'proper' subordinate position in the patriarchal family" are often supported by traditional religion and the state. The DAWN analysis stresses that traditions "have always been a double-edged sword for women." The role of traditional cultural norms in subordinating women and limiting their mobility and activity has already been noted. Furthermore, the demand "for cultural purity is often a thinly veiled attempt to continue women's subjugation in a rapidly changing society." Traditions and cultures also divide women from each other, because they vary across classes in the same society.[113]

DAWN identifies four key principles for action around cultural change. Although traditions are an important source of critical consciousness against cultural imperialism, they must be challenged at points where they are oppressive to women. First, traditional cultural forms such as music and dance need "to be harnessed for the struggle to raise the consciousness of both women and men," so that feminists are not seen as being "at loggerheads with the national and cultural stream." Second, *poor* women's problems must be a focus of change, since the reality of their daily lives so often "belies the fundamentalists' myth" about women's lives.

> Third, men's equal responsibility for upholding cultural traditions must be vociferously articulated. Whether in matters of dress, food and drinking habits, or as consumers of pornography, men are usually further removed than women from traditions and more responsible for cultural decline.[114]

Fourth, alliances should be made with progressive forces on specific issues and at the local level. An example cited by DAWN of a progressive movement which may be in women's interest is "liberation theology," although this movement is not without contradiction given

---

[113] DAWN, p. 69.

[114] Ibid., p. 69.

the opposition of the Catholic Church to contraception.[115] The fundamental basepoint in making alliances is concern for the wellbeing of women.

From Equality to Transformation:
Alternative Visions

DAWN clarified their understanding of feminism as part of the process of empowerment. They affirm the vision of feminism as striving "for the broadest and deepest development of society and human beings free of all systems of domination."[116] Feminism is "the political expression of the concerns and interests of women" from a variety of classes, nationalities, regions, and ethnic backgrounds; thus there is a diversity of feminisms, defined by these different women for themselves. The diversity builds on "a common opposition to gender oppression and hierarchy," but may be linked to struggles against oppression due to nationality, race, or class. As examples, they point to world-wide networks and movements to transform the subordination of women "and in the process to break down other oppressive structures" that had been forged during the Decade.[117]

The experience of grassroots organizations and women's groups needs to be crystallized into a clear vision of the kind of world women need and desire. DAWN's analysis is developed from the vantage point of poor women, whose well-being is at the core of the vision for change. It merits citation in full:

---

[115] Ibid., p. 70.

[116] Ibid., p. 13. They note that this vision was first articulated by women in international workshops in 1979 and 1980. See *Developing Strategies for the Future: Feminist Perspectives,* distributed by International Women's Tribune Center, New York City.

[117] DAWN, p. 15. The Women's Coalition for Nairobi - a multi-racial coalition of US women, the Association of African Women for Research and Development, the coalition of Latin American and Caribbean women at the Forum, and The Asian Women's Research and Action Network all argue for the necessity for such multifaceted movements in their reports to the Forum.

We want a world where inequality based on class, gender, and race is absent from every country, and from the relationships among countries. We want a world where basic needs become basic rights and where poverty and all forms of violence are eliminated. Each person will have the opportunity to develop her or his full potential and creativity, and women's values of nurturance and solidarity will characterize human relationships. In such a world women's reproductive role will be redefined: child care will be shared by men, women, and society as a whole. We want a world where the massive resources now used in the production of the means of destruction will be diverted to areas where they will help to relieve oppression both inside and outside the home. This technological revolution will eliminate disease and hunger, and give women means for the safe control of their fertility. We want a world where all institutions are open to participatory democratic processes, where women share in determining priorities and making decisions.[118]

DAWN argues that what is lacking in attaining such a vision is not resources, but "political will." However, they insist that "we cannot expect political will for systemic change to emerge voluntarily among those in power." Rather, political will must be developed by mass movements that emphasize the basic rights of the poor, and the reorientation of policies and projects toward that end. The opening of political processes and participation by poor people in decisions that affect their lives "at the macro and micro levels" is crucial. The "power and potential" of the women's movement could facilitate this process.[119]

To transform structures of subordination of women, DAWN endorses a multifaceted strategy:

changes in laws, civil codes, systems of property rights, control over our bodies, labour codes, and the social and legal institutions that underwrite male control and privilege are essential if women are to attain justice in society.[120]

---

[118] DAWN, p. 74.

[119] Ibid., p. 74.

[120] Ibid., p. 74.

The transformation of institutions that subordinate women and the basic rights of the poor are "inextricably linked" and "can be achieved together through the self-empowerment of women."[121]

An effective strategy for change will "integrate economic, political, legal, and cultural aspects." Long-run strategies "in the economic sphere" need to break down "the structures of inequity between genders, classes and nations, which act as barriers to development processes responsive to the needs of people." These include reorientation of production processes in agriculture, industry, and services to meeting the needs of the poor.

> In this context, recognition not just of poor women's work but of its *centrality* to such development processes is essential, as is the need to make poor women central to both planning and implementation.[122]

Requisites for such a change include "national liberation from colonial and neo-colonial domination, and national self-reliance, at least in the basic requirements such as food and energy sources, health care and water provision, and education."[123]

Other important strategies include a worldwide reduction in military expenditures and resource use, the control of multinationals, the transformation of internal inequities, genuine land reform with women having "equal status during and after the reforms." Organization of women agricultural workers and informal sector workers is a key short

---

[121] Ibid., p. 75.

[122] Ibid, p. 76. It is important that this emphasis on meeting basic needs is situated in a larger demand for participation by poor people and women in decision-making processes and redistribution of resources such as land. The International Council of African Women called for "another development perspective for women, one that views women as an underdeveloped, marginal class." Alternative strategies start with "a recognition of the common problems of women worldwide; informing, educating, and addressing these similarities, leading to self-reliance by using our creativity and combined resources to agitate actively for change in development strategies." *Women of Color Plan of Action*, p. 3.

[123] Other groups at the Forum, particularly Latin and Caribbean women and women of the Pacific Islands, also called for recognition of self-determination of peoples, land redistribution, and an end to militarization.

term strategy. Without these integrated efforts, some women question whether either a basic needs approach or a new international economic order would benefit women.[124]

Political mobilization, popular education, consciousness raising, and legal changes are core activities in the process of transformation. At the global level, support for the common goals of "a more just and equitable international order" and for disarmament is to be mobilized by a movement of women and the oppressed. At the national level mobilization of organizations of women and poor men to implement specific programs and around specific laws and civil codes have been effective. DAWN concluded that what is needed is not a social-political-economic program for women alone, but a program "for society from women's perspective."[125]

Conclusion: Our Struggle Continues

The impact of the Decade in terms of concrete improvements in women's lives is discouraging, as indicated in the first chapter of this study. As DAWN observed, "They appear to be as meagre as the resources that agencies and governments have actually directed to women."[126] But, DAWN added, the experiences of the Decade can be seen in another way. The research of the Decade confirmed how deeply ingrained and of what long historical standing is the subordination of women. Yet within the few years of the Decade world-wide networks and movements, "as never existed before," have been forged to develop a common vision as to how gender subordination and other oppressive structures may be transformed.

Many of the women who participated in the Decade meetings found the experience to be life transforming. A Caribbean participant spoke for many women:

---

[124] See ISIS, *Women in Development*, p. 20 and pp. 65-66 for discussion of this question.

[125] DAWN, p. 89.

[126] DAWN, p. 15.

For virtually all women who participated in the Forum the feeling we left with was one of being energized and strengthened for the long struggle ahead. We knew that for every one woman in Nairobi there were hundreds of others who would have liked to come. We learnt that most women are slowly coming to a similar understanding of the direction our struggle has to take. We are now aware of the potential power of the women's movement internationally as a force in the future direction of the world. We know also that those who fear justice, peace and true human liberation also now know these things. But ... the struggle continues.[127]

The growing consensus pointed to by this participant is the convergence of important strands of analyses that begin to account for the inequality of women and suggest strategies for change. The integration of sex-role theory with structural perspectives provides a multidimensional structural transformative approach best articulated by DAWN for Forum 85. This approach includes incorporating challenges to current notions of development, stressing the need for empowerment of women, and acknowledging the necessity for broad and deep structural transformation.

This emerging perspective has significant implications for the work of Christian economic ethics, which will be examined in the conclusion to this study. But first we need to assess the adequacy of various feminist analyses and proposals implicit in the Decade documents and some progressive Christian ethics in light of the accomplishments of the Decade. This assessment will clarify the most useful resources for analyzing and strategically engaging women's impoverishment.

---

[127] Rhoda Reddock, "Recollections on Forum '85," *Woman Speak!* Quarterly Newsletter About Caribbean Women, No. 18 (July/December 1985), p. 27.

CHAPTER FIVE

TAKING WOMEN'S LIVES SERIOUSLY:
TOWARDS A NEW PARADIGM

The best insights of the Decade for Women converge toward a theoretical perspective to illuminate adequately and engage strategically women's inequality and economic vulnerability. However, before we can examine the implications of this perspective. a testing of theoretical presuppositions implicit in the literature as to their usefulness in addressing the impoverishment of women is required. The level of integration demonstrated in the Decade documents does not yet characterize much of the debate about women's inequality. Here it is necessary to analyze further and critically evaluate the wider analytic literature and proposed strategies to test their adequacy from the multidimensional perspective emergent at Nairobi.

Texts which attempt to account for women's reality fall within a spectrum which may be described as liberal feminist, marxist, cultural feminist, and socialist feminist frameworks. My interest in this chapter is in noting how each framework accounts for the impoverishment of women. Almost all of the studies I review represent one of these specific theoretical frameworks clearly. Each of these studies addresses women's inequality from a global perspective and focuses on women's economic reality.   A critical review indicates the strengths and limitations of each of these perspectives and discloses movement toward a new paradigm.

Liberal Feminism:
Sex Roles and Equal Rights

I have already characterized liberal feminism as sex-role feminism, that is, it accounts for the inequality of women on the grounds of discrimination on the basis of sex-role stereotyping.   As I indicated, liberal feminism, neo-classical economic theory, and developmentalism all share the assumption that capitalist development is basically beneficial and only requires reforms to overcome discrimination against women.   The liberal program for change involves a direct attack on discrimination on the grounds of sex by advocating for equal rights for women.

As early as 1970 the negative effects of patterns of third world economic development on women in these developing countries was documented by Ester Boserup. In a pioneering work, she argued that gender is a significant socio-economic variable, that the labor force is not homogenous.   Her thesis is that an examination of the sexual division of labor is not only a legitimate but an essential focus of inquiry.   She insists on the existence of a sexual division of labor through history and globally: "even at the most primitive stages of family autarky there is some division of labor within the family, the main criteria for the division being that of age and sex."[1]

Boserup argued that although in both "primitive" and more developed communities "the traditional division of labor within the family is usually considered 'natural' in the sense of being obviously and originally imposed by the sex difference itself," the sexual division of labor actually is culturally determined and culturally specific. Although women tend to be concentrated in domestic labor, Boserup observed important differences in women's work. For example, she

---

[1] Ester Boserup, *Woman's Role in Economic Development* (New York: St. Martin's Press, 1970) p. 15.

notes the significant role African women play in food production, in contrast to a less significant role in Asia and Latin America.

Boserup also observed that the sexual division of labor varies over time in response to socioeconomic change. Boserup insists that women have been marginalized by the development process, losing access to resources and land and becoming relegated to low productivity types of employment that pay low wages. Boserup's contention is that women have lost status, prestige, and income as a result of colonialism and modernization. She held "European settlers, colonial administrators and technical advisers" responsible for the deterioration of women's status in the agricultural sector.

> In short, by their discriminatory policy in education and training the Europeans created a productivity gap between male and female farmers, and subsequently this gap seemed to justify their prejudice against female farmers.[2]

She found evidence that African women did not always accept the deterioration in their position without protest.

Boserup emphasized women's education as the strategy needed to integrate them more adequately into development and turn modernization to their advantage. Education would improve agricultural techniques in rural areas and enable women to compete in urban labor markets.[3]

Boserup's work made two fundamental contributions to social theory. Her insistence that the division of labor by sex is developed in all societies and her care in describing the variation in what was considered to be male or female tasks in different societies demonstrates that such a division is not "natural." Secondly, she documented the differential impact of recent patterns of development in the Third World on women and men, with the impact on women being more adverse.

Nevertheless, the explanatory power of her work is constrained by liberal assumptions. More specifically, this perspective does not account for the way capitalist accumulation and development creates

---

[2] Ibid., p. 57.

[3] Ibid., see especially pp. 211-25.

class inequalities as well as inequalities between women and men nor does it adequately account for the subordination of women.[4] Beneria and Sen point to these weaknesses in their critical evaluation of Boserup:

> Contrary to Boserup's implications, the problem for women is not only the lack of participation in this process as equal partners with men; it is a system that generates and intensifies inequalities, making use of existing gender hierarchies to place women in subordinate positions at each different level of interaction between class and gender.[5]

Some recent studies have demonstrated the use of existing gender hierarchies to marginalize women.

In her study of the development of cash crop production among the Yoruba, Simi Afonja contends that commercialization of land and the emphasis on individual property ownership gave women access to cash crop production. "Women in societies with bilateral kinship structure inherited cocoa farms and were able to use virgin land for commercial agricultural production." But this does not mean that women are as involved in cash-crop production as men. The predominance of men over women in cash-crop production is assured by male control of technology and capital.

---

[4] See Christine Obbo, *African Women: Their Struggle for Economic Independence* (London: Zed Press, 1980) for a more recent account of town migration of East African women to compare and contrast with Boserup. Obbo's account illumines class differences between women and traditional hierarchical gender relations and their impact on women's survival strategies.

[5] Lourdes Beneria and Gita Sen, "Accumulation, Reproduction, and Women's Role in Economic Development: Boserup Revisited," *Signs* 7, no. 2 (Winter 1981). This article is reprinted in the volume *Women's Work: Development and the Division of Labor by Gender,* ed. Eleanor Leacock and Helen Safa (South Hadley, MA: Bergin and Garvey Publishers, 1986), pp. 141-157. The citations in this chapter are from the latter volume. Beneria and Sen observe that although capitalist development might break down certain social rigidities which are oppressive to women, "these liberating tendencies are accompanied by new forms of subordination." Ibid., p. 150.

But the question is, What gave men and not women access to technology and capital? The answer to this lies in the control that men had over women's labor and reproduction in the subsistence economy, not solely in the opportunity given by the colonial administration, as Boserup suggests. Traditional values persist first because women's role in reproduction continues to be emphasized, and second because men were able to take advantage of their control of capital, land, and family labor in the subsistence economy when foreign technology was introduced.[6]

Traditional and colonial attitudes and practices contribute to the marginalization of Yoruba women.

Beneria and Sen also criticize Boserup for not having a clearly defined theoretical framework to interpret her empirical data. They identify her underlying analytical concepts as derivations of neo-classical theory.[7] Within the modernization/developmentalist paradigm Boserup accepts, capitalist institutions are taken as the norm. Many interpreters question whether economic growth under these conditions necessarily "trickles down" to many in the population. Thus Boserup is criticized for assuming that modernization is basically beneficial, and that its benefits are readily extended to women. One author even asks if modernization has "really been so beneficial to the majority of men?"[8] Beneria and Sen assert that Boserup's use of "the modernization approach" leads her to ignore processes of capital accumulation set in motion during colonialism and the effects of these processes on either

---

[6] Simi Afonja, "Changing Modes of Production and the Sexual Division of Labor Among the Yoruba," *Women's Work*, p. 131.

[7] To be more specific, I describe Boserup's presuppositions as developmentalist. Developmentalists point to social and cultural factors, such as persistent sex-role stereotypes, underlying women's social and economic marginalization in contrast to the more narrow focus of traditional neo-classical theorists on individual characteristics and personal choices. For a useful account of neo-classical economic theory in relation to the situation of women, see Nancy Barrett, "How the Study of Women Has Restructured the Discipline of Economics," *A Feminist Perspective in the Academy: The Difference it Makes* (Chicago: University of Chicago Press, 1983), pp. 101-9.

[8] Marilee Karl, "Women, Land, and Food Production," *Women in Development*, p. 74.

technical change or women's work. Nor does she analyze the effects of capital accumulation on women of different classes.

Further, Beneria and Sen argue that Boserup's proposal that women's education be the primary strategy for integration into development ignores two critical factors that an analysis based on concepts of accumulation and women's role in reproduction would highlight:[9]

> On one hand, it ignores the high incidence of unemployment among educated people in the Third World. Unless the systemic causes of unemployment are removed, women's education by itself is purely an individualistic solution; it attempts to alter the characteristics of the individual woman rather than those of the system of capital accumulation. On the other hand, even if there were dramatic changes, education by itself would not alter women's position, in that education cannot address issues of child care and domestic work. The high incidence of the double day in countries like the Soviet Union and China supplies ample evidence of this policy's limited success.[10]

The limitations of liberalism in accounting for women's impoverishment or proposing an adequate strategy for change are evident in this discussion of Boserup.

---

[9] Beneria and Sen note that "reproduction here refers not only to biological reproduction and daily maintenance of the labor force, but also to social reproduction - the perpetuation of social systems. Related is the view that in order to control social reproduction (through inheritance systems, for example) most societies have developed different forms of control over female sexuality and reproductive activities." They claim that "this control is the root of women's subordination." Beneria and Sen, p. 157. See Mary O'Brien, *The Politics of Reproduction* (Boston: Routledge and Kegan Paul, 1981) for a stunning exposition of this argument.

[10] Beneria and Sen, p. 156. Data presented in chapter one of this study established that "the double day" is a problem faced by women around the world. Although at this time it is too soon to draw definitive conclusions, some Eastern European women are arguing that with the collapse of socialism in the late 1980s, their situation has deteriorated as social programs such as subsidized child care are reduced or eliminated and job discrimination and unemployment have increased.

Marxist Perspectives:
Capitalism the Source of Women's Oppression

I have already indicated that marxist analyses of women and development view exploitation and oppression as structural features of international capitalism and point to the inadequacy of analyses, such as developmentalism, that isolate sexual inequality from socio-economic inequalities. I identified dependency theory as the perspective out of the broad Marxist theoretical tradition present in the Decade analyses.

The categories of analysis used by dependency theorists are sex-blind.[11] When advocates of dependency theory do address the situation of women, their inequality is perceived to be caused

> to a very large extent from mass poverty and general backwardness of the majority of the world's population caused by underdevelopment which is a product of imperialism, colonialism, neo-colonialism and also of unjust international economic relations.[12]

In this perspective, the development of a new international economic order is the primary program for overcoming underdevelopment, and thus the inequality of women.

Dependency theory has made a significant contribution to an adequate account of poverty and underdevelopment in illumining the class nature of capitalist development. It thus contributes to an account of the impoverishment of women, but it does not address the differential impact of underdevelopment on women nor explain why women

---

[11] For instance, in Andre Gunder Frank's classic text, *Capitalism and Underdevelopment in Latin America*, (New York: Monthly Review Press, 1967), there is no discussion of any differential impact of underdevelopment on women. In fact, there is no mention at all of women in this text. A sampling of texts on development written after much published research on women in development reveals the same situation. For example, neither *Decolonization and Dependency: Problems of Development of African Societies*, ed. Aguibou Y. Yansane, (Westport, CT: Greenwood Press, 1980) and *Dialectics of Third World Development*, ed. Vogeler and de Souze (Montclair: Allanheld. Osmun, 1980) include any substantive discussion of women.

[12] This sentence is from the Programme of Action adopted by the Copenhagen (1980) Decade for Women conference, *Report* (1980), paragraph 12.

experience a higher rate of poverty than men. *Asian Women Speak Out!* charged that "no model, neither the economic growth model nor the Marxist model, has addressed the problem of patriarchy. ... Women's oppression at home, at work and in society in general are not examined."[13]

Marxist feminists have expanded a strand of Marxist theory which attempts to more adequately account for the oppression of women. Like their male counterparts, they too argue that the status of women deteriorated with capitalist development. A key thesis in their analysis is that women make up a reserve labor supply for capitalist production.[14]

A Brazilian theorist, Heleieth Saffioti, elaborated an analysis of women in class societies to supplement a Marxist dependency perspective. She attempts to discern "among the structural contradictions of the social system those essential features of the system that will suffice to explain at once the roles of men, the roles of women, and the complementary functions they fulfill within each particular social formation."[15]

---

[13] *Asian Women Speak Out!* p. 3.

[14] See Tiano, pp. 2-10, for a useful comparison of modernization theory and marxist feminist theory. She also distinguishs between marxist feminists, who see class as the primary contradiction, and socialist feminists, who see class and gender as mutually reinforcing systems. I am following her usage in this study.

[15] Heleieth I.B. Saffioti, *Women in Class Society*, translated by Michael Vale, (New York: Monthly Review Press, 1978), p. 296. This pioneering book, which was written in 1967 but not published in English until 1978, is not well-known in this country. I am reviewing it rather extensively for her significant insights into the oppression of women from a Latin American perspective. In addition to the sections of the book mentioned in my text, she includes a illuminating analysis of science and ideology in the third section of her book, entitled "The Feminine Mystique and the Scientific Era," pp. 237-96. Drawing on anthropology, sociology and psychoanalytic theories in what she calls holism, she shows how socialization practices, personality attributes and ideological systems are shaped in conformity to the needs of capitalism. As Eleanor Burke Leacock says in her introduction to the book, "her discussion of science as ideology illuminates the conscious and unconscious processes whereby scientific knowledge is used to control rather than to liberate." Ibid., p. xx.

Saffioti's work includes a critique of Marx' and Engels' writings on women:

> Neither Marx nor Engels made an effort to analyze the specific functions that women fulfill in the family; thus neither was able to come up with even a theoretical solution to the woman problem; nor were they able to resist entirely the notion that the family structure in some way lagged behind the economic structure of capitalist society.[16]

Marx, she notes, never undertook a detailed analysis of women's condition in capitalist society. She criticizes Engel's claim that the institution of private property is responsible for the oppression of women. Saffioti warns that if socialist theory "persists in seeing the factors that bear on woman's condition as deriving solely from the economic structure" it will "lose sight of the partial autonomy that other structures tend to have, and will hence never be able to appreciate adequately the uniqueness of the feminine condition...."[17] "Everything ideological," Saffioti argues, "has repercussions on the female condition."

In this regard, Saffioti criticizes theorists who "viewed motherhood as a job in the economic sense," which she argues "provided arguments justifying the marginalization of women from the class structure." Women sought employment as their circumstances require it, "and in the last instance these are determined by the laws inherent to the particular mode of production." Employment, Saffioti asserts, "does less outrage to women than involuntary maternity, as "a job enables a woman to earn a living; in maternity she risks life itself." When societies give women no alternative to motherhood, they substitute

---

[16] Ibid., p. 81.

[17] Ibid., pp. 86, 89. In 1982 Lourdes Arizpe wrote that "the influence of dependency theory and Marxism on women's studies in Latin America and the Caribbean has clearly led to research into structural and particularly, economic, constraints on the advancement of women. But in the last few years, it has been argued that economic analysis is not enough; that there are ethnic and racial prejudices, cultural traditions and ideological prescriptions to be dealt with." Arizpe, "Women and Development in Latin America and the Caribbean," *Development Dialogue*, 1982: 1-2, p. 79.

women's reproductive function for their productive function, thus emphasizing women's identity as a "sexual being" and widening the social gap between women and men. Thus Saffioti insists that women's freedom is "closely tied to her freedom to choose whether or not to have children."[18]

The guiding assumption of Saffioti's study is that "women's situation in capitalist society can be elucidated by analyzing the relations existing between the sex factor and the essential characteristics of the capitalist mode of production." The main conclusion of her study is that

> Society uses gender to restrict the number of persons who are able to participate legitimately in the process of competition. Since the capitalist system is unable to absorb the total labor potential represented by all normal adult members in class society, it seeks to eliminate labor power from the market. To preserve itself without excessively exposing its internal contradictions, it uses biological and/or racial ethnic categories for this purpose; to justify the marginalization of large numbers of women from the class structure, for example, it stresses their traditional childbearing and childraising functions.[19]

Saffioti therefore argues that social stratification, regardless of the criteria on which they are based, are not just "fossilized vestiges of the former class relations in which they were rooted originally," but also "a discrete aspect of the concrete totality within which they stand..."[20]

Saffioti also analyzes women's position in relation to "the linkages between the kinship structure and the occupational structure." She noted two significant linkages: 1) sex role socialization, and 2) domestic

---

[18] Saffioti, p. 88.

[19] Ibid., p. 297.

[20] Ibid., p, 29. Thus, although Saffioti considers cultural factors as a critical dimension of women's "inferior social standing," she does not accept the view of those who see women's inequality as "a cultural atavism." Her chapter on "Class and Status in Stratified Society" is a particularly illuminating discussion of class and status. In contrast to liberal theorists who reduce class to status, she carefully articulates the class basis of social stratification. Ibid., pp. 13-30.

labor/paid labor. In regard to socialization and "the category of sex," she contends that

> The harmony of social life becomes contingent on the efficacy with which the system legitimates and controls the unequal participation of men and women in these two structures. In other words, not only are functional solutions to the problems of social existence indispensable for maintaining the structure of the system, but they also serve to reinforce the established order by furnishing its legitimacy.[21]

She observed that although the legitimation process does hold back sociocultural change, the ineffectiveness of these ideological solutions could "touch off processes of far-reaching change" as awareness of inequality grows and movements are organized to challenge them.

The second linkage between the occupation and kinship structures Saffioti analyzed is the relation between "the purely household labor of the woman and the paid labor of the husband." Saffioti contends that the unpaid labor of the housewife "actually increases the family's real income since it adds to the husband's wages an amount of labor that could be transformed into wages." She notes though, that the "monetary equivalent" of the household labor would not equal the wages a wife would earn "if she were gainfully employed in the dominant system of production."[22]

Saffioti dismisss the argument that justifies the role of the housewife by claiming that the "woman's wages are consumed in the payment of domestic services." Rather, the role of housewife could only be explained by "the coexistence of different modes of production."[23] In other words, those who are not employed in the dominant system of production as well as those who are actually unemployed are all "part of the reserve army of labor in modern capitalist economics." The housewife can be regarded as a part of this reserve army. She is not

---

[21] Ibid., p. 276.

[22] Ibid., p. 282.

[23] By including others marginalized from the dominant mode of production, Saffioti is more thorough in her analysis of non-wage work than later theorists who attempt to clarify how domestic labor relates to capitalist production.

directly engaged in the dominant system of production and she is not part of any class. Saffioti perceives the situation of the married woman as more complicated. Her social status is "the reflexion of her husband's economic status, which is itself the active reflexion of his class situation."[24]

In a further analysis of the domestic labor that women do, Saffioti argues that this work, although "nonproductive in that it does not create surplus value," is "indirectly productive in that it is necessary to men's productive work."[25] In capitalist society, women's labor power "sometimes appears as a commodity, and therefore with an exchange value, but sometimes it has only a use value." Female labor power, Saffioti asserts, "is a special type of commodity with no continuity, that is, it is not continually replaced to sustain objective alienation." If alienation under modern capitalism represents a form of false

---

[24] Ibid., pp. 283-4.

[25] Saffioti, pp. 292. The debate over domestic labor in socialist circles often becomes quite technical, but is significant for public policy and the well-being of women. See Hilda Scott, *Working Your Way to the Bottom: The Feminization of Poverty* (London: Pandora, 1984), pp. 129-46, for a discussion of the implications of this debate in the analysis of the impoverishment of women and for public policy.

For a summary of the debate, see Lise Vogel, *Marxism and the Oppression of Women: Toward a Unitary Theory* (New Brunswick, NJ: Rutgers University Press, 1983), pp. 17-24. There are three main positions in regard to the value of domestic labor. The first, exposited by Maria dalla Costa, is that unpaid household labor directly produces surplus value; this is the viewpoint of the Wages for Housework campaign.

The second, exposited by Ira Gerstein, contends that domestic labor is "simple commodity production," and creates only use value by transferring the values of the commodities purchased with the wage to the labor power borne by the worker. Gerstein's argument is cited extensively in Vogel, pp. 156-58. Another proponent is Vogel, whose argument rests in part on the questionable assumption that the family wage covers the consumption of two adults. There is a lack of attention in her discussion to the role the family plays in reproducing the labor force. Currently many women work because their husband's wages do not meet the needs of the family, yet they still retain responsibility for domestic labor.

The third view is the one reviewed here, articulated by Saffioti, that domestic labor indirectly produces surplus value. See Saffioti, "Women, Mode of Production, and Social Formations," *Latin American Perspectives* 4., nos. 1-2 (Winter - Spring, 1977), pp. 27-37, where she reasserts her position in relation to dalla Costa and Gerstein, whose work was published after her original study.

consciousness, and thus "a conservative force in capitalist society," women may not be "as conservative as has up to now been assumed" as they move between a relatively more alienated state when employed in the wage labor force and a less alienated state when not so employed. She contends, though, that a distinction between male praxis and female praxis is legitimate only in a general sense, and then only in measure as the class structure marginalizes women more than men.[26]

Saffioti's analysis of women's condition in Brazil, which follows her more general analysis of women and capitalism, is grounded in dependency analysis. She contends that "in countries with dependent economies," another factor is added in the use by market economies of "the sex factor socially as a means to marginalize the female labor force from the economy." Countries at the center of the world capitalist system, Saffioti argue, used international relations "as an outlet for the tensions generated by the class structure of these societies, thereby diminishing the need to utilize the sex factor" to marginalize the female labor force. For countries at the periphery, "even such a partial solution to the woman question is not so easy to find."[27]

Among the significant contributions of Saffioti's work are her analysis of race and sex as factors in social stratification systems which legitimate a reserve pool of labor; her articulation of the structural roots

---

[26] Some other theorists argue that different female and male praxis generates different forms of consciousness, which accounts for more than women's additional marginalization in class society. See Marie Mies, *Patriarchy and Accumulation on a World Scale: Women in the International Division of Labour* (London: Zed Books, 1986), pp. 44-73, who in attempting to account for the origins of the sexual division of labor develops an object-relations analysis of women's experience of their bodies as productive whereas men became productive through the development of tools, in particular weapons. This created the possibility of establishing relations of exploitation and domination through what Mies calls "a predatory mode of production." The question of origins is beyond the scope of this study. See Nancy Hartsock, *Money, Sex, and Power: Toward a Feminist Historical Materialism* (Boston: Northeastern University Press, 1983), pp. 231-63, for an account of contemporary differences in praxis between women and men and its significance for understanding power and class.

[27] Saffioti, p. 96. Cultural feminists, whose work will be reviewed next, would disagree with this contention.

of sex-role socialization; her analysis of women's domestic labor; and her insistence on the importance of both ideological and structural roots of women's marginalization. Thus she begins to account for some of the sources of women's impoverishment.

However, she does not discuss the politics of reproduction or sexuality. Thus her account of women's role in social reproduction and the household is only partial. She has not given a fully adequate analysis of the structural and ideological roots of women's marginalization. Nor does she propose a political program for overcoming the marginalization of women. In fact, she insists that there are serious limits to the changes in the relations of the sexes that can be made in nations at the periphery.

Cultural Feminism:
Patriarchy the Source of Women's Oppression

Cultural feminists contend that the root of women's oppression is men, who in the past overthrew egalitarian social orders and established patriarchal systems in which men now rule. Women have their own culture with their own sensibilities, perceptions and priorities, which is feared and reviled by patriarchal culture. According to cultural feminists, women must create and maintain cultural enclaves for support and nurture until (if ever) they decide to take over power from men to establish an egalitarian society.[28]

An early cultural feminist manifesto articulated this thesis:

> Women are an oppressed class. Our oppression is total, affecting every aspect of our lives.... Our proscribed behavior is enforced by the threat of physical violence.... Male supremacy is the oldest, most basic form of domination. All other forms of exploitation and oppression (racism, capitalism, imperialism, etc.) are extensions of male supremacy: men dominate women, a few men

---

[28] This description is drawn from my own reading of cultural feminists and the work of Carol Robb, "A Framework for Feminist Ethics," pp. 221-3. Cultural feminists usually refer to themselves as radical feminists. I am using the term cultural feminists in this study to avoid confusion between this feminist perspective and the radical social theory I describe and examine in the second part of this study.

dominate the rest.... *All men* receive economic, sexual, and psychological benefit from male supremacy. *All men* have oppressed women. [29]

This system of male supremacy is also called patriarchy and is said to be virtually universal. Women's role in reproduction is identified as the primary source of her oppression and the institutions of marriage, the family, and compulsory heterosexuality as the bases of oppression.[30]

The primary contribution of the cultural feminist perspective was to bring discussion of sexuality and violence against women into the debate about the oppression of women. There are two main limitations in this perspective. One is the ahistorical and universal character of the analysis of patriarchy; critics doubt that all societies have been patriarchal to the same degree and if all men have benefitted from it.[31]

---

[29] "The Redstocking Manifesto," *Sisterhood is Powerful: An Anthology of Writings from the Women's Liberation Movement*, ed. Robin Morgan (New York: Vintage Books, 1970), pp. 533-4, emphasis in original.

[30] Significant foundational texts for cultural feminism are Shulamith Firestone, *The Dialectic of Sex* (New York: Bantam Books, 1971) and Kate Millet, *Sexual Politics* (New York: Avon Books, 1971). For an analysis of compulsory heterosexuality, see Adrienne Rich, "Compulsory Heterosexuality and Lesbian Existence," *The Signs Reader: Women, Gender and Scholarship* (Chicago: University of Chicago Press, 1983), 139-168. See Linda Burnham and Miriam Louie, The Impossible Marriage: A Marxist Critique of Socialist Feminism, *Line of March*, # 17, Spring 1985, pp. 9-14, for a summary and critical assessment of this position.

[31] Burnham and Louie, who otherwise are very critical of cultural feminism, take over its account of the origins of women's oppression in her childbearing capacity. Their account of these origins also tends to be ahistorical and universal.

Burnham and Louis assert that "the sexual division of labor has its material basis in the intersection and conjunction between women's childbearing capacity and the broad socio-economic conditions that are the concrete expression of the mode of production." They then quote Kathleen Gough, who claims that "The family was made desirable by the early human combination of prolonged childcare with the need for hunting with weapons over large terrain. The sexual division of labor on which it was based grew out of a rudimentary pre-human division between male defense and female childcare. But among humans this sexual division of functions for the first time became crucial for food production and so laid the basis for future economic specialization and cooperation.... The extent of inequality varied according to the ecology and the resulting sexual division of tasks. But in any case, it was largely a matter of survival rather than of man-made cultural impositions."

The other is the lack of a political program for overcoming patriarchy. Separatism is the strategy of choice for many cultural feminists, with an emphasis on lifestyle options such as women's communities, lesbianism, and the creation of feminist cultural institutions. These weaknesses limit the ability of this perspective to adequately account for the growing impoverishment of women. Even so, its analysis of gender relations is a major source in the development of socialist feminism.

Socialist Feminism:
Capitalist Patriarchy the Source of Oppression

Socialist feminism attempts to overcome the ahistorical character of cultural feminism and the sex-blind categories of Marxism by synthesizing cultural feminism and central aspects of Marxist analysis of capitalism, thus identifying capitalist patriarchy as the source of oppression of women. Their conceptualization of the sexual division of labor attempts to integrate these two perspectives.[32]

Burnham and Louie, "The Impossible Marriage," p. 77.

This interpretation tends to be economistic and biologically reductionistic. It overestimates the contribution of men to subsistence in hunting and gathering societies and assumes that defense was a preoccupation of all early societies, and then universalizes from these questionable historical assumptions. Most disturbing is that this account turns women's capacity to reproduce the species into an inevitable and natural handicap, rather than a potential source of social power. Mary O'Brien, *The Politics of Reproduction*, and Beverly Harrison, *Our Right to Choose* (Boston: Beacon Press, 1983) offer analyses which stress the potential power of this capacity.

[32] Juliet Mitchell and Sheila Rowbotham are important theorists in the early development of socialist feminist theory. See Mitchell, *Women's Estate* (New York, Vintage Books, 1971) and Rowbotham, *Women's Consciousness, Man's World* (London: Penguin Books, 1973). Major collections of U.S. socialist feminist theory include Zillah Eisenstein, ed., *Capitalist Patriarchy and the Case for Socialist Feminism* (New York: Monthly Review Press, 1979) and Lydia Sargent, ed., *Women and Revolution: A Discussion of the Unhappy Marriage of Marxism and Feminism* (Boston: South End Press, 1981). For fuller critical accounts of the development of socialist feminism, see Burnham and Louie, "The Impossible Marriage," and Vogel, pp 13-40.

The synthesis of radical [cultural] feminism and Marxist analysis is a necessary first step in formulating a cohesive socialist feminist political theory, one that does not merely add together these two theories of power but sees them as interrelated through the sexual division of labor.[33]

Heidi Hartmann, a US theorist, argues that the sexual division of labor appears to be "universal throughout human history," although it is not always a hierarchical division. She contends that "the roots of women's present social status lie in this sex-ordered division of labor," which "must be eliminated if women are to attain equal social status with men..."[34]

According to Hartmann, men are the main beneficiaries of this division of labor. She and Ann Markusen define patriarchal gender relations as

a system of social relations between men and women, governing the production and reproduction of people and their gender identities.... Just as the division of labor between workers and capitalists connotes exploitation of surplus labor from workers by capitalists, so does the division of labor between women and men connote the exploitation of surplus labor from women for the benefit of men.[35]

These two semi-autonomous systems - the sex-gender system or patriarchy and the mode of production or capitalism - are seen as interconnected and mutually reinforcing.

This "dual systems theory," as it has come to be called, has been widely discussed and criticized.[36] Its primary contribution is its

---

[33] Zillah Eisenstein, "Developing a Theory of Capitalist Patriarchy and Socialist Feminism," in *Capitalist Patriarchy and the Case for Socialist Feminism*, p 6.

[34] Heidi Hartmann, "Capitalism, Patriarchy, and Job Segregation by Sex," *Women and the Workplace: The Implications of Occupational Segregation* (Chicago: University of Chicago Press, 1976), p. 137.

[35] Hartmann and Markusen, "Contemporary Marxist Theory and Practice: A Feminist Critique,' *Review of Political Economics* 12 (1980), pp. 87-94.

[36] *Women and Revolution: A Discussion of the Unhappy Marriage of Marxism and Feminism* contains several critical responses to the dual systems theory articulated by Hartmann in the lead essay of the volume.

exposition of the inadequacies of traditional Marxist analysis of what was identified as "the woman question" and its insistence on the importance of both gender and class relations as fundamental to an adequate analysis of women's oppression.

There are two main weaknesses in this perspective, as currently developed. One is its tendency to continue to analyze patriarchy in an ahistorical way. The second is its tendency to dualistic thinking, that is its failure to adequately articulate the relation of the two systems.

The socialist feminist understanding of the sexual division of labor has been criticized as ahistorical and universal because it does not adequately recognize the way class and race differentiate the lives of women. For instance, Leith Mullings in her study of class, race and gender in the United States before 1900 comes to a different set of conclusions than Hartmann:

> In all classes there was a sexual division of labor. But what gives any division of labor significance is its link to a structure of differential and unequal rewards. In this sense, the sex-ordered division of labor may have been greatest in the property-owning class and least among Afro-Americans, among whom for much of this period the sex division of labor was relatively minimal. But when we examine the concrete results of the division of labor - access to resources and the consequent ability to control one's life - the difference is perhaps greater among women (and among men) of different classes than between men and women of the same class. It seems clear that production relations ... determined the significance of reproductive relations....Although the ideology of the division of labor was universal, the way in which it was manifested in a given class was ultimately determined by the interests of the class in power.[37]

Mullings' critique also illumines Hartmann's failure to adequately show the interrelationship of reproductive and productive relations.

---

[37] Leith Mullings, "Uneven Development: Class, Race, and Gender in the United States Before 1900," *Women's Work: Development and the Division of Labor by Gender*, pp. 55-56. Also see Angela Davis, *Women, Race and Class* (New York: Vintage Books, 1981). Similar criticisms of British socialist feminist analyses of patriarchy and reproduction have been presented by Hazel Carby, "White women listen! Black feminism and the boundaries of sisterhood," and Pratibha Parmar, "Gender, race and class: Asian women in resistance," *The Empire Strikes Back: Race and racism in 70s Britain* (London: Hutchinson, 1982), pp. 212-75.

Social feminist analyses of the impoverishment of women in the United States have been criticized for a lack of attention to race and class. In their analysis of poverty in the United States, Stallard, Ehrenreich and Sklar contend that wage discrimination, occupational segregation, and the growing number of female headed households are the main causes of women's poverty. They also assert that virtually all women are vulnerable, as divorce or widowhood could throw middle-strata women into poverty.[38] Linda Burnham insists that this analysis misconstrues the factors contributing to the impoverishment of black women, overstates the vulnerability of white women to impoverishment, and ignores or underestimates the impoverishment of black men, as well as abandoning the thesis that the fundamental basis for the regeneration of poverty in the United States is working class exploitation.[39]

Other theorists contend that the sexual division of labor has not always been detrimental to women.

> The division of labor by gender has different meanings depending on its cultural and social contexts. The activities that women perform are variously defined in terms of both content and the social value attached to them. It cannot be said that women's labor is intrinsically inferior to that of men or that it is universally judged to be so.[40]

Some researches have argued that the sexual division of labor has at times actually been a source of power for women.

---

[38] Karin Stallard, Barbara Ehrenreich, and Holly Sklar, *Poverty in the American Dream,* (Boston: South End Press, 1983).

[39] Linda Burnham, "Has Poverty Been Feminized in Black America?" *The Black Scholar,* Vol. XVI, no. 2 (March/April 1985).

[40] Maria Patricia Fernandez Kelly, "Introduction," *Women's Work* , pp. 4-5. In a more sociologically oriented analysis, Jessie Bernard argues that the sexual division of labor has created separate male and female worlds, which are integrated in organic solidarity. As a result of the industrial revolution, the relations between the separate worlds have been challenged. The inequitable status quo is to be replaced with "equitable integration" with the male world through "affirmative action." Bernard, *The Female World from a Global Perspective* (Bloomington: Indiana University Press, 1987), especially chapters 2-3, 7-9. This work suffers not only from its developmentalist assumptions, but from a lack of attention to race and class dynamics.

For instance, in the Trobiands the domains of female and male power remain separate, yet tend to complement rather than oppose each other. Although men achieve political prominence, wealth created by women is critical to the reproduction and regeneration of social relations.[41] But there is evidence that even matrilineal societies, such as the Negeri Sembilan in Malaysia, have been unable to resist the marginalization of women with the incursion of colonialism and capitalist development, although the effects have been contradictory, uneven, and complex.[42]

Another limitation of socialist feminist theory as so far developed in Europe and the United States has been its general lack of attention to colonialism and imperialism in its analyses. Bina Agarwar, an Indian feminist, acknowledges the contribution of developments in "Western

---

[41] Annette B. Weiner, "Forgotten Wealth: Cloth and Women's Production in the Pacific," in *Women's Work*, pp. 96-110. Valentina Borreman discusses the protection the sexual division of labor offered women from individual competition with men, in her analysis of the impact of development and what is called appropriate technology. Borreman, "Technique and Women's Toil," *Cross Currents*, (Winter 1982-3), pp. 420-29. For other analyses of the variety of types of gender relations, see Peggy Sanday, *Female Power and Male Dominance: On the Origins of Sexual Inequality* (Cambridge: Cambridge University Press, 1981). Sanday, who uses insights from symbolic anthropology, distinguishes three broad types of societies: 1) egalitarian, where the environment is seen as friendly, women and men cooperate in many activities and women's power is emphasized; 2) dual sex, where women have distinctly separate but complementary domains; and 3) male dominant societies, where the environment is viewed as hostile and animals are the primary source of food. See also Lisa Leghorn and Katherine Parker, *Woman's Worth: Sexual Economics and the World of Women* (Boston: Routledge & Kegan Paul, 1981). These authors identify three main types of economic organization or societies throughout the world: 1) minimal power for women, 2) token power for women, and 3) negotiating power for women. The following criteria were used to gauge women's status: a) valuation of women's fertility and physical integrity, b) women's access to and control over crucial resources, including property, paid and collective labor, training and education, and c) women's networks.

[42] Maila Stivens, "The fate of women's land rights: gender, matriliny, and capitalism in Rembau, Negeri Sembilan, Malaysia," *Women, Work, and Ideology in the Third World*, edited by Haleh Afshar (London: Tavistock Publications, 1985). This is a useful collection of essays from a women and development study group at the University of Liverpool.

feminist theory" such as the analysis of the relationship between class and patriarchy, production and reproduction. She also observes that

> feminist theorizing in the First World is done in the particular context of advanced capitalism, of a highly industrialized urban society. Women in the First World fail to recognize the relationship of imperialism and colonization in their theoretical writings. This is, therefore, one of the challenges to feminist writing in the Third World-to take account of our particular situation and make links.[43]

In response to this challenge, a more recent work by Maria Mies, a European sociologist, attempts to develop a historical analysis of capitalist-patriarchy which takes account of colonialism and imperialism.

> Whereas the concept patriarchy denotes the historical depth of women's exploitation and oppression, the concept capitalism is expressive of the contemporary manifestation, the latest development of this system. ...It is my thesis that capitalism cannot function without patriarchy, that the goal of this system, namely the never-ending process of capital accumulation, cannot be achieved unless patriarchal man-woman relations are maintained or newly created.[44]

---

[43] Quoted in *Connexions: An International Women's Quarterly* No. 17-18(Summer/Fall, 1985), p. 24. Beneria and Roldan also note this in their discussion of socialist feminism. Citing Michele Barrett's *Women's Oppression Today,* (London: Verso Editions, 1980) as a more integrated analysis which incorporates radical feminist insights to understand the ideological aspects of gender formation and Marxist concepts and methods to understand women's subordination, they note that it is grounded in conditions prevalent in Britain and thus not directly applicable to the great variety of experiences that characterize women's lives in the periphery. Lourdes Beneria and Martha Roldan, *The Crossroads of Class and Gender* (Chicago: University of Chicago Press, 1987), pp. 9-10.

Lise Vogel's analysis of the reproduction of labor power is another example of this error. She assumes that the options are generational replacement or the introduction of migrant labor. *Marxism and the Oppression of Women*, p. 150. Her lack of attention to the international division of labor as an aspect of capitalist production causes her to overstate the capital's need for the participation of women in the labor force and to underestimate the contribution of their unpaid labor to the reproduction of labor power.

[44] Mies, p. 38. Mies sees her work as going beyond socialist feminism, in that she does not just add "the woman question" to another social theory, pp. 12-3. As this review indicates, Mies does make a significant contribution toward this aim. Yet as I demonstrate, she has not overcome some of the limitations of socialist

Mies further argues that what she calls "the general production of life," or subsistence production, is the necessary basis for the capitalist wage labor relation.

She considers the capitalist production process to comprise "the superexploitation of nonwage labourers (women, colonies, peasants) upon which wage labour exploitation is then possible." Nonwage labor is superexploited because it is not based on the appropriation by the capitalist of the surplus labor, that labor which is over and above the necessary labor for the reproduction of the worker, but of "the time and labour necessary for people's own survival or subsistence. It is not compensated for by a wage ... but is mainly determined by force or coercive institutions."[45]

Violence, Mies contends, is the form of primitive capital accumulation. Historically violence against women during the European witch hunts and violence against blacks in the development of the slave trade contributed to the accumulation of the capital needed to launch the industrial revolution, as wealth and property were expropriated from some "witches" and slave traders made a profit from providing "free" laborers.   Violence   was   necessary   because   of   resistance   to marginalization and enslavement by women and blacks. Mies argues that the witch hunt and the slave trade were the beginnings of dynamics of "housewifization" and colonization which remain necessary to the accumulation of capital needed to perpetuate the growth model of international development.[46]

Mies asserts that the development of an alternative economy, based on self-reliance and subsistence production, is necessary to overcome the exploitation of women, colonies, and nature. The center of the whole restructuring process required of a transformed society must be the sexual division of labor based on man the breadwinner and woman

---

feminism as now articulated.

[45] Ibid., p. 48. See also Maria Mies, Veronkia Bennholdt-Thomsen, and Claudia Von Werlhof *Women: The Last Colony*, (London: Zed Books, 1988).

[46] Ibid., pp. 74-110. Mies interprets the rash of bride-burnings and dowry murders in India as a form of primitive capital accumulation. See pp. 157-62.

the housewife. For this to happen the violence that characterizes capitalist-patriarchal relations will need to be abolished by men, who will also share responsibility for "the immediate production of life ... childcare, housework the care of the sick and the old, relationship work..."[47] Intermediate steps include a consumer liberation movement of housewives and a movement by workers for democratization of the production process.

Mies' work makes two important contributions to feminist social theory. One is her analysis of the relation between the oppression of women and the development of colonialism and imperialism, and the necessity of nonwaged labor to capitalist relations of production. The second is her analysis of the ongoing role of violence in the capital accumulation process. Even so, her work continues some of the limitations of previous socialist feminist theory, particularly its universalizing tendencies which obscure race and class differences among women.

By not paying adequate attention to class and race differences between women, Mies overestimates the vulnerability of middle-strata women to impoverishment. She also underestimates the impoverishment and marginalization of poor and working class men.[48] Mies program for change is also questionable on several counts. Although she calls for a massive return to the land, she does not say how the masses of people driven from the land should return to it. Her expectation that men will be the ones to end violence against women is unrealistic, as is her expectation that middle-strata housewives in a consumer's liberation movement can begin to transform the international

---

[47] Ibid., pp. 221-2.

[48] For instance, Mies argues that all men benefit from the exploitation of women and that women, in contrast to men, are made to pay with their human dignity or their lives "for the 'honour' of being either prostitute or housewife. This is not an adequate description of the reality of many Afro-American men or South African black men, among others. Nor is her argument that poor Third World women are the 'image of the future' for women in the industrialized countries accurate, particularly in relation to white ruling class women. She is perpetuating the limitations of radical feminist theory universalizing women's experience too greatly. Ibid., p. 143.

division of labor. Further, her proposal that the center of the restructuring process will be the transformation of the existing sexual division of labor (breadwinner/housewife) assumes that the ideology of that division is the reality.[49]   In point of fact, increasingly more "housewives" are entering the paid labor force.

Emerging Women's Voices: Movement Towards A Multidimensional Transformative Perspective

I have already argued that to adequately account for the impoverishment of women we need to begin our analysis from the vantage of poor women, as the DAWN collective has contended. From this perspective the structural roots of poverty are seen to "lie in unequal access to resources, control over production, trade, finance, and money, and across nations, genders, regions, and classes."[50]   The theoretical articulation of the relations between these different categories is an historical one. Our theory must reflect the nuances of careful historical attention to how these dynamics shape the lives of various communities of women.

In an essay on development and the sexual division of labor, Maria Patricia Fernandez Kelly briefly summarizes the impact of capitalist development on subsistence activities:

---

[49] See Mullings critique of Hartmann, above, on this same point. In other parts of her text Mies argues that this relation is not the reality. Hilda Scott develops an analysis of unpaid labor in *Working Your Way to the Bottom* that is similar to Mies. Yet she does not see a return to the land or the rejection of technology as a viable alternative. Instead, she rejects the dichotomy between "productive" and "nonproductive" work and aims "for the recognition of unpaid work as real work on its own terms, productive of value, [and] we clear a space for it." Ibid., p. 146. Bell Hooks makes a similar proposal in her chapter "Rethinking the Nature of Work," in *Feminist Theory: from margin to center* (Boston: South End Press, 1984). Their suggestions will be discussed in more detail in the conclusion of this study.

[50] DAWN, p. 73.

In peripheral and semiperipheral nations, capitalist investments have accentuated dependency on the highly industrialized core nations. In nineteenth century Europe (and later in other parts of the world) the transition from a subsistence to a market economy based on the use of wage labor caused a net loss of autonomy for kin-based groups and households. Individuals become more dependent on external political, economic, and ideological forces. A profound contradiction resulted from the increasing individuation of the labor force and the need to maintain collective mechanisms for the reproduction of the working class through preexisting but constantly evolving patterns of family, household and kinship organization. In other words, the advance of capitalism created a dynamic opposition between productive and reproductive spheres.[51]

According to Kelly, the creation of a wage-labor market often undermines the preexisting division of labor within the household.

This division has different meanings, dependent on its social and cultural contexts. The activities women perform are defined both in terms of their content and the social value assigned them. Kelly asserts that "it cannot be said that women's labor is intrinsically inferior to that of men or that it is universally judged to be so. When the household is forced to release one of its members to the wage-labor market, "the family's productive relations must be reorganized, in terms of both task reallocation and labor time expended in each task." This reorganization will affect household size, migratory flows, and the distribution of various tasks on the basis of gender.[52]

Kelly argues that culture alone cannot explain the sexual division of labor, although it has "a measure of autonomy."

Cultural norms sanctioning women's confinement to the household are more than ideological constructions. They express an objective reality in which domestic work is a mechanism subsidizing accumulation. Excluded from the realm of remunerated work, large groups of women have historically been

---

[51] Kelly, "Introduction," *Women's Work*, p. 2.

[52] Ibid., p. 4-5, 8. An example of Kelly's point is the study by Mona Hammam, "Capitalist Development, Family Division of Labor, and Migration in the Middle East," *Women's Work*, pp. 158-73, asserts that the participation of Arab women in the labor force is not a result only of culture or Islamic traditions, but of an interplay of social and economic forces, at the base of which is the household sexual division of labor.

transformed at various times into reserves of cheap labor. Paradoxically, women are subordinated, not because their work is socially inferior or unimportant, but precisely because of its importance. Women's labor both in production and reproduction is fundamental to the maintenance of economic and social systems.[53]

Thus one can argue that the subordination of women can be accounted for, at least in part, by analyzing gendered divisions of labor to see who controls women's labor power and who benefits from it.

Inequitable sexual divisions of labor, such as that described by Kelly, contribute to the marginalization and impoverishment of women. As we have seen, ideological justifications of women's primary responsibility for domestic work contribute to women's lower pay in the paid labor force while her responsibility for domestic work will lead to a double day if she is also involved in paid labor. Yet, as is evident from our discussion this far, any specific sexual division of labor is shaped by the mode of production and appropriation of surplus going on in particular societies. Thus one cannot fully account for women's impoverishment without an analysis of processes of accumulation and class relations, nationally and internationally.

Further, racial divisions of labor or racial stratification of the labor force, nationally and internationally, must be analyzed. Concrete analysis has shown that race is a critical factor in impoverishment and marginalization of both women and men of color particularly in the United States, western Europe, and South Africa.[54] Thus one cannot make generalizations about all women from an analysis of a sexual division of labor, but must also analyze race, class, and the global accumulation processes and the international division of labor.

DAWN's analysis of the impact of the global economy on the agricultural, service, and informal sectors must be supplemented by an analysis of the industrial sector. Swasti Mitter offers such an analysis in her study of women and the changing structure of employment in

---

[53] Kelly., p. 6.

[54] In addition to the sources already cited in the discussion of socialist feminism, see Swasti Mitter, *Common Fate, Common Bond*, and Arthur Brittan and Mary Maynard, *Sexism, Racism and Oppression* (Oxford: Basil Blackwell, 1984).

what has been called the new international division of labor. According to Mitter, the major features of this new division are the centralization of market and technology in core countries and the decentralization of production, not only to the peripheries but in the casualization of the labor force in core countries in home based production. Casualization entails creation of a peripheral work force, with low wages, few benefits, and little job security. This division is a new management strategy which aims "to nullify the rights and privileges that organized labor had won, especially in the West, through years of struggle."[55]

The outcome of this strategy has been a "massive integration" of women and blacks - and in several sectors black women workers - into the global economy in a new way.

> These workers are precisely the ones who have so far been marginalized in the mainstream labour movement. Their very vulnerability made them a preferred labour force in an evolving pattern of business organization that tends to rely on flexible and disposable workers. The transnational corporations (TNCs), with their immense resources, engineer access to such workers by restructuring labour nationally as well as globally on the basis of race and gender. Colour and sex have thus become the main principles behind the most recent international division of labour.[56]

A small core of men, "generally white men," maintain a monopoly over a small number of "elite 'core' jobs."[57]

The patriarchal values of both the state and the family are drawn on to create "a largely female marginalized workforce." Mitter argues that this experience of marginalization "has been instrumental in fostering a common bond," from which international networks of women workers are beginning to challenge "the politics of international capital."

> The common experience of male attitudes has brought about, especially in the 1980s, a sense of solidarity among female workers, a new awareness of a bond that transcends racial and geographic boundaries. The new technology has been

---

[55] Mitter, p. 6.

[56] Ibid., p. 6. Mitter uses the term black as the British do, to mean all people of color and not just Africans or African-Americans, as Americans would.

[57] Ibid., p. 2.

instrumental in fragmenting the production process to the advantage of the TNCs, but it has also, by facilitating improved communication and transport, helped women workers to exchange their experiences.[58]

These women workers call for alternative economic strategies including a fresh definition of the working class to include home based and "casual" workers. They advocate provision of work for all those who want to work in jobs that are geared to meeting social needs and the use of technology to "reskill labour." They demand sharing of childcare through flexible patterns of employment and shorter working hours. They envision a "more caring, sharing and co-operative economic structure." Mitter describes this agenda as a transnational socialism which builds on municipal socialist experiences and cooperation of trade unions and grassroots organizations of women and black workers.[59]

Conclusion

This multidimensional structural transformative perspective, although not yet a fully articulated paradigm, moves towards a new paradigm in its identification of the critical categories - gender, race, ethnicity, class, nationality - to be analyzed historically and globally.[60] This perspective proposes a program for change based in fundamental structural transformation of the exploitative and oppressive international and national class relations and male dominant gender relations, guided by principles of negotiated interdependence, self-reliance and self-

---

[58] Ibid., p. 145. Mitter focuses one of her chapters on these organizations of "women working worldwide."

[59] Ibid., pp. 156-62. These women are advocating a form of socialism which does not center power in the state or limit working class power to "core" workers.

[60] See Beneria and Roldan, "Introduction and Theoretical Framework," *The Crossroads of Class and Gender*, pp. 1-16, for a discussion of the challenge to "conceptualize a paradigm to include all factors having an influence on the complexity" of the lives of women in the periphery and to "capture the dynamics" of the totality of real life without losing sights of its different elements - "multiple relations of domination/subordination - based on race, age, ethnicity, nationality, sexual preference - interact dialectically with class and gender relations."

determination, and equitable access to and control of productive resources and democratic decision-making processes.[61] Empowerment of women is a central strategy.

This approach integrates the strengths of the various frameworks discussed in this chapter and is in continuity with them, particularly the socialist feminist perspective. The multidimensional structural approach overcomes most of the limitations of each of these perspectives through broadening and deepening their analyses.   In contrast to liberal feminism, this approach does not see the oppression of women as chiefly ideological nor does it contend that amelioration of the existing system is adequate to overcome that oppression, although it does advocate legislation as one part of its program for change. In contrast to cultural feminism, it does not insist that gender is the primary contradiction or patriarchy an invariably universal structure. Nor does it assert that cultural or lifestyle changes alone are adequate, although it acknowledges the role of culture and ideology and the need for cultural transformation. In contrast to marxism, it does not see class as the primary contradiction with gender relations only ideological. Nor does it contend that a transition to socialism alone is adequate, although it advocates a form of transnational socialism.

In contrast to socialist feminism, its deeper incorporation of a global historical perspective and a more central analysis of racism yields a more complex analysis of the sexual division of labor and the relation of social reproduction and production. More specifically, it does not make universal claims about the sexual division of labor nor does it see it as autonomous from the mode of production. This perspective broadens the conception of work and the working class. Its program for change is also distinctive, in that it calls into question growth models of development, particularly in situations of gross class and

---

[61] These principles are from the Dakar Declaration on Another Development with Women, issued by the participants in a seminar in June of 1982 sponsored by The Association of African Women in Research and Development and the Dag Hammerskjold Foundation. The Declaration and several of the papers from the seminar were published in *Development Dialogue* 1982: 1-2. The work of this seminar informed the DAWN project; it was a significant part of the process of the formation of the multidimensional structural perspective.

gender inequities, advocates participatory processes and limiting the power of the state, emphasizes strategies of self-reliance and reorganization of production and reproduction to meet basic needs, and insists on an end to hierarchies of domination and exploitation, including structures of male domination, through the empowerment of women and other oppressed peoples.[62]

Thus I contend that the multidimensional transformative perspective is able to most adequately account for the growing impoverishment of women, without ignoring poor men, and to propose a program for overcoming poverty. It also opens the way to deeper solidarity among women by enabling us to identify commonalities among women around the globe and to specify our differences more precisely. As Asoka Bandarage has asserted:

> Women's subordination is a systematic feature of the world's political economy and ideology. The struggle against women's subordination must also be international in character. It is in this common struggle against those aspects of women's subordination rooted in the "world system" that different groups of women and their culturally specific movements come together.[63]

What would it mean for Christian economic ethics to attend to the insights of this approach? This is the question which will be examined in the conclusion to our study.

---

[62] Mies has an insightful discussion of the discontinuities between what she calls "new feminism" and the feminist frameworks grounded in liberalism or marxism. She identifies three in particular: "body politics," "a new concept of politics," and "women's work." Mies, pp. 24-34.

[63] Asoka Bandarage, "Toward International Feminism," *Brandeis Review* 3 (Summer 1983).

CONCLUSION

PLACING WOMEN AT THE CENTER:
THE DIFFERENCE IT MAKES IN OUR ETHICS
TO RENDER THE INVISIBLE VISIBLE

In concluding this study, it is essential to return to the question of the difference it would make if women's economic reality is placed at the center of Christian economic ethics. This assessment needs to be informed by the learnings derived from evaluating theoretical assumptions in previous chapters. The problems discovered from a critical reading of Christian economic ethics in light of women's economic reality in part one of this study need to be reviewed with a view to propose presuppositions, criteria and normative principles for a more adequate socio-ethical method for economic justice.

The marginality and invisibility of women's economic reality in much contemporary progressive literature in Christian economic ethics has been documented in the second part of this study. Its inadequacy in accounting for or engaging the economic vulnerability and

243

impoverishment of women was illumined and some of the theoretical presuppositions which obscure women's reality identified.

As I demonstrated, most Roman Catholic social teaching is constrained by an organic normative view of male and female nature that obscures the existing economic relations of many contemporary women. Roman Catholic teaching rarely acknowledges that the pattern it presents as normative - male breadwinner, female homemaker - has never been the empirical reality for many of the world's peoples nor that it is no longer the reality today. Nor does this teaching generally note the presence and plight of many female-headed households around the globe.

The normative position of this economic teaching supports both the economic dependency of women and the patriarchal authority of men.[1] Social teaching grounded in organic understanding of gender relations contributes to and legitimates the growing economic vulnerability of women. Our survey makes clear that some recent Catholic social teaching begins to move away from static natural law understandings of male and female "nature." This teaching has used either a dependency perspective, as in the Puebla documents, or a liberal sex-role perspective, as in the US Catholic bishops letters.

In the previous chapter I argued that these perspectives still do not enable Christian ethics to fully focus the economic vulnerability and impoverishment of women. Both share a tendency to account for the inequality of women as primarily ideological, thus obscuring the structural sources of women's economic vulnerability. Yet both begin to recognize the reality of women's inequality, so may provide an opening towards a deeper structural analysis.

As I have noted, World Council of Churches insensitivity to women's economic suffering has a different source. Its social ethics has tended to embrace classical liberal presuppositions about the autonomy of so-called public and private spheres of political economy and

---

[1] Although Roman Catholic social teaching no longer appeals to a natural hierarchy in which men have authority over women, teaching about the initiating character of masculinity and the receiving character of femininity suggests that males are the ones in authority and that females are to accept that authority.

interpersonal life. World Council social ethics usually addresses issues in politics and economics - the so-called "public sphere," without analyzing their relation to households and families - the presumed "private sphere." It is assumed that women's experience in the "public sphere" is the same as men's, while gender diversion in the domicile is "natural." So too women's economic reality remained invisible and unanalyzed in most World Council social ethics. Even when more recent statements from the Nairobi and Vancouver Assemblies of the Council have addressed the oppression of women, here too the public/private dichotomy has been operational and the connection between women's work in the household and their labor force participation is not analyzed. Furthermore, these analyses of gender oppression have yet to be fully integrated into the analysis developed in the statements on political economy. Thus women's economic vulnerability remains marginalized in the social ethics of the Council.

The Difference It Makes in Our Analysis: Illuminating Concrete Suffering

Placing women's economic reality, particularly poor women's, at the center of an ethical analysis requires us to face the limits of liberal, cultural, Marxist, and socialist-feminist perspectives in addressing the impoverishment of women. [2] Just as taking seriously increasing poverty in the third world challenges developmentalism and requires a shift to a liberationist paradigm,[3] taking women's poverty seriously exposes the need for a more authentically multidimensional structural perspective. Merely compounding a liberal account of women's subordination with a radical analysis of how poverty is engendered by existing political economy, in the way that the best recent Christian economic ethics has done, still does not illumine adequately or engage strategically women's economic vulnerability. A unified multi-dimensional structural

---

[2] This thesis was defended in chapters four and five of this study.

[3] Ellison convincingly defended this thesis in his *The Center Cannot Hold*.

perspective is needed to account for and address the growing global inequality and impoverishment of women and their dependent children.

Placing poor women at the center of an analysis will deepen the progressive religious critique of capitalist growth models of development. In addition to noting the growing inequalities and impoverishment these generate, an analysis which incorporates the experience of poor women illumines the way that social reproduction becomes marginalized with capitalist development. By taking systematic account of the reality of women, their critical role in survival is clarified and strategies can be formulated to more effectively meet basic human needs. Including the sexual division of labor as a category of analysis, along with the social and the international division, more fully illumines the dynamics, costs, and benefits of different development strategies.

Criteria for Adequacy
of Social Analysis

The multidimensional transformative perspective emerging from sources discussed in part three of this study enables us to begin to understand criteria for the theoretical framework that enables us to test the adequacy of any specific analysis. Placing poor women at the center of analysis generates the following criteria for adequacy for any socio-economic analysis in economics ethics:

1) All socio-economic analysis must be set within a global perspective, as our social and economic reality is shaped by a global economic system; this means analyzing the international division of labor and processes of capital accumulation as they are conditioned by four and five below.

2) Gender must be addressed intentionally and systematically throughout an analysis; this means accounting for the differential participation of women in the economy and the differential impact of economic development on them.

3) Both the material and ideological bases of women's subordination and their interrelation must be accounted for; it is inadequate to treat women's oppression simply as cultural. Yet the ideological and cultural dynamics must also be recognized and proposals for cultural change advocated.

4) An effective integration of race, sex, and class as simultaneous social dynamics is necessary, as neither racism nor class exploitation is reducible to gender, nor is sexism reducible to either racism or class oppression.

5) All analyses of social or economic trends must be placed into concrete historical perspective; this means the concrete history of slavery, of colonialism, of racial-ethnic oppression, of the subordination of women, and of working-class exploitation.

To sum up, an adequate theory needs to account concretely for the structures and practices which create conflict and oppression, historically and globally, to fully illumine concrete conflict and suffering; this includes relations of production and reproduction and processes of accumulation and legitimation.

I would argue that this multidimensional structural perspective correlates well with the needs of a theological ethic, that it meets the criterion of critically breaking open our experience.[4] Such an analysis reveals that relations that are perceived as "natural" are in fact socially constructed and open to change. To take the experience of poor women as our starting point also correlates methodologically with the option for the poor claimed in both Roman Catholic social teaching and World Council of Churches teaching. It clarifies the sources of oppression of poor women of color without denying the reality of the oppression and suffering of poor men. Christian economic ethics will not reach the

---

[4] Beverly W. Harrison proposes this criterion in "The Role of Social Theory in Religious Social Ethics," *Making the Connections*, pp. 75- 80. The multidimensional structural perspective I am arguing for draws on the radical social theory Harrison is proposing for use in religious social theory, but it more fully addresses the socio-economic reality of women.

goal of illuminating concrete suffering until the nature of poor women's economic vulnerability is given this centrality.

The Difference It Makes
in Our Normative Moral Principles:
Claiming Women's Moral Agency

Both Roman Catholic social teaching and World Council social ethics claim human dignity as their fundamental norm. Although this norm would seem to be gender neutral, my research suggests that as yet the experience of males is normative. In Roman Catholic social teaching a "difference in kind," grounded in static natural law assumptions, limits women's human dignity and moral agency. In this view, women are destined by nature to be mothers. Supposedly, this destiny shapes their whole being in contradistinction to that of men; "femininity" is conceptualized as receiving, "masculinity" as initiating. As I demonstrated, this conception of "woman's nature" is appealed to in social teaching as a constraint on women's equality, dignity and moral agency. As the teaching does not constrain men's equality, dignity or moral agency by appeals to a distinctive male nature, it is apparent that male experience is normative for conceptions of human dignity.

A different set of assumptions informs World Council teaching and contributes to male experience being normative for conceptions of human dignity. These assumptions are grounded in the liberal social theory from which much World Council ethics draws. As I demonstrated in chapter three of this study, both a public/private dichotomy and universalist assumptions are operational in this teaching. Although seldom specifically articulated in World Council teaching, the public sphere is conceived as a male arena with universal principles whereas women are relegated to the private sphere of particular relations. As social ethics address the "public" sphere, male experience is de facto normative for conceptions of human dignity and moral agency. Some implications of this partial conception will become evident as our discussion proceeds.

As I disclosed, in World Council teaching and to some extent in Roman Catholic teaching, women's actual maternal practice and domestic labor are most always invisible.[5]   These activities of women are not perceived as economic contributions or domains involving moral agency and decision-making; they are devalued both materially and morally. Furthermore, both World Council and Roman Catholic social teaching tend to sacralize family relations and thus refuse to conceive of the possibility of exploitation, oppression or abuse within the family. Thus family relations are not addressed as an arena of justice, particularly within the World Council. As the overwhelming evidence is that women are most always the ones who are exploited, oppressed and abused within the family, women are the ones who suffer most from this "conspiracy of silence."

When women's moral voice and integrity are taken seriously, our understanding of moral agency and human dignity must shift. We must reconceive the conditions for human dignity in terms of persons in community. Conceptions of the self as moral agent must shift from "an autonomous, detached, rational subject" into "an integrated, other connected self" who incorporates "a sense of moral imagination, moral empathy and moral feeling." Second, distinctions between the so-called public and private domains must be blurred. Finally, "genuine womanly virtues" must be reclaimed as "fully human virtues." [6]

As we have seen, the blurring between the so-called public and private domains is a central dynamic in the Decade documents. Moral norms such as equity and social justice, usually confined to the "public sphere" are claimed to be normative in the family and household, the "private sphere." [7] As part of this continuing task, we need to develop

---

[5] While Roman Catholic teaching emphasizes women's destiny to motherhood, it spiritualizes and thus obscures the labor involved in mothering and homemaking. I also demonstrated that this teaching obscures the agency and labor of childbearing in conceptualizing it as a natural generative process.

[6] Morgan, pp. 224-5. In her essay, Morgan focuses on the person. In my discussion, I am attending to communities as well. In addition to the work of Morgan, my discussion here also draws on the work of Christian feminist ethicists such as Beverly Harrison and Ruth Smith.

[7] E. A. Cebatorev describes an interesting approach to development in which the family/household is the "entry point" through which equity and social justice are brought about in society. "The Family and Social Change," *The Ecumenist*, May-

an ethic of rights and obligations for interpersonal relations which includes sexual relations and for family relations which takes seriously the actual domestic labor which supports family life.

Womanly virtues which have been relegated to "the private sphere" need to be reclaimed as morally valuable characteristics for public life. DAWN asserts that the women's movement has "an ethic drawn from women's daily lives," which can strengthen and empower us.

> At its deepest it is not an effort to play "catch up" with the competitive, aggressive "dog-eat-dog" spirit of the dominant system. It is rather, an attempt to convert men and the system to the sense of responsibility, nurturance, openness, and rejection of hierarchy that are part of our vision. [8]

In this assertion, womanly virtues such as nurturance and openness are reclaimed as human virtues.

Responsibility and nurturance are certainly normative in a Christian social ethic.   Nurturance is an obligation for care.   Rejection of hierarchy may seem to correlate with claims to equality as normative in Christian social ethics. However, when proposing norms for economic activity Christian social ethics has tended to affirm property rights and patriarchal rights.[9]   When DAWN invokes anti-hierarchalization as a

---

June 1987, pp. 55-58.

[8] DAWN, p. 72. DAWN also advocates for empowerment of women; thus this call for conversion of men and the system is not primarily an appeal to the powerful for change. Nor does this assertion ground these womanly virtues in a biologically different nature, rather they are grounded in women's daily lives. They thus avoid the danger of "biologistic reductionism, of reinstituting traditional male-female dichotomies in a new guise" that characterizes some feminist theory. Martha A. Ackelsberg, "Communities, Resistance, and Women's Activism," *Women and the Politics of Empowerment*, ed. Ann Bookman and Sandra Morgen (Philadelphia: Temple University Press, 1988), p. 309. This essay is a useful discussion of the limits of liberal and Marxist political conceptions and an examination of the implications of women's activism for an adequate conception of democratic politics which focuses on the politics of relationship generated by concerns of daily lives.

[9] Herbert Gintis illumines the contradictions between equality, property rights and patriarchal rights in his article "Social Contradictions and the Liberal Theory of Justice," *New Directions in Economic Justice*, pp. 91-112. Gintis locates these contradictions not in any inherent deficiencies in a philosophy of natural rights, but

moral principle, the intent is to make it operational in all areas of life and to advocate participation and inclusiveness as conditions for dignity for persons in community. [10]

I would argue further than when an account is taken of women's experience as well as that of men, the interpretation of norms shared by Christian ethics and feminist ethics will be different. The moral norms that are appealed to in a multi-dimensional transformative perspective correlate with these moral norms in progressive Christian social teaching: justice, equality, participation, self-determination, solidarity, and the preferential option for the poor. One might say that these norms will be transformed when they are grounded in an other-connected self rather than an individualistic autonomous self.

Beverly Harrison has pointed to the transformation of moral norms which is required when they are grounded in a communitarian conception of human nature in liberation ethics.

> Implicit in the experience of liberation struggle is ... a radically relational understanding of justice as rightly ordered relationships of mutuality within the total web of our social relations. The givenness of reciprocal, interdependent social relations must be presupposed in liberation moral theory. All of our norms must be reciprocal, stressing mutuality both of responsibility and control. [11]

An understanding of justice as "rightly ordered relationships of mutuality" resonates with the moral understanding of a multidimensional transformative perspective, particularly the normative principle of mutually beneficiary and negotiated interdependence.

---

rather in the "cultural project of legitimating societies in which this diversity of rights does exist and is central to social reproduction." He argues convincingly that "a reasonable case can be made for a philosophy of natural rights in which only rights vested in individuals as members of the social community are fundamental. Other rights may be sustained, but only insofar as they reinforce and enhance the rights of persons in the social community." Ibid., p. 91.

[10] Riane Eisler makes a useful distinction between hierarchies of domination and hierarchies of actualization, which are a progression toward a more complex level of function. *The Chalice and the Blade: Our History, Our Future* (San Francisco: Harper and Row, 1987), pp. 105-6. In their full text, DAWN speaks specifically of hierarchies of domination and subordination.

[11] Harrison, "The Role of Theological Reflection in the Struggle for Liberation," p. 253.

Another example of this transformation of normative principles is in regards to the norm of participation. Generally this norm is not articulated in such a way as to take account of the conditions which hamper the participation of women. One of the Forum documents clarified these conditions in their assertion that

> Their long day of home, children and work, added to the debilitating dictates of culture, rein women more tightly into a constricted world and shut them more effectively out of the public arena of decision-making.[12]

Thus a social ethic for which participation is a foundational moral norm must analyze and address those factors which constrain the participation of women. [13]

As was demonstrated in our discussion of the Decade documents in chapter four, equality must be interpreted as equal access to power and resources rather than just legal equality of opportunity for education and employment. A condition for this access is empowerment of women, particularly in grassroots organizations. The need for empowerment has implications for interpretation of norms of solidarity and the option for the poor. To be in solidarity, to opt for the poor, is to participate in struggles for justice in which the poor are empowered as they seek to meet their basic needs and to transform hierarchies of domination and subordination. The participation of women in these struggles is of critical importance.

A foundational moral norm absent from most progressive Christian ethics examined in this study that is claimed by many who value women's lives is women's right to control over their reproductive powers. The Decade documents contend that this right is a condition for "real equality" between women and men, a necessary prerequisite to the self-determination of women.

DAWN interprets "control over reproduction" as a basic need as well as a basic right "for all women." Citing the links between reproduction, social structures of religion and state control, and private profit as well as women's health and social status, DAWN asserts that

---

[12] *Asian Women Speak Out!*, p. 9

[13] Marie Giblin insightfully discusses the constraints on Tanzanian peasant women's participation and the impact this has on peasant well-being. *Toward Justice, Equality, and Participation*, pp. 75-111.

the right to control reproduction is "best understood and affirmed" from the vantage point of poor women.

> Women know that child-bearing is a social, not a purely personal, phenomenon; nor do we deny that world population trends are likely to exert considerable pressure on resources and institutions by the end of this century. But our bodies have become a pawn in the struggles among states, religions, male heads of households, and private corporations.... [14]

DAWN further asserted that "the requirements of a genuine, people-oriented development necessitate the acknowledgement of this fundamental need and right," thus grounding their claim in both women's well-being and the well-being of the community.

Although not interpreted to support reproductive rights, bodily integrity has been claimed as a fundamental right in Roman Catholic social teaching.[15] Harrison has developed an ethic for procreative choice which appeals to bodily integrity as "a foundational condition of human well-being and dignity."[16] Such a shift in Catholic social teaching would require recognition of women's full moral agency, which as I have argued is denied by restrictive conceptualizations of femininity.

The World Council obscures women's full moral agency through the invisibility of moral domains. As I have already demonstrated, women's maternal practice and domestic labor are invisible in World Council ethics. Roman Catholic teaching limits women's human dignity by absolutizing our capacity to give birth whereas this capacity and practice is ignored in World Council teaching. Women are claiming their capacity to act as fully moral persons in all areas of life. The task before us is to formulate a theological anthropology informed by this practice which affirms the human dignity and well-being of women and men in community.

---

[14] DAWN, p. 42

[15] Bodily integrity is included in a listing of personal rights identified by John XXIII in *Pacem in Terris*, para. 11.

[16] Beverly W. Harrison, *Our Right to Choose: Toward a New Ethic of Abortion* (Boston: Beacon Press, 1983), p. 196. Also see Betsy Hartmann, *Reproductive Rights and Wrongs: The Global Politics of Population Control and Contraceptive Choice* (New York: Harper and Row, 1987).

The Difference It Makes
in Our Strategic Policy Directions for Action:
Basic Needs from Margin to Center

Moral norms can be expressed as principles of action."[17] Placing
women's experience, particularly poor women's experience, at the
center of economic ethics will also make a difference in our policy
principles. Most importantly, this will mean that our commitment and
accountability is to the well-being of poor and oppressed women and
their dependent children. In some instances this will mean insisting that
present action guides are applicable to women as well as men. In other
instances it will mean the formulation of some new action guides.

Christian economic ethics has advocated equitable access to
resources, participation in decision making, and equitable benefits as
foundational policy norms in overcoming economic dependency. As
indicated in part two of this study, these norms have not been
specifically applied to women and there is some evidence that they are
meant to apply only to men, either for themselves or as heads of
households. When poor women's experience is at the center of our
ethic, these norms will apply to both women and men.[18]

Criteria for Adequacy
for Policy Proposals

Placing women's experience at the center of our analysis has
exposed the critical links that actually exist between production and
social reproduction, both in regard to economic growth and social well-
being. When this linkage and women's key contribution to meeting
basic needs are recognized, policy norms will need to be formulated
with this in mind. Based on the perspectives reviewed in part three of

---

[17] Since norms are conceptual formulations of envisioned values, they may be
expressed as principles of action." Harrison, "The Role of Theological Reflection,"
p. 253. Values are states to be realized. Virtues, which are qualities of character,
can also be expressed as principles of action.

[18] The primary grounds for insisting that all norms apply to women is the full
personhood of women. However, the fact that women do not always benefit from
their husband's income or that many women are themselves heads of households are
further reasons for insisting that all norms apply to women.

this study, the following criteria of adequacy must be used to evaluate any normative policy proposals within an economic ethic.

1) Every proposal for economic development must be scrutinized for the impact it would have on the cultural system, the social infrastructure, and the environment, with particular attention to whether the proposed change would further marginalize women or enhance their participation.

2) The impact of any new imposition of wage labor on the existing subsistence base of economies in transition must be taken into account, and plans made to avoid increasing women's work load.

3) All areas of work must be open to women and more equitable value assigned to sectors which have been devalued, such as service work traditionally assigned to women.

4) Basic needs must become an inviolable priority, with explicit budgetary provisions, in developed and underdeveloped countries.[19]

5) In any proposals for change, the care of children and domestic work must be impacted so that they are shared by women and men in families and by the larger society.

6) The capacity to impact the self-determination of peoples, both women and men, must be understood in the formulation and adoption of specific socio-economic goals and policies and assessed in this light. Processes for ensuring people's role in setting goals and policies must be developed.

7) Mutually beneficial and negotiated interdependence between women and men, classes, racial ethnic groups, and nations is to replace relations of domination and dependence.

---

[19] For a useful discussion of the role of a basic needs approach in achieving economic justice, see Denis Goulet, "Overcoming Injustice: Possibilities and Limits," *Poverty and Economic Justice*, pp. 113-158. For support of a basic needs approach in developed countries such as the United States, see Rochelle Lefkowitz and Ann Withorn, "Introduction," *For Crying Out Loud*, p. 7.

8) Empowerment of marginalized groups must be a key part of any proposal for socio-economic development.

Any proposals should aim toward structural transformation from a system with inequitable access and control of resources and production and reproduction to one with more equitable access and control. Specific strategies need to be evaluated in regard to these principles.

For instance, the principle of shared parenting and social responsibility for children cannot be implemented without social transformation:

> To change fundamentally the relations of men with children would have profound effects on capitalism, on the relations between the sexes and in the very construction of gender, and is inconceivable at present, because it would affect all those processes fundamental to capital accumulation. Occupational segregation and the social/sexual division of labour with its accompanying constructions of masculinity and femininity are deeply embedded not only in the process of capital accumulation but also in the legitimation of capitalism as an economic and social form. [20]

Thus strategies for shared parenting and social responsibility for children need to be part of a larger project of social transformation. [21]

This is also the case with strategies for pay equity. Lourdes Beneria cautions that even if pay equity is gained within a given job structure, jobs and occupations may be redesigned in such a way that a high proportion of women are still at the bottom "of a constantly created labor hierarchy." She argues that "a more egalitarian structure of production, and particularly one that reflects the interests of those who work within it, would be more conducive to attaining gender equality."[22]

---

[20] Burton, p. xv.

[21] Rosemary Ruether has described some of the changes that would need to be made in the capitalist organization of work in order for child care and domestic work to be shared. "Working Women and the Male Workday," *Christianity and Crisis*, 1977, reprinted in *Women, Faith, and Economic Justice*, ed. Jackie Smith (Philadelphia: Westminster Press, 1985), pp. 53-56.

[22] Beneria, "Introduction," *Women, Households, and the Economy*, ed. Beneria and Stimpson (New Brunswick: Rutgers University Press, 1987), pp. xxiii-xxiv.

The Difference It Makes
in Our Vision of the Good Society:
Rethinking Work

Many women share with the churches the vision of a just and peaceful social order which honors the integrity of creation.[23]   Yet just as placing women's lives at the center of our social ethics transforms moral norms and policy proposals, so too will our vision of the good society be transformed. Society must be envisioned so that maternity, maternal values, and social reproduction are not marginal values but central to the common good. As the Peruvian Christian feminist circle "Talitha Cumi" claims, motherhood is a relation open to the whole world, to all who promote the communication and transmission of life.[24]

Such a reorganization will mean a change in how work is understood, organized and rewarded. Bell Hooks, an African-American theorist, insists that "rethinking the nature of work is essential for feminist movement in the United States." Women - and men as well - must learn to value the work they do, whether paid or unpaid, "as a significant and meaningful gesture of power and resistance."[25] Rethinking work in this way, Hooks asserts, will make feminism relevant to all women. Working class and poor women in particular

---

[23] Justice, Peace and the Integrity of Creation is the program emphasis which emerged from the Vancouver Assembly of the World Council of Churches. The Roman Catholic Church is participating fully with the World Council in the process of commitment for justice, peace and the integrity of creation. The WCC declared that "the foundation of this emphasis should be confessing Christ as the life of the world and Christian resistance to the demonic powers of death in racism, sexism, caste oppression, economic exploitation, militarism, violations of human rights, and the misuse of science and technology. WCC, *Justice, Peace and the Integrity of Creation Resource Materials*, 1.2, September 1987. D. Preman Niles discusses the history and meaning of the JPIC call in "Covenanting for Justice, Peace and the Integrity of Creation: An Ecumenical Survey," *The Ecumenical Review* 39 (October 1987), pp. 470-484.

[24] Circulo de Feministas Cristianas "Talitha Cumi," *La Maternidad, Tarea de Todos*, Dia de la Madre, 1987, Lima, Peru. I am grateful to Ada Maria Isasi-Diaz for making this available to me.

[25] Bell Hooks, *Feminist Theory*, p. 103.

have much to offer to such a reconceptualization, as their contributions have been critical to their families' survival.[26]

Hilda Scott, a European-American theorist, observes that claiming women's values as human values "means simply a strengthening of the use values of caring, humanizing activities which are done largely by women."[27] She has sketched "a political economy of unpaid work" that would elevate unpaid work "to a place in the economy equal to that of paid work," making "improved human welfare in the general sense an economically practical goal."

> Income would no longer be tied entirely to paid work. Needs would be judged individually, not according to family status. At least some services would no longer be income-related. Recompense for voluntary work could include health insurance, old age and disability pensions, and credit for relevant experience when applying for a job in the monetized sector. Those who gave their time free might also be entitled to free or low-cost access to other facilities, including restaurants, public transportation, recreation and entertainment.[28]

The possibilities for developing coalitions of grassroots organizations around such a vision of personal and community well-being are immense. Such a vision also resonates with the values of the best of progressive Christian ethics.

---

[26] I am grateful to Joan Martin for this insight. In her panel presentation at the American Academy of Religion, she argued that black women's experience as domestic workers symbolizes those who can create new resources for work that has to be done but can be transformed through recognition of its contribution to survival. "Whose Experience Counts?" Panel, November 20, 1988, (Chicago). See also Bonnie Thornton Dill, "'Making Your Job Good Yourself': Domestic Service and the Construction of Personal Dignity," *Women and the Politics of Empowerment*, pp. 33-52.

[27] Hilda Scott, *Working Your Way to The Bottom*, p. 154.

[28] Ibid., pp. 162-3. Scott notes that such an economy will require changes in our value system, in its structures, and in the way political confrontation occurs. Marilyn Waring suggests a useful conceptual approach to an economy of paid and unpaid work in the last chapter of her book, "Glimpsing the Whole: A New Model for Global Economics," in *If Women Counted: A New Feminist Economics* (San Francisco: Harper and Row, 1988).

Challenge to the Praxis of the Church:
Solidarity with Women

Women's inequality and economic vulnerability are issues of profound import not only morally, but also theologically and ecclesiologically. I agree with Sheila Briggs that

> To ask about the nature of the church requires that we ask about the social practice by virtue of which the church is the church. The church is a community of practice; it cannot avoid being a community of practice. The crucial question becomes what is its praxis. Is the praxis of the Christian church in continuity with and an authentic imitation of the praxis of Jesus of Nazareth?[29]

The contemporary women's movement in the churches has been rediscovering the radically egalitarian praxis of the Jesus movement, as indicated in part two of this study, and is challenging the churches today to imitate that praxis.

The churches have begun to realize that their social teaching has implications for their own internal life. The U.S. Bishops indicated in their pastoral on the U.S. economy that the church must apply its normative principles for economic justice to its own practices in regard to employment, investments, and participation in policy-making. The World Council has made some significant strides in increasing the participation of women in its ongoing life.

However, the churches have barely begun to take account of their own role in legitimizing the oppression of women. During the Decade for Women, women themselves have become ever more vocal in identifying the negative impact of the churches here. It is time for the churches to hear the message from women on this count, whether those within its life or without.

Churches could play a significant role in challenging and transforming beliefs and ideologies which perpetuate sex-based stereotyping and oppressive gender identities, as part of a larger project

---

[29] Sheila Briggs, "Church Theology," *The Kairos Covenant: Standing with South African Christians*, ed. Willis H. Logan (New York: Friendship Press, 1988), p. 81. This stance resonates with the understanding of the church in the Anabaptist tradition from which I come.

of transformation of hierarchies of domination and exploitation.[30] The critical evaluation of scripture, theology, ethics, church history, ministry, liturgy and other areas of religious teaching and practice undertaken by feminist and womanist scholars and activists needs to be continued. This work, primarily done in the early stages by white women and racial-ethnic women in the first world, needs increasingly to be in dialogue with the emerging voices of third world women.

Third world women theologians gathered in their first intercontinental conference claimed theologizing as a way in which women struggle for their right to life, to liberation from oppression. The theologizing of third world women, they noted, arises from experiences of discrimination as women and as people of the Third World. "Spiritual experience rooted in action for justice" constitutes an integral part of their theologizing.[31]

These women movingly articulated the contribution they bring to the doing of theology. Their profound insights present a significant challenge to all theology, as they note, and thus bear citing in full:

> The passionate and compassionate way in which women do theology is a rich contribution to theological science. The key to this theological process is the word LIFE. We perceive that in the three continents women are deeply covenanted with life, giving and protecting life. The woman in our streets always appears surrounded and weighed down with children: children in her body, in her arms, on her back. Thus, even physically, she extends and reaches out to other lives, other human beings born from her body, sustaining their lives. In doing theology, we in the Third World find ourselves committed and faithful to all the vital elements that compose human life. Thus without losing its scientific seriousness, which includes analyzing the basic causes of women's multiple oppression, our theologizing is deeply rooted in experience,

---

[30] Madeline Munnik, an African theorist, identified tasks that remained at the end of the Decade for Women. "Although the Decade has seen a number of changes in the laws that have been enacted and the projects that have been launched for the benefit of women, the formidable task remains of transforming societies and specifically the structure of relationships between women and men. It is not only the material and technical obstacles that must be removed for women's full potential to be utilized, but the psychological obstacles that are perpetuated through education and culture." "Editorial" in *African Insight* 16 (1986), p. 3. Religions play a significant role in cultural transmission.

[31] "Final Document: Intercontinental Women's Conference," Virginia Fabella and Mercy Oduyoye, eds., *With Passion and Compassion: Third World Women Doing Theology* (Maryknoll, NY: Orbis Books, 1988), p. 186.

in affection, in life. We as women feel called to do scientific theology passionately, a theology based on feeling as well as on knowledge, on wisdom as well as on science, a theology made not only with the mind but also with the heart, the body, the womb. We consider this a challenge and an imperative not only for doing theology from women's perspective, but also for all theology.[32]

The church is called to do theology passionately and compassionately, rooted in experience, affection and life. Can we begin to imagine the difference it would make to do theology passionately and compassionately, committed "to all the vital elements that compose human life?" This is a significant challenge to the praxis of the church.

These women further claim that the goal of theologizing "is to bring a new dimension to the struggle for justice and for promoting God's reign." This new dimension comes "both by the voices of our people clamoring for justice and by God." This struggle for justice will benefit not only women, but "humanity as a whole."[33]

This is one of the most critical challenges before the churches today: to engage in a praxis of liberation of women that stands to benefit all humanity through the birthing of a more just and a more caring global community. Our struggle continues ...

---

[32] Ibid., p. 188.

[33] Ibid., p. 189.

SELECTED BIBLIOGRAPHY

Sources in Religious Studies

Ethical and Theological Studies

Andolsen, Barbara H., Christine E. Gudorf, Mary D. Pellauer, ed. *Women's consciousness, Women's conscience: A Reader in Feminist Ethics*. Minneapolis: Winston Press, 1985.

Bam, Brigalia H. and Lotika Sarkar. *New Perspectives for Third World Women*. Madras: The Christian Literature Society, 1979.

Birch, Bruce C. and Larry L. Rasmussen. *Bible and Ethics in the Christian Life*, revised and expanded edition. Minneapolis: Augsburg, 1989.

Briggs, Sheila. "Church Theology." *The Kairos Covenant: Standing with South African Christians*, ed. Willis Logan. New York: Friendship Press, 1988.

Chopp, Rebecca S. *The Praxis of Suffering: An Interpretation of Liberation and Political Theologies*. Maryknoll, NY: Orbis Books, 1986.

Ellison, Marvin Mahan. *The Center Cannot Hold: The Search for a Global Economy of Justice*. Washington, DC: University Press of America, 1983.

Fabella, Virginia and Mercy Oduyoye, ed. *With Passion and Compassion: Third World Women Doing Theology*. Maryknoll, NY: Orbis Books, 1988.

Fiorenza, Elisabeth Schussler. *In Memory of Her: A Feminist Theological Reconstruction of Christian Origins*. New York: Crossroad, 1983.

_____. "Liberation, Unity and Equality in Community: a New Testament Case Study." *Beyond unity-in-tension: Unity, renewal and the community of women and men*, ed. Thomas F. Best. Geneva: WCC Publications, 1988.

Goulet, Denis. "'Development' ... or Liberation?" *International Development Review* XII, no. 3 (1971/3): 6-10.

Robert H. Hartman, ed. *Poverty and Economic Justice: A Philosophical Approach*, New York: Paulist Press, 1984.

Harrison, Beverly W. *Making the Connections: Essays in Feminist Social Ethics.* Edited by Carol S. Robb. Boston: Beacon Press, 1985.

_____. *Our Right to Choose: Toward A New Ethic of Abortion.* Boston: Beacon Press, 1983.

Holland, Joe and Peter Henriot, S.J. *Social Analysis: Linking Faith and Justice,* revised and enlarged edition. Maryknoll, NY: Orbis Books, 1983.

Lebacqz, Karen. *Justice in an Unjust World: Foundations for a Christian Approach to Justice.* Minneapolis: Augsburg, 1987.

Maguire, Daniel. *The Moral Choice.* Minneapolis: Winston Press, 1978.

Morgan, Kathryn Pauly. "Women and Moral Madness." *Canadian Journal of Philosophy*, Supplementary Volume 13: 201-226.

Pobee, John S. and Barbel von Wartenberg-Potter, eds. *New eyes for reading: Biblical and theological reflections by women from the third world.* Oak Park, IL: Meyer-Stone Books, 1986.

Robins, Wendy S. ed. *Through the eyes of a woman: Bible studies on the experience of women.* London: World YWCA, 1986.

Smith, Jackie, ed. *Women, Faith, and Economic Justice.* Philadelphia: Westminster Press, 1985.

Russell, Letty M., ed. *Feminist Interpretation of the Bible.* Philadelphia: Westminster Press, 1985.

_____. "Partnership in Models of Renewed Community." *Ecumenical Review* 40 (January 1988): 16-26.

Smith, Ruth L. "Reinhold Niebuhr and History: The Elusive Liberal Critique." *Horizons* 15 (1988): 283-98.

Williams, Delores. "The Color of Feminism: Or Speaking the Black Woman's Tongue." *The Journal of Religious Thought* 43 (Spring-Summer, 1986): 42-58.

Wills, David. "Racial Justice and the Limits of American Liberalism." *Journal of Religious Ethics* 6 (1978):187-220.

Wogaman, J. Philip. *The Great Economic Debate: An Ethical Analysis.* Philadephia: The Westminster Press, 1977.

Roman Catholic Social Teaching

Aman, Kenneth. "The Pope and 'Social Concerns.'" *Christianity and Crisis* 48 (1988): 177.

Antoncich, Ricardo. *Christians in the Face of Injustice: A Latin American Reading of Catholic Social Teaching.* Translated by Matthew J. O'Connell. Maryknoll, NY: Orbis Books, 1987.

Baum, Gregory. *The Priority of Labor: A Commentary on Laborem Exercens.* New York: Paulist Press, 1982.

Byers, David M., ed. *Justice in the Marketplace: Collected Statements of the Vatican and the U.S. Catholic Bishops on Economic Policy, 1891-1984.* General Introduction and Document Introductions by Rev. John T. Pawlikowski. Washington, DC: United States Catholic Conference, 1985.

Canadian Bishops Commission. "Alternatives to Present Economic Structures." *Origins* 12 (1983): 522-27.

Chinigo, Michael, ed. *The Pope Speaks: The Teachings of Pius XII.* New York: Pantheon, 1957.

Cormie, Lee. "The U.S. Bishops on Capitalism." From the working papers of the American Academy of Religion, 1985.

Curran, Charles. *American Catholic Social Ethics.* Notre Dame: University of Notre Dame Press, 1982.

Dorr, Donal. *Option for the Poor: A Hundred Years of Vatican Social Teaching.* Maryknoll: Orbis Books, 1983.

Eagleson, John and Philip Scharper, ed. *Puebla and Beyond: Documentary and Commentary.* Maryknoll, NY: Orbis, 1979.

Giblin, Marie. *Toward Justice, Equality, and Participation: Issues for the Church Concerning Tanzanian Women and Men Peasants.* Union Theological Seminary, unpublished dissertation, 1986.

Gremillion, Joseph, ed. *The Gospel of Peace and Justice: Catholic Social Teaching Since Pope John.* Maryknoll, NY: Orbis Books, 1976.

Gudorf, Christine. *Catholic Social Teaching on Liberation Themes.* Washington, DC: University Press in America, 1981.

Henriot, Peter J., Edward P. DeBerri, and Michael J. Schultheis. *Catholic Social Teaching: Our Best Kept Secret*. Maryknoll, NY: Orbis Books, 1988.

Hobgood, Mary E. *Catholic Social Teaching and Economic Theory: Paradigms in Conflict*. Philadelphia: Temple University, 1991.

Houch, John and Oliver Williams, ed. *Catholic Social Teachings and the United States Economy: Working Papers for a Bishops' Pastoral*. Washington, DC: University Press of America, 1984.

Isasi-Diaz, Ada Maria. "Silent Women Will Never Be Heard." *Missiology: An International Review* VII (1979): 295-301.

John XXIII. "Ad Petri Cathedram." *The Pope Speaks* 5 (1959): 359-73.

_____. "Woman and Society." *The Pope Speaks* 7 (1961): 344-46.

_____. "The Woman of Today at Home and at Work," *The Pope Speaks* 7 (1961): 171-3.

_____. "Woman's Work." *The Pope Speaks* 6 (1960): 329-31.

John Paul II. *Mulieris Dignitatem* (On the Dignity and Vocation of Women) *Origins* 18, (1988): 261-283.

_____. *Sollicitudo Rei Socialis. Origins* 17 (1988): 641-60.

Land, Phil, S.J. "On Human Work: What's in it for Women?" *Center of Concern* Issue 49 (July 1982): 5-6.

Latin American Episcopal Council. *The Church in the Present Day Transformation of Latin America in Light of the Council* II: Conclusions. Washington, DC: US Catholic Conference, 1970.

Paul VI. "Women in the Life of Society." *The Pope Speaks* 22, (1977): 22-5.

Rasmussen, Larry. "Economic Policy: Creation, Covenant and Community." *America* 152 (1985): 341-50.

"Reflections of Peruvian Women on the Occasion of the Visit of Pope John Paul II." *Women in the Church*, The New LADOC "Keyhole" Series, no. 2, 2-3. Lima, Peru: Latin American Documentation, 1986.

Seven Great Encyclicals. Glen Rock, NJ: Paulist Press, 1939.

Tabb, William K. "The Shoulds and the Excluded Whys: The U.S. Catholic Bishops Look at the Economy." *Churches in Struggle: Liberation Theologies and Social Change in North America*, ed. William K. Tabb, 278-90. New York: Monthly Review Press, 1986.

Tedesco, Giglia. "Laborem exercens: A Handicap for Women." *NTC News* (Rome) Vol. 8, nos. 11-12 (November-December 1981): 1-4.

United States Conference of Catholic Bishops. *Economic Justice for All: Catholic Social Teaching and the U.S. Economy*. Washington, DC: United States Catholic Conference, 1986.

Ecumenical Social Ethics

Abrecht, Paul. "From Oxford to Vancouver" Lessons from Fifty Years of Ecumenical Work for Economic and Social Justice." *The Ecumenical Review* 40, (1988): 147-68.

Barot, Madeleine. *Cooperation of Men and Women in Church, Family and Society*. Geneva: WCC, 1964.

Bell, G.K.A., ed. *The Stockholm Conference 1925*. London: Oxford University Press, 1926.

Bennett, John. "Breakthrough in Ecumenical Social Ethics: The Legacy of the Oxford Conference on Church, Community, and State (1937)." *The Ecumenical Review* 40 (1988): 132-46.

Best, Thomas F. "The Community Study: Where Do We Go From Here." *The Ecumenical Review* 40 (1988): 48-56.

Bliss, Kathleen. "Personal Relations in a Technical Society. *The Church and the Disorder of Society: An Ecumenical Study*, 83-8. Geneva: World Council of Churches, 1948.

Bock, Paul. *In Search of a Responsible World Society: The Social Teachings of the World Council of Churches*. Philadelphia: The Westminster Press, 1974.

C.O.P.E.C. Commission Reports. London: Longmans, Green and Co., 1924.

Couch, Beatriz Melano. "New Visions of the Church in Latin America: A Protestant View." *The Emergent Gospel: Theology from the Underside of History*, Sergio Torres and Virginia Fabella, ed., 193-226. Maryknoll, NY: Orbis Books, 1978.

Derr, Thomas Sieger. "The Economic Thought of the World Council of Churches." *This World* 1 (Winter/Spring 1982): 20-33.

Dickinson, Richard D. N. *Poor, Yet Making Many Rich.* Geneva: WCC, 1982.

Duchrow, Ulrich. *Global Economy: A Confessional Issue for the Churches?* Geneva, WCC, 1987.

Duff, Edward. *The Social Thought of the World Council of Churches.* New York: Association Press, 1956.

"Ecumenical Decade 1988-98: Churches in Solidarity with Women." *Women in a Changing World* 23 (June 1987): 3-23.

Gaines, David. *The World Council of Churches: A Study of its Background and History.* Peterborough, NH: Richard R. Smith, 1966.

Gill, David, ed. *Gathered for Life - Official Report VI Assembly of the World Council of Churches.* Geneva: WCC, 1983.

Goodall, Norman, ed. *The Uppsala Report 1968.* Geneva: WCC, 1968.

Gruber, Pamela, ed. *Fetters of Injustice.* Geneva: WCC, 1970.

Gustafson, James M. "An Analysis of Church and Society Ethical Writings. *The Ecumenical Review* 40 (1988): 267-78.

Herzel, Susannah. *A Voice for Women: The women's department of the World Council of Churches.* Geneva: WCC, 1981.

Lindqvist, Martti. *Economic Growth and the Quality of Life: An Analysis of the Debate within the World Council of Churches.* Helsinki: Finnish Society for Missiology and Ecumenics, 1975.

May, Melanie. *Bonds of Unity.* Atlanta: Scholars Press, 1989.

McCreary, David. "John Bennett on Oxford '37." *The Christian Century* (October 28, 1987): 942-4.

McFarland, Charles S. *Steps Towards the World Council.* New York: Fleming H. Revell, 1938.

Mulholland, Catherine, compiler. *Ecumenical Reflections on Political Economy.* Geneva: WCC, 1988.

Oduyoye, Mercy. "Comments from Three Continents: Africa." *The Poverty Makers*, David Millwood, 61-3. Geneva: WCC, 1977.

Oldham, J.H. *The Oxford Conference: Official Report*. Chicago: Willett, Clark & Co., 1937.

Parvey, Constance. "The Community Study: its Mixed Messages for the Churches." *Beyond unity-in tension*, ed. Thomas F. Best, 34-43. Geneva: WCC, 1988.

_____, ed. *The Community of Women and Men in the Church*. Philadelphia: Fortress Press, 1983.

Paton, David M., ed. *Breaking Barriers: Nairobi 1975*. Grand Rapids: Eerdmans, 1976.

Santa Ana, Julio de. "The Economic Debate in the Ecumenical Movement." *The Ecumenical Review* 37 (1985): 98-105.

Shillito, Edward. *Life and Work*. London: Longmans, Green and Co, Ltd 1926.

Shin, Sun. "A Vision of the Women's Committee." *In God's Image* (June 1988).

Shinn, Roger L. "The churches' search for a peace policy." *Christianity and Crisis* (April 2, 1984): 105-111.

Sub-Unit on Women in Church and Society. *Ecumenical Decade 1988-1998: Churches in Solidarity with Women*. Geneva: World Council of Churches, 1988.

Thompson, Betty. *A Chance to Change: Women and Men in the Church*. Philadephia: Fortress Press, 1982.

Traitler, Reinhild. "An Oikoumene of Women?" *The Ecumenical Review* 40 (1988).

Universal Christian Conference on Life and Work. *Minutes of the Continuation Committee*, 9/5-9/19/1929. N.p.

Van der Bent, Ans J., ed. *Breaking Down the Walls: World Council of Churches' Statements and Actions on Racism, 1948-1985*. Geneva: WCC, 1986.

_____. *Vital Ecumenical Concerns: Sixteen Documentary Surveys*. Geneva: WCC, 1986.

Van Leeuwen, Arend Theodor. *Development Through Revolution*. New York: Charles Scribner's Sons, 1970.

Visser't Hooft, W. A. *The Genesis and Formation of the World Council of Churches.* Geneva: WCC, 1982.

_____. "The historical significance of Stockholm 1925. *The Gospel for all realms of life: reflections on the Universal Christian Conference on Life and Work,* 1-16. Geneva: WCC, 1975.

_____, ed. *The Evanston Report.* London: SCM Press, Ltd. 1955.

_____, ed. *The First Assembly of the World Council of Churches: Official Report.* London: SCM Press, Ltd, 1949.

_____, ed. *The New Delhi Report.* Geneva: WCC, 1962.

Webb, Pauline. "Gender as an Issue." *The Ecumenical Review* 40 (1988): 4-15.

West, Charles C. "Ecumenics, Church and Society: The Tradition of Life and Work." *The Ecumenical Review* 39 (1987): 462-84.

World Council of Churches. *Faith and Science in an Unjust World: Report of the World Council of Churches' Conference on Faith, Science and the Future* I and II. Geneva, WCC, 1980.

_____. *Justice, Peace and the Integrity of Creation: Resource Materials,* Packets 1-4. 1987-89.

_____. *Men and Women in Church and Society.* Geneva: WCC, 1956.

_____. *Sex, Love and Marriage in the Caribbean.* Geneva: WCC, 1965.

_____. *Sexism in the 1970's: Discrimination Against Women.* Geneva: WCC, 1975.

_____. *Solidarity with the Poor for Justice, Peace and the Integrity of Creation.* Commission on the Churches' Participation in Development (CCPD) Documents - Justice and Development no. 9. 1987.

_____. *Women Under Racism.* Programme to Combat Racism Reports and Background Papers no. 19. 1984.

_____. *Women, Work and Economic Injustice.* CCPD Documents - Justice and Development no. 5. 1985.

_____. *World Conference of Church and Society (Geneva 1966) - Report: Christians in the Technical and Social Revolutions of Our Time.* Geneva: WCC, 1967.

Sources from the Decade for Women

"Africa task force meets." *African Women Link: A Development Newsletter* 1, no. 3, (1985): 2-3.

Anker, Richard. "Female labour force participation in developing countries: A critique of current definitions and data collection methods." *International Labour Review* 122, (Nov.-Dec., 1983): 712.

Asian Women's Research and Action Network. *Asian Women Speak Out!A 14-Country Alternative Asian Report On the Impact of the UN Decade for Women.* N.p., 1985.

Bandele, Safiya. "The UN World Conference and World Forum on Women." *African Women Rising* 2 (Winter-Spring 1986): 1,12.

Beneria, Lourdes. "Accounting for Women's Work." *Women and Development: The Sexual Division of Labour in Rural Societies*, ed. Lourdes Beneria. New York: Praeger Publishers, 1982.

Bunch, Charlotte. *Bringing the Global Home*. Denver: Antelope Publications, 1985.

Bunch, Charlotte and Shirley Castley. *Developing Strategies for the Future: Feminist Perspectives.* New York: International Women's Tribune Center, 1980.

Chatterji, Jyotsna. *The Women's Decade 1975-1985: An Assessment.* Banhi Series. Delhi: ISPCK, 1985.

"Decade for Women Not Beneficial for Pakistani Women." *Depthnews Women's Feature* (May 5, 1985): 1-4.

"Decade - Mujer." *Alternativas*, Organo de Dirusion del Centro de Promocion y Accion de la Mujer, Lima, Peru, no date.

Elliott, Carolyn. "Theories of Development." *Signs* 3 (Autumn 1977): 1-8.

Fahnbulleh, Fanbutteh. "The UN Women's Decade: an Offer We Couldn't Refuse." *Third World Women's News* 1 (1986): 17-22.

Forum 85 (Nairobi), Wednesday, July 10 -Friday, July 26, 1985.

Fraser, Arvonne S. *The U.N. Decade for Women: Documents and Dialogue.* Boulder: Westview Press, 1987.

Garabaghi, Ninou. "A New Approach to Women's Participation in the Economy." *International Social Science Journal* 35 (1983): 659-82.

Ghurayyib, Rose. "Reviewing the Decade for Women in Arab Countries." *Al-raida* (February 1, 1985): 7-9.

Hinojosa, Claudia. "Forum 80, Forum 85: Things Have Changed." *Connexions*, No. 17-18 (Summer/Fall 1985): 7-9.

Hobbs, Loretta. "Equality, Development, and Peace through Our Eyes." *African Women Rising* 2 (Winter-Spring 1986): 3.

Huston, Perdita. *Third World Women Speak Out: Interviews in Six Countries on Change, Development, and Basic Needs.* New York: Praeger Publishers, 1979.

The International Council of African Women. "Women of Color Plan of Action." *African Women Rising* 1 (Spring 1985): 1-5.

The International Women's Studies Institute in Kenya. San Francisco: IWSI, 1985.

International Women's Tribune Center. *Images of Nairobi*, Decade for Women Information Resources #5. New York: IWTC, 1986.

ISIS Women's International Information and Communication Service. *Women in Development: A resource guide for organization and action.* Boston: New Society Publishers, 1984.

"The Kenyan Women: A Decade of Oppression." *Connexions* 17-18 (Summer/Fall 1985).

Mehran, Farhad. "Measurement of women's work." *Women at Work* 2 (1983).

Morgan, Robin, ed. *Sisterhood Is Global: The International Women's Movement Anthology.* Garden City, NJ: Doubleday, 1984.

Munnik, Madeline. "Editorial: Equality, Development and Peace." *African Insight* 16 (1986): 2-3.

"Our Struggle Continues." *Womanspeak: Quarterly Newsletter about Caribbean Women* 18 (July/December 1985): 27-28.

Parpet, Jane L. *African Women and Development: Gender in the Lagos Plan of Action.* Working Papers on Women in International Development, no. 87. East Lansing: Michigan State University, December 1981.

Pezzullo, Caroline for the NGO Planning Committee. *For the Record ... Forum '85.* New York: IWTC, 1986.

Post-Nairobi Donors' Meeting on Women and Development, 1985. N.p.

Ravindran, Sundari. "Looking forward from Nairobi." *ISIS International,* Women's Journal Supplement no. 4: 18.

Reddock, Rhoda. "Recollections on Forum '85," *Woman Speak!* Quarterly Newsletter About Caribbean Women, No. 18 (July/December 1985): 26-7.

"Report of the AAWORD Working Group on Women and Reproduction in Africa," *Echo* 1, no. 1 (1986): 5-6.

Santa Cruz, Adriana. "Ten Years of Progress - But Still more to be Achieved," *Third World Women's News* 1 (1986): 24-26.

Sen, Gita with Caren Grown. *Development, Crises, and Alternative Visions: Third World Women's Perspectives.* New Delhi: Institute of Social Studies Trust, 1984; reprint, New York: Montly Review Press, 1986.

Sivard, Ruth L. *Women ... a world survey.* Washington, D.C.: World Priorities, 1985.

The State of the World's Women 1985. Oxford: New Internationalist Publications, 1985.

Stephan, Wafa.' "Editorial: Arab Women and the Women's Decade." *Al-raida* 3 (February 1, 1985): 2-3.

Tadesse, Zenebeworke. "Editorial." *Echo,* Bilingual Quarterly Newsletter of the Association of African Women for Research and Development (AAWORD) 1, no. 1, (1986): 2.

United Nations. *Minutes of the General Assembly, Thirty-fourth Session.* 1979. 34/180.

_____. *Review and Appraisal of Progress Achieved and Obstacles Encountered at the National Level in the Realization of the Goals and Objectives of the United Nations Decade for Women: Equality, Development and Peace.* 1985. A/CONF.116/5/Add.1-14.

_____. *Review and Appraisal of Progress Achieved and Obstacles Encountered by the United Nations System at the Regional and International Level in the Realization of the Goals and Objectives of the United Nations Decade for Women: Equality, Development and Peace.* 1985. A/CONF.116/8.

_____. *Report of the World Conference of the International Women's Year.* 1975. E/CONF.66/34.

_____. *Report of the World Conference of the United Nations Decade for Women: Equality, Development and Peace, Copenhagen, 24-30 July 1980.* 1981 . A/CONF.94/35.

_____. *Report of the World Conference to Review and Appraise the Achievements of the United Nations Decade for Women: Equality, Development, and Peace, Nairobi, 15-26 July 1985.* 1985. A/CONF.116/28/Rev.1.

_____. *World Survey on the Role of Women in Development.* 1986. A/CONF.116/4/Rev.1.

United Nations Development Fund for Women. *Development Co-operation with Women.* 1985.

United Nations, ILO/INSTRAW. *Women in Economic Activity: A Global Statistical Survey.* 1985.

Wages for Housework International Campaign Journal. Summer 1985.

The Women's Coalition for Nairobi. *The Effects of Racism and Militarization on Women's Equality.* N.p., 1985.

"World Crisis and Women: Risk of Dispossession or an Opportunity for Empowerment." *Compass*, Newsletter of the Society for International Development, Number 27 (April 1986): 1-2.

Sources in Economics and Women's Studies

Abrahams, Kenneth. "Poverty in Namibia." *Namibian Review Publications* 5 (March 1985).

Arizpe, Lourdes. "Women and Development in Latin America and the Caribbean." *Development Dialogue*, (1982: 1-2): 74-84.

Afshar, Haleh, ed. *Women, Work, and Ideology in the Third World.* London: Tavistock Publications, 1985.

Barrett, Nancy. "How the Study of Women Has Restructured the Discipline of Economics." *A Feminist Perspective in the Academy: The Difference it Makes*, ed. Elizabeth Langland and Walter Gove, 101-9. Chicago: University of Chicago Press, 1983.

Benhabib,, Seyla and Driculla Cornell, eds. *Feminism as Critique: Essays on the Politics of Gender in Late-Capitalist Societies*, Cambridge, UK: Polity Press, 1987.

Beneria, Lourdes and Martha Roldan. *The Crossroads of Class and Gender*. Chicago: University of Chicago Press, 1987.

Bernard, Jessie. *The Female World from a Global Perspective*. Bloomington: Indiana University Press, 1987.

Bookman, Ann and Sandra Morgen, eds. *Women and the Politics of Empowerment*. Philadephia: Temple University Press, 1988.

Borreman, Valentina. "Technique and Women's Toil." *Cross Currents* (Winter 1982-3): 420-29.

Boserup, Ester. *Woman's Role in Economic Development*. New York: St. Martin's Press, 1970.

Brittan, Arthur and Mary Maynard. *Sexism, Racism and Oppression*. Oxford: Basil Blackwell, 1984.

Burnham, Linda. "Has Poverty Been Feminized in Black America?" *The Black Scholar* XVI, no. 2 (March/April 1985): 14-25.

Burnham, Linda and Miriam Louie. "The Impossible Marriage: A Marxist Critique of Socialist Feminism." *Line of March*, # 17, Spring 1985.

Burton, Clare. *Subordination: Feminism and Social Theory*. Sydney: George Allen and Unwin, 1985.

Carby, Hazel. "White women listen! Black feminism and the boundaries of sisterhood." *The Empire Strikes Back: Race and racism in 70s Britian*, Centre for Contemporary Cultural Studies, 212-35. London: Hutchinson, 1982.

Cebatorev, E.A. "Women, Work and Employment: Some Attainments of the International Women's Decade. *The Decade for Women: A Special Report*, Canadian Congress for Learning Opportunities for Women. N.p., 1985.

Circulo de Feministas Cristianas "Talitha Cumi." *La Maternidad, Tarea de Todos*, Dia de la Madre, 1987, Lima, Peru. N.p.

"The Dakar Declaration on Another Development with Women." *Development Dialogue*, (1982: 1-2): 11-16.

Davis, Angela. *Women, Race and Class*. New York: Vintage Books, 1981.

Eisenstein, Zillah, ed. *Capitalist Patriarchy and the Case for Socialist Feminism*, New York: Monthly Review Press, 1979.

Eisler, Riane. *The Chalice and the Blade: Our History, Our Future*. San Francisco: Harper and Row, 1987.

Firestone, Shulamith. *The Dialectic of Sex*. New York: Bantam Books, 1971.

Gallin, Rita, Patricia Whittier, and Margaret Graham. *Research and Policy: An Analysis of the Working Papers on Women in International Development*, WID Forum 85-V. East Lansing: Michigan State University, December 1985.

Gordon, David. *Problems in Political Economy*, 2nd ed. Lexington, MA: D.C. Heath and Company, 1977.

Harrington, Michael. *The New American Poverty*. New York: Penguin Books, 1986.

Hartmann, Betsy. *Reproductive Rights and Wrongs: The Global Politics of Population Control and Contraceptive Choice*. New York: Harper and Row, 1987.

Hartmann, Heidi. "Capitalism, Patriarchy, and Job Segregation by Sex." *Women and the Workplace: The Implications of Occupational Segregation*, ed. Martha Blaxall and Barbara Reagan. Chicago: University of Chicago Press, 1976.

Hartmann, Heidi and Ann Markusen. "Contemporary Marxist Theory and Practice: A Feminist Critique." *Review of Political Economics* 12 (1980): 87-94.

Hartman, Nancy. *Money, Sex, and Power: Toward a Feminist Historical Materialism*. Boston: Northeastern University Press, 1983.

Hooks, Bell. *Feminist Theory: from margin to center*. Boston: South End Press, 1984.

Hunt, E.K. and Howard J. Sherman. *Economics: An Introduction to Traditional and Radical Views*, 5th ed. New York: Harper and Row, 1986.

Jaggar, Alison, and Paula Rothenberg Struhl. *Feminist Frameworks*, 2nd ed. New York: McGraw-Hill, 1984.

Leacock, Eleanor, and Helen Safa, eds. *Women's Work: Development and the Division of Labor by Gender*, South Hadley, MA: Bergin and Garvey Publishers, 1986.

Lefkowitz, Rochelle and Ann Withorn, ed. *For Crying Out Loud: Women and Poverty in the United States.* New York: Pilgrim Press, 1986.

Leghorn, Lisa and Katherine Parker. *Woman's Worth: Sexual Economics and the World of Women..* Boston: Routledge & Kegan Paul, 1981.

Mies, Maria. *Patriarchy and Accumulation on a World Scale: Women in the International Division of Labour.* London: Zed Books, 1986.

Millet, Kate. *Sexual Politics.* New York: Avon Books, 1971.

Mitchell, Juliet. *Women's Estate.* New York, Vintage Books, 1971.

Mitter, Swatsi. *Common Fate, Common Bond: Women in the Global Economy.* London: Pluto Press, 1986.

Morgan, Robin, ed. *Sisterhood is Powerful: An Anthology of Writings from the Women's Liberation Movement* . New York: Vintage Books, 1970.

Oakley, Ann. *Subject Women: Where Women Stand Today - Politically, Economically, Socially, Emotionally.* New York: Pantheon Books, 1981.

Obbo, Christine. *African Women: Their Struggle for Economic Independence.* London: Zed Press, 1980.

O'Brien, Mary. *The Politics of Reproduction.* Boston: Routledge and Kegan Paul, 1981.

Parmar, Pratibha. "Gender, race and class: Asian women in resistance." *The Empire Strikes Back: Race and racism in 70s Britian*, Centre for Contemporary Cultural Studies, 236-75. London: Hutchinson, 1982.

Pateman, Carole and Elizabeth Gross, eds. *Feminist Challenges: Social and Political Theory.* Boston: Northeastern University Press, 1986.

Peattie, Lisa and Martin Rein. *Women's Claims: A Study in Political Economy.* Oxford: Oxford University Press, 1983.

Phillips, Anne, ed. *Feminism and Equality.* New York: New York University Press, 1987.

Rich, Adrienne. "Compulsory Heterosexuality and Lesbian Existence." *The Signs Reader: Women, Gender and Scholarship*, 139-68. Chicago: University of Chicago Press, 1983.

Rowbotham, Sheila. *Women's Consciousness, Man's World*. London: Penguin Books, 1973.

Saffioti, Heleieth I.B. *Women in Class Society*. Translated by Michael Vale. New York: Monthly Review Press, 1978.

_____. "Women, Mode of Production, and Social Formations." *Latin American Perspectives* 4 (Winter - Spring, 1977): 27-37.

Sanday, Peggy. *Female Power and Male Dominance: On the Origins of Sexual Inequality*. Cambridge: Cambridge University Press, 1981.

Sargent, Lydia, ed. *Women and Revolution: A Discussion of the Unhappy Marriage of Marxism and Feminism*. Boston: South End Press, 1981.

Sarvasy, Wendy and Judith Van Allen. "Fighting the Feminization of Poverty: Socialist-Feminist Analysis and Strategy." *Review of Radical Political Economics* 16, no. 4 (1984): 89-110.

Scott, Hilda. *Working Your Way to the Bottom: The Feminization of Poverty*. London: Pandora, 1984.

Sidel, Ruth. *Women and Children Last: The Plight of Poor Women and Children in Affluent America.*. New York: Viking Press, 1986.

Stallard, Karin, Barbara Ehrenreich, and Holly Sklar. *Poverty in the American Dream*. Boston: South End Press, 1983.

Thurow, Lester C. "A Surge in Inequality" *Scientific American* 256 (May 1987).

Tiano, Susan. The Separation of Women's Remunerated and Household Work: Theoretical Perspectives on "Women in Development." *Working Papers on Women in International Development*, no. 2. East Lansing: Michigan State University, December 1981.

Vogel, Lise. *Marxism and the Oppression of Women: Toward a Unitary Theory*. New Brunswick, NJ: Rutgers University Press, 1983.

Waring, Marilyn. *If Women Counted: A New Feminist Economics*. San Francisco: Harper and Row, 1988.

The Wellesley Editorial Committee, ed. *Women and National Development: The Complexities of Change*. Chicago: University of Chicago Press, 1977.

"Women: Protagonists of Change." *Development*, Journal of the Society for International Development (1984:4).